Student Success in College

Student Success in College

Creating Conditions That Matter

GEORGE D. KUH
JILLIAN KINZIE
JOHN H. SCHUH
ELIZABETH J. WHITT
AND ASSOCIATES

JOSSEY-BASS
A Wiley Imprint
www.josseybass.com

Published by Jossey-Bass
A Wiley Imprint
989 Market Street, San Francisco, CA 94103-1741   www.josseybass.com

Jossey-Bass books and products are available through most bookstores. To contact Jossey-Bass
directly call our Customer Care Department within the U.S. at 800-956-7739, outside the U.S.
at 317-572-3986 or fax 317-572-4002.

Jossey-Bass also publishes its books in a variety of electronic formats. Some content that appears in
print may not be available in electronic books.

Library of Congress Cataloging-in-Publication Data

Student success in college : creating conditions that matter / George D. Kuh ... [et al.].— 1st ed.
    p. cm.
  Includes bibliographical references and index.
  ISBN 0-7879-7914-7 (alk. paper)
  1. College student orientation—United States. 2. Documenting Effective Educational Practice
(Project) I. Kuh, George D. II. Documenting Effective Educational Practice (Project)
  LB2343.32.S79 2005
  378.1'98—dc22   2004027912

Printed in the United States of America

FIRST EDITION

HB Printing 10   9   8   7   6   5   4   3   2   1

CONTENTS

PREFACE

SOME MONTHS AGO, faculty and administrators from a dozen different colleges and universities came together to discuss the institutional policies and practices they believe are associated with student success. During the three-day meeting, one person attributed his institution's relatively strong graduation rates and other indicators of quality to the good fortune of having many "gifted amateurs" as colleagues. He quickly added he wasn't sure how long his college would be able to maintain its excellence relying on well-intentioned "amateurs," given the profound changes occurring in the student body, the disciplines, pedagogical approaches, and so on. His worry is well placed.

The college-going stakes are higher today than at any point in history, both in terms of costs and potential benefits to students and society. Indeed, virtually all forecasters agree that to be economically self-sufficient in the information-driven world economy, some form of postsecondary education is essential, with a baccalaureate degree being much preferred. This realization has hit all demographic groups, bringing waves of historically underserved students to campus. The task is to do something at a scale never before realized—to provide a high-quality postsecondary education to more than three-quarters of the adult population. Yet many students are not as well prepared academically as faculty members would like. Many students find the social as well as academic environments somewhat foreign—if not unfriendly—and challenging to navigate. In the face of escalating costs and lagging state support, institutions are under mounting pressure from state and federal oversight agencies to demonstrate that they are doing everything possible to keep college affordable and to graduate students in a timely manner. Accreditation agencies require evidence that students are learning what colleges intend.

This is a pretty complicated scenario for gifted amateurs to manage. The times require reflective, student-centered professionals, expert to be sure in their respective disciplines but also knowledgeable and skilled in areas required by the management functions they perform. They must also be familiar with policies and practices that are linked to student success, broadly defined to include satisfaction, persistence, and high levels of learning and personal development of the increasingly diverse students enrolling at their institution. There is no single best curriculum or career path to prepare for this work. There are, however, places to turn to get some good ideas for what to do. One approach is to creatively swipe—in the organizational management guru Tom Peters's (1987) words—what seems to be working at high-performing institutions. That's what this book is about—the search for policies and practices associated with student success in college.

PURPOSE OF THE BOOK

The project on which this book is based follows in the tradition of previous efforts to document noteworthy performance in postsecondary settings. Several widely disseminated volumes lay out many of the key concepts associated with student success and strong institutional performance, including *Involvement in Learning* (Study Group on the Conditions of Excellence in American Higher Education, 1984), and "The Seven Principles for Good Practices in Undergraduate Education" (Chickering & Gamson, 1987). A handful of other reports flesh out these and related factors and conditions in more detail, among them Peter Ewell's synthesis produced for the Education Commission of the States' (1995) *Making Quality Count*. Other major studies of educational effectiveness are mentioned in Chapter One. Taken together, these reports point to the following institutional conditions that are important to student development:

- A clear, focused institutional mission
- High standards for student performance
- Support for students to explore human differences and emerging dimensions of self
- Emphasis on early months and first year of study
- Respect for diverse talents
- Integration of prior learning and experience
- Ongoing practice of learned skills
- Active learning
- Assessment and feedback
- Collaboration among students
- Adequate time on task
- Out-of-class contact with faculty

Many of these practices have taken root to varying degrees in different colleges and universities across the country. For example, thanks to the pioneering work of John Gardner and his colleagues, first at the University of South Carolina and more recently at the Policy Center on the First Year of College, most institutions are now concentrating resources on first-year students. Learning communities are becoming increasingly popular, though they vary widely in terms of their structure, coherence, length, and other design elements as recent reports produced by the Washington Center show. Study abroad is receiving additional attention as an enriching educational experience. Service learning and related forms of community involvement appear to benefit both students and the local agencies and people they touch. The national movement to incorporate more active and collaborative learning activities continues to gain momentum. Indeed, we were initially surprised after the first round of National

Survey of Student Engagement (NSSE) results five years ago with the amount of active and collaborative learning students were reporting. However, the few large-scale studies of the phenomena provide only a surface reading of the frequency with which these activities are used, not necessarily the quality of the experiences or their effectiveness, relative to other activities and pedagogical techniques.

These effective educational practices have been around long enough that even casual readers of the professional higher education literature are familiar with them. They are working their way into discipline-based journals as disparate as communication studies, economics, and engineering, as well as periodicals that focus more broadly on the liberal arts and sciences, such as *Liberal Education* and *Daedulus*. Absent from the literature is a comprehensive, systematic study of institutions that reach many students with these practices. In other words, what does an educationally effective college or university look like at the turn of the 21st century? The twenty institutions that are the basis of this book serve that purpose nicely.

HOW TO READ AND USE THIS BOOK

The book is divided into four parts. Part One sets the stage, discussing in more detail why we undertook the Documenting Effective Educational Practice (DEEP) project. As we explain in Chapter One, we set out to identify and document what strong-performing colleges and universities do to promote student success, which we defined as higher-than-predicted graduation rates and better-than-predicted student engagement scores on the NSSE. In addition, we summarize how and why we selected this particular set of schools. We also introduce the concept of student engagement and describe its relationship to college student success. Appendix A summarizes the research approach we used to collect information from the participating institutions.

In Part Two (Chapters Two through Seven) we discuss the six overarching features we found to be common to the 20 DEEP colleges and universities. Chapter Two is especially important, as it includes descriptive information about each institution's mission and context, which is needed to understand and interpret how and why the specific policies and practices illustrated later work so well together to promote student success. As we emphasize throughout, the noteworthy level of performance achieved by these colleges and universities is a product not only of the various programs and practices they have in place, but the *numbers* of students touched in meaningful ways by one or more, the *quality* of the respective initiatives, and the *synergy* and *complementarity* of these efforts that create a success-oriented campus culture and learning environment. Chapter Six includes some illustrative examples of the circumstances and triggering events that put several DEEP schools on a path toward institutional improvement that created these conditions.

Chapters Eight through Twelve in Part Three present examples of policies, programs, and practices that can be adapted by other institutions to enhance student engagement in each of the five areas of effective educational practice measured by the National Survey of Student Engagement. Even with a book of this length, it's not possible to describe every noteworthy initiative at these 20 schools. We present a mix of some of the more common examples along with a sprinkling of novel, boutique-like programs to illustrate that institutions can effectively reach fairly large numbers of students with high-quality initiatives while also tailoring other efforts to address the varying needs of different groups of students. We're convinced that many of these practices can be productively adapted by other institutions, whether or not they are similar in mission, size, and so forth.

In Part Four, we summarize and interpret our findings at a somewhat more abstract level of analysis. Chapter Thirteen synthesizes the principles that guide the work of large numbers of faculty and staff members at DEEP colleges. Chapter Fourteen offers recommendations for colleges and universities that are committed to enhancing student success. In addition to these general recommendations, almost every page of Chapters Two through Twelve contains one or more ideas for improving educational practice. Thus, the book's utility will increase upon subsequent readings, after the reader absorbs the big picture of what makes for effective educational practice. Indeed, as will become evident, the foundation of strong performance is a multilayered tapestry of enacted mission, coherent operating philosophy, and promising practices woven together and reinforced by key personnel in a consistent, caring way to create a compelling, coherent environment for learning.

Finally, in an effort to make the book reader-friendly, we use research notes and references sparingly throughout the middle sections of the book, as we want readers to focus on what these institutions *do* by way of effective educational practices. As we indicated earlier, we have benefited from the ground-breaking work of those who have gone before and cite relevant work, especially early in the book and again when summarizing and synthesizing our findings in Chapters Thirteen and Fourteen.

We talked with more than 2,700 people across the 20 campuses during the course of this two-year project, many of them more than once. Though everyone we spoke with contributed to the insights we gleaned about effective educational practice, we mention by name only a few people in the book; most were senior administrators at the time of the study. This enables us to focus mainly on the institutions per se, as opposed to individuals. Even so, as will become clear early on, DEEP colleges are special places precisely because of the people who work, live, and study there.

Indeed, the more time we spent on these campuses, delving into what they do and how they do it, the more we were impressed with the range and quality of their initiatives. This can become mildly problematic, should the high regard we developed for the good work being done at these colleges and universities make it appear that we are proselytizing on their behalf. That's not our intent, though we admire the convictions that animate these institutions and their willingness—even enthusiasm—for experimenting with promising pedagogical approaches and organizational arrangements. Another reason the text may seem overly generous is that our prose is intentionally descriptive, not evaluative. That is, because we sought to discover and feature what is working well on these campuses, we do not dwell on their shortcomings. No organization is perfect, including these fine colleges and universities. They grapple everyday with many of the same challenges facing most institutions, and we address some of these matters in Chapters Two and Thirteen. For better or worse, we say little about other issues bedeviling these and other colleges today, such as the proper role of athletics and helping students meet the rising cost of college, both of which affect whether various groups of students will benefit to the fullest extent from the college experience. But as we explain later, one of the qualities that makes the DEEP schools distinctive is the way they address issues such as these while keeping their eye on the prize of student success.

ACKNOWLEDGMENTS

A project such as this has many intellectual debts, not the least of which is to the inspirational students, faculty, and staff at the institutions we visited and the scholars whose prior work continues to inform our understanding of effective practice. Our working partners in this and related initiatives are colleagues at the American Association for Higher Education (AAHE), including Vice President for Programs Barbara Cambridge, President Clara Lovett, and Project Manager Lacey Leegwater. AAHE staff coordinated a series of roundtables in 2003–2004 with different constituent groups around the country that helped inform our understanding of how institutions were using student engagement data in various ways to improve educational practice. These reports are available at (www.aahe.org/DEEP/roundtables.htm).

We are indebted to Sam Cargile and Susan Conner at Lumina Foundation for Education for their keen interest and unwavering support for a study of high-performing colleges. Another key partner is the Center of Inquiry in the Liberal Arts (CILA) at Wabash College, especially President Andrew Ford, Dean Mauri Ditzler, and Professor Charles Blaich, who early on saw promise in how the project could be used to inform liberal arts education and liberal arts colleges. Without the support of Lumina and CILA, this study would have remained just a potentially informative endeavor.

Offering sage advice behind the scenes from beginning to end were past and present members of the NSSE National Advisory Board (http://www.iub.edu/~nsse/html/advisory_board.htm) and DEEP Advisory Panel (http://education.indiana.edu/~nsse/nsse_institute/ deep_project/ student _success/advisory_board.htm). The latter group does double duty, serving also as advisors to the Building Engagement and Attainment of Minority Students project, a multiple-year initiative also funded by Lumina Foundation for Education.

We owe a special word of gratitude to three friends of student engagement who continue to influence our thinking and work. C. Robert Pace, UCLA professor emeritus, is the progenitor of what we today call student engagement. Bob introduced the concept of quality of effort in the early 1970s, and with Spencer Foundation support launched the College Student Experiences Questionnaire (CSEQ) research program. Many of the questions on the NSSE survey are from the CSEQ. We think of Peter Ewell as the godfather of NSSE, for he chaired the design team that developed the survey and remains a trusted advisor. Russ Edgerton had the foresight and courage to invest in the premise and promise of student engagement when he directed the education program at the Pew Charitable Trusts. Without Russ's leadership and Pew support, we'd be nowhere near this far along in changing the nature of the public dialogue about what matters to collegiate quality.

In every possible way, we were buoyed by our colleagues and friends at the Indiana University Center for Postsecondary Research. They covered for us during our many trips to DEEP schools, for which we are most grateful. To a person, they are a superbly talented and productive group. Our work and lives are enriched immeasurably by being around them.

Last but certainly not least, the rich and varied expertise of the DEEP research team (Appendix B) made this project a career highlight. Represented as "Associates" in the list of authors, they are co-investigators and key contributors to this volume in every sense of the word. Their insights and excellent field work appear on every page. Equally important, collectively they brought a breadth and depth of perspective and experience that may be heretofore unmatched in studies of colleges and universities. We are deeply appreciative of what they brought and gave to this project and book. Thanks, DEEP team!

February 15, 2005

George D. Kuh
Bloomington, Indiana

Jillian Kinzie
Bloomington, Indiana

Student Success
in College

PART I

Introduction

On other campuses, I hear they just read from the book and discuss the material in the abstract. Here we tell how the reading relates to our life—our history and background. It is much more personal and has feeling. I would not be able to relate otherwise; that is what made the education engaging for me.
—California State University at Monterey Bay first-year student

The one thing that really helped me to get through college was the faculty. They have this philosophy that the first thing that comes to mind is the student. They have an open door and open ears to what students want to do in college and what they want to learn.

—University of Texas at El Paso senior

I never thought I would study abroad because I am such a homebody. . . . I heard about the London Review in a presentation in one of my business classes and I thought I should look into it. I went on the two-week trip and then decided to spend an entire semester abroad.

—University of Kansas senior

Wabash has made me a man. Instantly there's a lot going on and you're expected to jump in headfirst. It breeds confidence. You think, "Hey, I can do this, too." You get the sense that you can achieve anything.

—Wabash College junior

The people here have helped me develop who I am. No one ever encouraged me in science before. Internships and study abroad got me into environmental activism. I've learned how the majority of the world lives, and that you don't need all the stuff you think you need. There are so many opportunities here and once I started, I just never quit!

—Wheaton College senior

The whole education at UMF is about constant reflection. You develop a deliberate, thinking state of mind. Thinking critically becomes second nature. They're tricky like that!

—University of Maine at Farmington senior

The number one thing I like here is the interaction in the classroom. We have intimacy and respect with the faculty. They don't baby-sit you, but you get a lot of attention. You're asked to reflect on yourself and your character, and it broadens your understanding of life. I'm a better leader because of it.

—Longwood University junior

Students are so empowered here to be engaged. We truly have ownership of our lives and so we just assume we'll be in charge of things. It's amazing how motivated that makes you to take on responsibility and succeed.

—Miami University sophomore

There are many challenges here. You have to challenge yourself academically, challenge yourself to understand people from diverse backgrounds, and challenge yourself to understand the community and the world.

—Macalester College junior

These students seem to be thriving in college. They describe experiences that challenged them to develop skills, awareness, and confidence. Although the colleges the students attend are very different, the institutions perform well on two important measures. That is, when the institutions' resources and student characteristics are taken into consideration, all graduate more students than might be predicted, and their students partake more frequently than predicted in activities that encourage learning and development.

What accounts for these achievements? And what can other colleges and universities learn from them to enhance their own effectiveness?

The Educationally Effective Colleges Quiz includes some clues. (Hint: Review the student quotes earlier.) The answers are at the end of Chapter Two. If you read straight through to that point, without skipping the pages in between, you should do well on the quiz. What will become apparent early on is that the colleges and universities represented in the questions are very different in size and educational mission. Some on the list might surprise you. What they all have in common is that they take undergraduate education very seriously and have implemented policies and practices and cultivated campus cultures that encourage their students to take advantage of a variety of educational opportunities.

To find out more about these institutions and what they do to promote student success, read on!

Exhibit 1. Educationally Effective Colleges Quiz.

1. What college uses peer evaluations, external assessors from the local community, and student self-evaluations to assess student learning?
2. What university located on a former military base requires all students to complete two service-learning courses?
3. At what institution do groups of students and faculty members decide together what to study for an extended period of time using an inter-disciplinary approach?
4. What public Historically Black College or University (HBCU) increased its first-to-second-year retention in five years by instituting a wave of student success initiatives?
5. What mid-Atlantic public university where more than 40% of the undergraduates are students of color or international students systemically incorporated electronic technology when redesigning 100+ courses?
6. At what Jesuit university do students annually coordinate and perform about 30,000 hours of community service?
7. What medium-sized university revised and connected its general education program more tightly to students' out-of-class experiences to pursue its mission of Preparing Citizen Leaders?
8. What liberal arts college emphasizes internationalism and multicul-turalism in its mission and has more than half of its students study abroad?
9. At what public university do all 15,000 undergraduates have a cap-stone experience that requires them to integrate liberal learning with specialized knowledge?
10. At what women's college do students take at least three writing inten-sive courses and begin each academic year by marching to the top of a nearby hill to the founder's grave site for a remembrance cere-mony?
11. What public research university annually bestows on 20 faculty mem-bers at the beginning of each academic year prestigious $5,000 awards to honor outstanding teaching?
12. What small public university improved its persistence rates by creating campus jobs for more than half of its students?

Student Success in College

Exhibit 1. (*Continued*)

13. What major public research university ranks in the top 10 among its peers in terms of external grants and contracts but also did six major studies of the quality of the undergraduate experience of its students since 1986?
14. At what 10,000-acre liberal arts college campus do faculty members and many students still wear academic robes to class?
15. What Hispanic-serving university is one of the six Model Institutions for Excellence (MIE) identified by the National Science Foundation?
16. At what liberal arts college does the academic dean host a biweekly colloquium to introduce new faculty members to key issues at the college by talking with senior colleagues?
17. At what liberal arts college is the entire student code of conduct only 24 words long?
18. What former women's college became "consciously coeducational" in the late 1980s and offers a "gender-balanced" curriculum?
19. What university designates sections of the freshman seminar for students interested in specific majors and expects the faculty member teaching the course to serve as a mentor and academic advisor to the students in their section?
20. What is the smallest college playing Division I football where the interdisciplinary learning communities for first-year students are designed and led by faculty and student preceptors?

The DEEP Schools

Alverno College
California State University at
    Monterey Bay
Evergreen State College
Fayetteville State University
George Mason University
Gonzaga University
Longwood University
Macalester College
Miami University
Sewanee, University of the South

Sweet Briar College
University of Kansas
University of Maine at Farmington
University of Michigan
University of Texas at El Paso
Ursinus College
Wabash College
Wheaton College (Massachusetts)
Winston-Salem State University
Wofford College

Student Engagement

A Key to Student Success

FOR DECADES, the college graduation rate has hovered around 50% (Astin, 1975; Braxton, 2000; Pascarella & Terenzini, 1991; Tinto, 1993). Until the 1970s, graduation rates were calculated on a four-year metric. Today the standard denominator is six years, which acknowledges the college-going patterns of contemporary undergraduate students, many of whom attend college part time. Nearly one out of five four-year institutions graduates fewer than one-third of its first-time, full-time, degree-seeking first-year students within six years (Carey, 2004). Even if baccalaureate completion estimates are low, as some claim (Adelman, 2004), everyone agrees that persistence and educational attainment rates, as well as the quality of student learning, must improve if postsecondary education is to meet the needs of our nation and our world. Indeed, as we write, the House subcommittee drafting the reauthorization legislation for the Higher Education Act has included language requiring colleges and universities to report degree completion rates for certificates and degrees for students who start at the institution or who transfer to it. Although not everyone agrees as to the most appropriate way to compute graduation rates, it is clear that increasing persistence and degree completion is a high priority for many institutions. The best predictors of whether a student will graduate or not are academic preparation and motivation (Adelman, 2004; Pascarella & Terenzini, 1991). Thus, the surest way to increase the number of "successful" students—those who persist, benefit in desired ways from their college experiences, are satisfied with college, and graduate—is to admit only well-prepared, academically talented students (Kuh, 2001a).

The problem with this approach is obvious. More people, from a wider, deeper, and more diverse pool of undergraduates, are going to college (Keller, 2001). Moreover, in the coming decade, four-fifths of high school graduates will need some form of postsecondary education to acquire the knowledge, skills, and competencies necessary to address the complex social, economic, and political issues they will face (Kazis, Vargas, & Hoffman, 2004).

Because admitting only the most talented and well-prepared students is neither a solution nor an option, are there other promising approaches to enhancing student success? Decades of research studies on college-impact and persistence suggest a promising area of emphasis: student engagement.

WHY EFFECTIVE EDUCATIONAL PRACTICE MATTERS

What students *do* during college counts more in terms of what they learn and whether they will persist in college than who they are or even where they go to college. That is, the voluminous research on college student development shows that the time and energy students devote to educationally purposeful activities is the single best predictor of their learning and personal development (Astin, 1993; Pascarella & Terenzini, 1991; Pace, 1980). Certain institutional practices are known to lead to high levels of student engagement (Astin, 1991; Chickering & Reisser, 1993; Kuh, Schuh, Whitt, & Associates, 1991; Pascarella & Terenzini, 1991). Perhaps the best-known set of engagement indicators is the "Seven Principles for Good Practice in Undergraduate Education" (Chickering & Gamson, 1987). These principles include student-faculty contact, cooperation among students, active learning, prompt feedback, time on task, high expectations, and respect for diverse talents and ways of learning. Also important to student learning are institutional environments that are perceived by students as inclusive and affirming and where expectations for performance are clearly communicated and set at reasonably high levels

(Education Commission of the States, 1995; Kuh, 2001b; Kuh et al., 1991; Pascarella, 2001).

All these factors and conditions are positively related to student satisfaction, learning and development on a variety of dimensions, and persistence (Astin, 1984, 1985, 1993; Bruffee, 1993; Goodsell, Maher, & Tinto, 1992; Johnson, Johnson, & Smith, 1991; McKeachie, Pintrich, Lin, & Smith, 1986; Pascarella & Terenzini, 1991; Pike, 1993; Sorcinelli, 1991). Thus, educationally effective colleges and universities—those that add value—channel students' energies toward appropriate activities and engage them at a high level in these activities (Education Commission of the States, 1995; Study Group on the Conditions of Excellence in American Higher Education, 1984).

In sum, student engagement has two key components that contribute to student success. The first is the amount of time and effort students put into their studies and other activities that lead to the experiences and outcomes that constitute student success. The second is the ways the institution allocates resources and organizes learning opportunities and services to induce students to participate in and benefit from such activities. What the institution does to foster student success is of particular interest, as those are practices over which a college or university has some direct influence. That is, if faculty and administrators use principles of good practice to arrange the curriculum and other aspects of the college experience, students would ostensibly put forth more effort. Students would write more papers, read more books, meet more frequently with faculty and peers, and use information technology appropriately, all of which would result in greater gains in such areas as critical thinking, problem solving, effective communication, and responsible citizenship.

Many colleges claim to provide high-quality learning environments for their students. As evidence, schools point to educationally enriching opportunities they make available, such as honors programs, cocurricular leadership development programs, and collaboration with faculty members on a research project. Too often, however, such experiences are products of serendipity or efforts on the part of students themselves—the first component of engagement. Moreover, for every student who has such an experience, there are others who do not connect in meaningful ways with their teachers and their peers, or take advantage of learning opportunities. As a result, many students leave school prematurely, or put so little effort into their learning that they fall short of benefiting from college to the extent they should.

Are low levels of engagement by many students inevitable? Or can institutions fashion policies, programs, and practices that encourage students to participate in educationally purposeful activities—so that a greater number of students may achieve their potential?

In the for-profit sector, a time-honored approach to improving effectiveness is identifying and adapting the practices of high-performing organizations. If we can identify colleges and universities that "add value" to their students' experiences, might we be able to learn from them ways to create powerful learning environments for all students? These questions led us to the study we describe next.

DOCUMENTING EFFECTIVE EDUCATIONAL PRACTICE (DEEP)

The research team set out to identify colleges and universities that perform well in two areas: student engagement and graduation rates. First, we used a regression model to identify baccalaureate-granting institutions that had higher-than-predicted scores on the five clusters of effective educational practice used by the National Survey of Student Engagement (NSSE). The clusters are level of academic challenge, active and collaborative learning, student interaction with faculty members, enriching educational experiences, and supportive campus environment (see Exhibit 1.1). Many research studies show that participating in activities related to these clusters is linked with desired outcomes of college. We used a second regression model to determine the predicted graduation rates of these schools, and compared those rates with their actual six-year graduation rate.

Both regression models took into account student characteristics and institutional features such as size, selectivity, and location. Thus, "higher-than-predicted" means that the institutions generally performed better than they were expected to, given their student and institutional characteristics (Appendix A). More information about the prediction

Exhibit 1.1. Summary of the NSSE Clusters of Effective Education Practice.

Level of Academic Challenge

Challenging intellectual and creative work is central to student learning and collegiate quality. A number of questions from NSSE's instrument, *The College Student Report,* correspond to three integral components of academic challenge. Several questions represent the nature and amount of assigned academic work, some reflect the complexity of cognitive tasks presented to students, and several others ask about the standards faculty members use to evaluate student performance. Specifically these questions are related to

- Preparing for class (studying, reading, writing, rehearsing)
- Reading and writing
- Using higher-order thinking skills
- Working harder than students thought they could to meet an instructor's standards
- An institutional environment that emphasizes studying and academic work

Active and Collaborative Learning

Students learn more when they are intensely involved in their education and have opportunities to think about and apply what they are learning in different settings. And when students collaborate with others in solving problems or mastering difficult material, they acquire valuable skills that prepare them to deal with the messy, unscripted problems they will encounter daily during and after college. Survey questions that contribute to this cluster include

- Asking questions in class or contributing to class discussions
- Making class presentations
- Working with other students on projects during class
- Working with classmates outside of class to prepare class assignments
- Tutoring or teaching other students
- Participating in community-based projects as part of a regular course
- Discussing ideas from readings or classes with others

(*Continued*)

Exhibit 1.1. Summary of the NSSE Clusters of Effective Education Practice. (*Continued*)

Student Interactions with Faculty Members
In general, the more contact students have with their teachers the better. Working with a professor on a research project or serving with faculty members on a college committee or community organization lets students see first-hand how experts identify and solve practical problems. Through such interactions teachers become role models, mentors, and guides for continuous, lifelong learning. Questions in this cluster include

- Discussing grades or assignments with an instructor
- Talking about career plans with a faculty member or advisor
- Discussing ideas from readings or classes with faculty members outside of class
- Working with faculty members on activities other than coursework (committees, orientation, student-life activities, and so forth)
- Getting prompt feedback on academic performance
- Working with a faculty member on a research project

Enriching Educational Experiences
Educationally effective colleges and universities offer many different opportunities inside and outside the classroom that complement the goals of the academic program. One of the most important is exposure to diversity, from which students learn valuable things about themselves and gain an appreciation for other cultures. Technology is increasingly being used to facilitate the learning process and, when done appropriately, can increase collaboration between peers and instructors, which actively engages students in their learning. Other valuable educational experiences include internships, community service, and senior capstone courses that provide students with opportunities to synthesize, integrate, and apply their knowledge. As a result, learning is deeper, more meaningful, and ultimately more useful because what students know becomes a part of who they are. Questions from the survey representing these kinds of experiences include

- Talking with students with different religious beliefs, political opinions, or values
- Talking with students of a different race or ethnicity

Exhibit 1.1. (*Continued*)

- An institutional climate that encourages contact among students from different economic, social, and racial or ethnic backgrounds
- Using electronic technology to discuss or complete assignments
- Participating in:
  - Internships or field experiences
  - Community service or volunteer work
  - Foreign language coursework
  - Study abroad
  - Independent study or self-designed major
  - Cocurricular activities
  - A culminating senior experience

Supportive Campus Environment
Students perform better and are more satisfied at colleges that are committed to their success and cultivate positive working and social relations among different groups on campus. Survey questions contributing to this cluster describe a campus environment that

- Helps students succeed academically
- Helps students cope with nonacademic responsibilities (work, family, and so forth)
- Helps students thrive socially
- Promotes good relations between students and their peers
- Promotes good relations between students and faculty members
- Promotes good relations between students and administrative staff

models used to identify the institutions in this study is available at (http://education.indiana.edu/~nsse/nsse_institute/deep_project/student_success/research_methods.htm).

Higher-than-predicted levels of engagement and graduation represent something meaningful beyond what students bring to college. Arguably, at such colleges and universities students are taking advantage of the opportunities the institutions provide for their learning. In addition, the institutions themselves are presumed to be doing something that encourages students to take part in effective, educationally purposeful activities.

The 20 institutions in this study are among a larger number that met the criteria for higher-than-predicted student engagement and graduation. They are not necessarily the "most engaging" institutions in the country, nor do they necessarily have the "highest" graduation rates. Nevertheless, they are performing at a level that is better than expected, taking into account a variety of factors.

We selected this particular group of colleges and universities in part to represent the diversity of baccalaureate-granting institutions. Nine are private; 11 are public. Some are large research-intensive universities; others focus exclusively on undergraduate education. Some are residential; others enroll substantial numbers of commuting and part-time students. One has fewer than 700 undergraduate students (Sweet Briar College), whereas others enroll more than 20,000 (University of Kansas, University of Michigan). Two are historically black colleges and universities (Fayetteville State University and Winston-Salem State University). Two are Hispanic-serving institutions—California State University at Monterey Bay (CSUMB) and the University of Texas at El Paso (UTEP). Two are women's colleges (Alverno and Sweet Briar). One is a men's college (Wabash).

At all but a few, the range of student ability and academic preparation is substantial. While standardized test scores place the University of Michigan and Miami University among the most selective public universities in the country, other institutions, such as Fayetteville State University and UTEP, provide educational access to many students marginally prepared for college-level work. The private liberal arts colleges in the study practice selective admissions to varying degrees.

Commuter and part-time students are numerous at some DEEP colleges, such as UTEP, CSUMB, and George Mason. Others, such as Macalester, Sweet Briar, University of Michigan, and Wabash, enroll almost an entirely residential, full-time student body. Miami, Wofford, Gonzaga, and George Mason University are among the top 10 universities in proportion of students who study abroad during college.

The DEEP institutions are diverse in mission, selectivity, size, control, location, and student characteristics (see Table 1.1). Thus, other colleges and universities will be able to identify philosophical underpinnings and

Table 1.1. DEEP Schools

Institution	Year Founded	Institutional Type	Tuition in-state (out-of-state)	Student-Faculty Ratio	Total Full-Time Undergrad Population	Part-Time Students	Transfer Students
Alverno College	1887	Private women's college	$12,150	13:1	907	94%	51%
California State University Monterey Bay	1994	Public Hispanic-serving university	$1,815 ($9,195)	19:1	1,791	11%	15%
The Evergreen State University	1967	Public liberal arts college	$3,097 ($10,837)	20:1	3,901	14%	56%
Fayetteville State University	1867	Public historically black university	$1,770 ($9,692)	20:1	3,126	22%	31%
George Mason University	1957	Public research university	$3,792 ($12,696)	15:1	15,312	29%	50–60%

(Continued)

Table 1.1. DEEP Schools (Continued)

Institution	Year Founded	Institutional Type	Tuition in-state (out-of-state)	Student-Faculty Ratio	Total Full-Time Undergrad Population	Part-Time Students	Transfer Students
Gonzaga University	1887	Private Jesuit university	$19,400	13:1	3,485	6.2%	11%
Longwood University	1839	Public master's university	$4,226 ($9,946)	19:1	3,440	4%	5%
Macalester College	1874	Private liberal arts college	$22,608	10:1	1,773	4%	4%
Miami University	1809	Public research university	$7,666 ($16,390)	17:1	14,720	3%	2%
Sewanee: University of the South	1857	Private liberal arts college	$22,370	10:1	1,308	1.5%*	3.2%
Sweet Briar College	1901	Private women's college	$18,010	10:1	682	8%	3%
University of Kansas	1864	Public research university	$2,333 ($9,260)	15:1	17,475	11%	7.2%

Institution	Year	Type	Tuition	Ratio	Enrollment		
University of Maine at Farmington	1863	Public liberal arts university	$3,990 ($9,750)	16:1	2,000	16%*	25%
University of Michigan	1817	Public research university	$7,340 ($22,932)	10:1	23,063	6%	19.3%
University of Texas at El Paso	1913	Public Hispanic-serving university	$2,208 ($8,000)	20:1	10,013	37%	10%
Ursinus College	1869	Private liberal arts college	$26,200	12:1	1,310	1%	2.4%
Wabash College	1832	Private men's liberal arts college	$19,837	10:1	853	1%	1.75%
Wheaton College (MA)	1834	Private liberal arts college	$23,140	13:1	1,478	1%	2.4%
Winston-Salem State University	1892	Public historically black university	$1,168 ($9,039)	16:1	2,320	20%	7.6%
Wofford College	1854	Public liberal arts college	$18,515	14:1	1,082	2%	2%

These data are reported for the 2002–2003 academic year, when the data collection for this project began.

*From Barron's Profiles of American Colleges (25th ed., 2003).

educational policies and practices that they can adapt in order to enhance their educational effectiveness.

The primary purpose of this project was to discover what a diverse set of institutions does to promote student success so other colleges and universities that aspire to enhance the quality of the undergraduate experience might learn from their example. As we began the study, however, we did not assume these colleges were aware of the reasons for their effectiveness; indeed, there are disadvantages to being successful without knowing why. In *Good to Great,* a study of organizations that attained and then sustained a level of superlative performance for at least 15 years, Collins (2001) warned that knowing what good firms have in common with others is not nearly as important as knowing what distinguishes them from others. Not knowing what contributes to exceptional performance makes an institution vulnerable to losing over time what made it successful in the first place. Thus, a secondary purpose of the study was to help strong-performing institutions better understand what they do that has the desired effects.

Toward these ends, the DEEP research team conducted two multiple-day visits to each of the 20 campuses. We reviewed countless documents and Web sites prior to, during, and after the site visits. We visited more than 50 classrooms and laboratories, observed faculty and staff meetings, spent more than 1,000 hours on campus, and talked in all with more than 2,700 people—many of them more than once—to learn what these schools do to promote student success.

Appendix A provides more information about the selection processes for these schools and describes our data collection and analysis procedures. Additional details about the project can be found at (http://education. indiana.edu/~nsse/nsse_institute/deep_project/student_success/research_ methods.htm).

KEEP IN MIND

• We do not claim that these 20 institutions are the "best" or the "most educationally effective" of the more than 700 four-year colleges and universities that had used NSSE by 2003. At the same time, their performance is noteworthy, and they offer many examples of promising practices that could be adapted and used profitably at other institutions.

• Our examination focused exclusively on four-year colleges and universities. This is because NSSE was designed for use by the four-year sector of colleges and universities. A counterpart survey for two-year colleges, the Community College Survey of Student Engagement, was established in 2003. Though by necessity we could include only four-year colleges and universities that administered NSSE between 2000 and 2002, many of these lessons may well apply to most four-year institutions and are worthy of consideration in two-year institutions and to postbaccalaureate programs as well.

• Because we cannot describe every educationally effective policy and practice employed by the 20 DEEP colleges and universities that warrant attention, we have focused on examples that have potential for use at other institutions.

• Whatever the path each of these 20 institutions followed to achieve effectiveness, each stands confidently, rejecting imitation. Each has its own cultural traditions, history, and motivations for improvement that differ somewhat from the others. In addition, each tailors its own educationally purposeful activities to accommodate the students it attracts. Therefore, we hope readers will adapt and apply relevant lessons from these descriptions to their own institutional context.

Although we emphasize characteristics shared by most of the schools (Chapters Two through Seven), we also occasionally refer to aspects that describe only some. For example, what works at Wabash College, a men's college, might not work for men at coeducational institutions. Also, some institutions enjoy advantages provided by their location and surrounding communities that are not possible to replicate: George Mason University and the greater Washington, D.C. area, the Evergreen State College and the nearby Puget Sound, and the University of Maine at Farmington and the rural, forested landscape.

• Many effective practices we illustrate are familiar. For example, hundreds of colleges and universities offer learning communities, first-year seminars, service learning, or study abroad opportunities. At every institution, some students and faculty members get to know one another quite well. What sets these 20 schools and other educationally effective institutions apart from the majority is *how well* they implement their programs and practices and the meaningful ways one or many of these initiatives have touched a *large number* of students. To get a sense of the extent to which your college or university approximates what DEEP schools do to promote student success, think about the following as you read about what these institutions do:

- How well do we promote student success?

- How many students do our efforts reach in meaningful ways and what is our evidence for this?

- To what extent are our programs and practices complementary and synergistic, thereby having a greater impact than the sum of each individual initiative?

- To what extent are our initiatives sustainable in terms of financial and human resources?

- What are we doing that is *not* represented among the policies and practices described here, and what evidence justifies doing it?

- What are we not doing that we should? How might we adapt certain policies and practices for our unique context and circumstances?

NO SINGLE BLUEPRINT FOR STUDENT SUCCESS

A final issue to keep in mind is that there are many roads to becoming an educationally engaging institution. These institutions have many similar policies and practices, yet differences exist. Each of the 20 colleges and universities in the study found its own way to educational effectiveness, experimenting with some homegrown ideas and frequently adapting promising practices discovered at other institutions. At some schools— the Evergreen State College, Macalester College, University of Michigan, and Ursinus College—the curriculum is the focal point for promoting student success. Gonzaga University, Longwood University, Miami University, and University of Maine at Farmington (UMF) use out-of-class activities to enhance student learning by connecting students in productive ways to their studies and to the institution. Sometimes a convergence of external forces such as changing accreditation standards and an authentic desire to improve student learning move schools to assess systematically aspects of the student experience and institutional performance; Alverno College and California State University at Monterey Bay (CSUMB) are examples. At some schools, such as UMF, University of Texas at El Paso, Fayetteville State, and George Mason, visionary leaders pointed the way. At others—CSUMB, Evergreen State, Michigan, Sewanee, Sweet Briar, and Wabash—a salient founding mission and strong campus culture are touchstones for student success. At all DEEP schools, a unique combination of external and internal factors worked together to crystallize and support an institutionwide focus on student success. No blueprint exists to reproduce what they do, or how, in another setting.

The absence of such a blueprint and the fact that many roads lead to student success are, in fact, good news for those who desire to enhance student learning and engagement at their own institutions. Many of the programs, policies, and practices at DEEP schools are potentially transportable to any college or university. As you read what we found, consider how these examples might be adapted to address the educational needs of your students and to fit the mission, people, and cultures of your institution.

PART II

Properties and Conditions Common to Educationally Effective Colleges

Gemstone: A precious or semi-precious stone, especially before it is cut and polished for use as a gem. (Funk & Wagnalls Standard College Dictionary, 1963, p. 555)

Like gemstones, the 20 colleges and universities in this study are attractive in some ways. At the same time, they differ at least on the surface one from another when set side by side. Some have polished reputations and considerable national visibility. Others might be considered diamonds in the rough. All have minor flaws that are easy to overlook, given their other attractive attributes. Gemstones are not just necessarily pretty but have enduring qualities that can be arranged in a variety of settings or combined to create distinctively different visual effects. They have both sentimental and financial value that increase over time. All are precious to those who own them. Most important for our purposes, gemstones represent something to be admired—natural materials that become even more appealing because of the hard work put into polishing and arranging their properties so that under scrutiny their character and appeal are striking.

The 20 DEEP colleges and universities are, by almost any measure of student success, gemstones. They share six features that foster student engagement and persistence:

- A "living" mission and "lived" educational philosophy
- An unshakeable focus on student learning
- Environments adapted for educational enrichment
- Clearly marked pathways to student success
- An improvement oriented ethos
- Shared responsibility for educational quality and student success

Although we discuss each separately, these features are not independent or mutually exclusive. That is, elements of one can be found in others, and they work together to shape the effectiveness of the whole. Like a gemstone that derives its beauty and value from a combination of cut, clarity, and color, these schools perform as well as they do precisely because their policies and practices are linked in complementary ways to promote student success. Moreover, as we explain in Chapter Thirteen, the impact on student success is multiplied when institutions create these conditions and expose students to a variety of synergistic, effective, educational practices.

"Living" Mission and "Lived" Educational Philosophy

E VERY ONE of the 20 DEEP colleges and universities has its own particular mix of mission-driven educational practices. But all share two characteristics: (1) clearly articulated educational purposes and aspirations, and (2) a coherent, relatively well understood philosophy that guides "how we do things here." Together, the mission and philosophy provide a rationale for the institution's educational programs, policies, and practices. Some of the DEEP colleges and universities have maintained a consistent approach over time in terms of their educational goals. Others changed their mission, such as embracing coeducation. Over time, all have tweaked their educational purposes, philosophy, and offerings in order to respond in purposeful ways to changing times and student characteristics and educational needs.

MISSION

Mission refers to the overarching purposes of the institution—what it is and stands for as well as what it aspires to be (Keeton, 1971; Kuh, Schuh, Whitt, & Associates, 1991). The mission establishes the tone of a college and conveys its educational purposes, whether based on religious, ideological, or educational beliefs, giving direction to all aspects of institutional life, including the policies and practices that foster student success.

Every college has two missions. The one that comes immediately to mind is the *espoused* mission. Typically, this is what a school writes about itself—its mission statement. Large public universities usually have broad, expansive mission statements that promise something to almost everyone, as is expected by the taxpayers who support them. Many smaller colleges—especially denominational colleges and special purpose institutions such as single-sex colleges and engineering and technology institutions—have espoused missions that specifically delineate their educational priorities.

The second mission is the school's *enacted* mission—what the institution actually does and who it serves. The enacted mission is arguably more important to student success than the espoused mission because it guides the daily actions of those in regular contact with students—in classrooms, in residence halls, and on playing fields—as well as those who set institutional policy, make strategic plans and decisions, and allocate resources. The enacted mission often differs from what the institution says or writes about itself. A university's mission statement might, for example, feature a commitment to teaching undergraduates, but its enacted mission focuses human and fiscal resources on graduate students and research. A college might claim in its mission statement to be concerned with "the education of the whole student" but, in fact, provide few opportunities for intellectual or social development outside of the classroom.

DEEP institutions are distinctive because the gap is smaller between their espoused mission and their enacted mission than at most other schools. At these colleges, the mission is not just a record of incorporation for periodic review by accreditors and legislators, but also a stable, yet somewhat elastic educational foundation examined routinely to ensure its continued relevance. The mission is stable in that it provides a constancy of purpose and direction. The mission is elastic because it can be modified to accommodate changing external circumstances, curricular innovation, and students' needs and educational objectives.

As we noted in Chapter One, the missions of DEEP schools range from educating students of a particular race, ethnicity, or sex to educating large and diverse student populations. The missions of some refer explicitly to research and graduate education; others specify teaching undergraduates. Some are proudly public and open-access; others are unabashedly private

and selective. In addition, several are both public and selective. Despite their
great differences, however, DEEP schools have one characteristic in common: their mission is "alive." Faculty members, administrators, staff, students, and others use it to explain their behavior and to talk about what the
institution is, the direction it is heading, and how their work contributes to
its goals. For example, administrators, faculty, and staff at California State
University at Monterey Bay refer to the vision statement to guide everyday
practice at the institution and use the term "Vision Students" to refer to the
population of students the institution is committed to serving—those who
historically have been denied educational opportunity due to their socioeconomic or racial and ethnic backgrounds. Because of the widespread use
of shared language and commonly understood terms, most people at a
DEEP campus describe their school's mission in similar ways.

OPERATING PHILOSOPHY

Over time, and consciously or not, a college develops a philosophy that
guides thought and action as it pursues its educational mission. The institution's philosophy is knitted into what Schein (1992) called the "hidden"
layer of culture. That is, the philosophy is composed of tacit understandings about what is important to the institution and its constituents and
unspoken but deeply held values and beliefs about students and their education. Institutional philosophies serve as a compass, keeping the institution on track as it makes decisions about resources, curriculum, and
educational opportunities. They are threads woven into the institution's
conscience that help people determine how to spend their time and energy
in pursuit of the institution's mission and purposes.

The philosophies of DEEP schools differ, which is to be expected given their different missions and student characteristics. Nevertheless, they all have developed approaches to foster student success that complement their specific context and address their students' needs. Miami University, Fayetteville State University, and Sewanee emphasize status distinctions. At Fayetteville State, for example, students are taught early on to revere faculty members as aspirational figures and role models because of their achievements. Thus, the social and academic distance between faculty members and students spurs students to greater academic efforts. This is in stark contrast to the egalitarian ethic that pervades Evergreen State, the University of Maine at Farmington, and Alverno College. Evergreen State has held fast from its beginnings to a belief that faculty and students are both learners. Because of the interdisciplinary nature of the academic program, it is not unusual for some students to have a better grasp of some aspects of the topic under study than some faculty. The faculty models inquisitiveness and a commitment to continuous, lifelong learning, an attitude that students quickly pick up and adopt as their own. Although the FSU and Evergreen philosophies are very different, they work well in their respective contexts.

The missions of Winston-Salem State University and the University of Texas at El Paso emphasize that every person has the potential to learn. These institutions, along with many other DEEP schools, are dedicated to expanding educational opportunity for students who by traditional measures are not expected to succeed in higher education. These universities value diversity, high-quality undergraduate teaching, and support for all students. They promote social responsibility by encouraging students to give back to their communities. Moreover, these values are enacted by open-door admissions, emphasis on undergraduate teaching, first-year transition and orientation courses that help students acquire study skills and self-confidence, and rewards for meaningful student-faculty interaction.

MEET THE DEEP SCHOOLS

Because mission and operating philosophy affect virtually all aspects of institutional performance, we briefly introduce all 20 DEEP schools in this section to provide a context for understanding how the remaining five properties and conditions work together to foster student success. In addition to summarizing some key aspects of their missions and philosophies, we identify one or more salient aspects of their educational programs that begin to account for their ability to engage students at relatively high levels in effective educational practices and to graduate students at higher-than-predicted rates. Indeed, because of the complex web of complementary policies and programs that each of these institutions has in place, it is not possible to fully appreciate how and why they work so well without an appreciation for the mission and educational philosophy that guide these activities. Thus, we urge readers to resist the impulse to focus only on those colleges and universities that are most like their own and become acquainted with each of the DEEP schools. Meaningful insights into student success can be gleaned from every one.

Alverno College: A Sisterhood in More Ways than One

Much has been written in recent years about Alverno College in Milwaukee, Wisconsin, especially about its groundbreaking work on assessing student learning. Such attention is well earned. However, Alverno also is distinctive because of its mission: promoting the personal and professional development of women. Founded in 1887 as St. Joseph's Normal School to educate the School Sisters of St. Francis, it later developed into a teachers college. In 1946, the institution became a four-year liberal arts college. The Alverno mission statement acknowledges its affiliation with the Catholic Church, yet the college's inclusive culture makes it feel nondenominational. Indeed, inclusiveness and respect for all religious denominations are pervasive institutional norms.

Alverno's mission statement highlights its unique niche in higher education: "Alverno exists to promote the personal and professional development of women." The statement goes on to describe the college's operating philosophy: "[Our mission] defines both our long-term aims and daily pursuits. To accomplish our mission, we must work constantly [to create] a community of learning [in] the pursuit of knowledge and the development of students' abilities." As one faculty member told us, being a women's college is "central to everything we do." Students talk about the college as "a sisterhood—a sisterhood goes along with being at a women's college." One student pointed out, "All the cultural messages are about women, about cultural expectations of women." Another told us, "Here I don't have anyone undermining my learning. You remove that factor and it builds self-esteem."

Grounded in egalitarian ideals and an ethic of social justice, the college by constitution and action is committed to cultivating the intellect and leadership potential of women who often have been ignored or overlooked by higher education. Approximately 2,000 women enrolled in 2002. More than 70% are first-generation college students. Approximately 28% are African American and 8% Latina. Alverno's weekday college is primarily a commuter liberal arts college; only about 8% of weekday students live on campus. Its Weekend College, established in 1977, is not unlike a community college in that it offers working adult women flexible class schedules leading to degrees in fields such as business, professional communication, and nursing. A large percentage of students are from the surrounding area, and most students return to their communities to work upon completion of their degrees.

The Alverno learning environment provides academic challenges and personal support to encourage students to perform interdependent work. Emblematic of these efforts is the way classrooms are physically arranged. Tables and chairs are set in small clusters, referred to as "pods" by one faculty member, to facilitate collaborative work in class. Especially important is that Alverno students evaluate one another's performance as well as their own. These peer evaluations give everyone a chance to review others' contributions to the group's overall performance. Pods and the practice of peer evaluation encourage students to learn from one another and to form meaningful relations with people they probably would not otherwise interact. Connecting authentically with peers enriches the learning process and also deepens students' loyalty to the college. In addition, peer evaluation helps instill in each student the sense that she is expected to contribute in meaningful ways to the learning environment.

> Established in 1977, Alverno's Weekend College was the first program of its kind in the Milwaukee area to reach out to working women. Over 70% of its students are first generation.

California State University at Monterey Bay: Realizing a Vision of Excellence

Founded in 1994, California State University at Monterey Bay organizes its academic programs according to principles of interdisciplinary and outcomes-based education. In 1999, the university embarked on a series of "vision dialogues" that gave university stakeholders an opportunity to review its vision statement and to seek more effective ways to enact the vision in educational practice. A revised vision statement resulted: "To build a multicultural learning community founded on academic excellence from which all partners in the educational process emerge prepared to contribute productively, responsibly, and ethically to California and the global community."

Four broad strategic planning themes illustrate the university's core values: a pluralistic academic community, student learning, support for learning, and an engaged campus. Administrators and faculty use the vision as an orienting device—a compass of sorts. "When I see something that doesn't reflect our vision then I'll challenge it," explained an administrator. Another administrator has the vision statement printed on the back of his business cards as a reminder of his commitment. Another said, "Our vision is like a virus. . . . Here everyone gets infected."

Students, staff, and faculty are considered equals. This egalitarian model is rooted in the early years of the university, when everyone had to "roll up their sleeves" and "work on whatever needed to be done." During this period, position or title meant little; faculty members were accustomed to supporting students in the face of a lean student affairs staff. One faculty member expressed the belief that equality is a founding principle of the institution. "This university is about creating a safe and respectful space for learning, where equality is valued." In the process, CSUMB has become an educational sanctuary for many students from the region who have struggled and given up in other postsecondary settings.

> CSUMB's campus sprawls across more than 1,300 acres, just a five-minute drive to the beach. Formerly the site of Fort Ord military base, the grounds are spacious enough so that a majority of students, faculty, and administrators can live on campus.

CSUMB's outcomes-based education (OBE) model places student learning at the center of the institution, replacing the all-too-familiar credit hours and seat time as measures of learning with systematic assessments of authentic student learning. Learning outcomes are explicitly articulated and drive course design, general education and major field requirements, pedagogy, and assessment. Faculty members understand that for OBE to work well they must clearly communicate desired outcomes to students at the beginning of every class to guide student effort. In addition, the university encourages faculty to accept different types of evidence of learning. Although faculty require students to demonstrate their knowledge related to the course outcomes, students may choose to do so in ways consistent with their own learning styles and interests. That is, students may represent their learning by leading class discussions, making presentations, writing papers, taking exams, or contributing to group projects. Assessment is integral to OBE, and the Center for Teaching, Learning, and Assessment provides faculty with tools and guidance to assess student learning effectively. This approach lends itself to increased student-faculty interaction via assessment, promotes active and collaborative learning efforts as students select the best approach to demonstrate their learning, and supports diverse students by allowing students to build from their strengths.

The enthusiasm associated with being a young campus with a great deal of promise is palpable at CSUMB. The pioneering zeal of the founding faculty pushed the development of effective educational programs and fostered a strong sense of ownership for the institution. The president and provost model the institution's values and aspirations to provide a distinctive, high-quality undergraduate education. The energy generated by building a culture of innovation, collaboration, and pluralism contributes to CSUMB's educational effectiveness.

The Evergreen State College: An Authentic Learning Community

Created in 1967 by the Washington State Legislature, Evergreen opened in 1971 as a regional college that featured experimentation, interdisciplinary study, cooperation, and freedom from traditional standards and practices. Its mission changed in the 1980s to recognize and sharpen its focus on the liberal arts. Nonetheless, over the years the college has retained its innovative, iconoclastic spirit, remaining true to its founding principles.

In 1989, the college adopted five foci for teaching and learning to more effectively organize students' academic and social experiences: (1) interdisciplinary learning, (2) learning across significant differences, (3) personal engagement with learning, (4) linking theory to practice, and (5) collaborative learning. The primary means to implement teaching and learning at Evergreen are the Coordinated Study Program, Group Contracts, Individual Learning Contracts, and Internships. Others (Kuh et al., 1991; Tagg, 2003) have described these components, several of which are also described later in this book. Here we briefly summarize salient aspects of the Coordinated Study Program (also known as "the Program"), Evergreen's best-known and arguably most influential pedagogical vehicle to demonstrate why learning is an all-encompassing experience for Evergreen students.

The Program employs a range of effective educational practices that make a substantial claim on student time and energy, both inside and outside the classroom. Instead of a 16-credit course load of four or five different courses, students can enroll in one Program for the full 16 credits of a quarter. The college offers many Program sections for a full year; some run for one or two quarters. The Program, which is akin to a small college, is the locus of community for students, substituting for the primary peer affinity group at most other institutions. A Program typically includes a common reading list, labs, lectures, workshops, individual projects; some include internships. Students and faculty devote all their time and attention at school to this shared work, which usually is organized around a theme or problem and examined from a variety of disciplinary perspectives. No matter the specific focus of a Program, a good deal of reading and writing is required.

> Evergreen's Upside Down Degree program enables students with certain technical degrees to complete a bachelor's degree, inverting the traditional model of general coursework followed by specialized training.

Students regularly participate in small book seminars in which they read and discuss a book related to their program. The seminar discussion format is very different from what most Evergreen students were exposed to in high school or elsewhere. In addition to reading and discussing key texts, the seminar helps students learn how to work together by paying attention to issues of equivalent participation and faculty authority. Seminars also are highly interactive as students customarily take responsibility for the reading and discussion.

Written feedback is another Evergreen cornerstone. The college does not award letter grades. Instead, faculty evaluate student performance by using descriptive narratives. Students respond in kind, providing narrative feedback to faculty about their performance. All this two-way feedback demands a significant amount of reflection and writing on the part of both students and faculty.

Because of its founding ideals and values, the college's academic and management structures and operating philosophy are different from those at most state-supported colleges and universities. An unusual and functional egalitarianism and a special level of caring and community are two more distinctive qualities. Students and faculty members alike are infectiously enthusiastic about their academic and intellectual pursuits. They practice an approach to learning that is so old that it can seem experimental, even radical: students should receive as much individual attention as possible, and in the process assume as much responsibility as possible for their own education.

Fayetteville State University: "Meeting Students Where They Are"

In 1867, seven African American men purchased a small piece of land in Fayetteville, North Carolina, for $136 and built a school to educate African American youth. Over the years, the institution evolved from a school for former slaves to the State Colored Normal School to Fayetteville State Teachers College to, in 1969, Fayetteville State University (FSU). Now part of the University of North Carolina System, the core of its mission has not changed: preparing students who thought college was out of reach to become creative thinkers and societal leaders. Most Fayetteville students (85%) are the first in their families to attend college. More than 70% are African American, 21% are Caucasian, and 4% are Latino. Over 60% come from Cumberland County, FSU's home county. Given that many first-year students come from families whose annual incomes are less than $20,000, most (82%) receive some type of financial aid. A host of integrated programs and services for first- and second-year students designed to promote student success support a core curriculum of liberal arts and professional training.

FSU's Chancellor's Scholars are required to complete a minimum of six hours of community service each week. They work as peer tutors, lab assistants, computer lab helpers, or library assistants. Some are tutors and mentors in Fayetteville's public schools.

One such initiative is FSU's version of the federal TRIO program. (Federal TRIO programs include six outreach and support programs targeted to serve and assist low-income, first-generation college students, and students with disabilities to progress through the academic pipeline from middle school to postbaccalaureate programs.) The Student Support Services (SSS) program is a highly structured and demanding initiative that helps first-generation, low-income, high-risk students meet the academic and personal challenges of college. Students must participate in 20 hours of tutoring per week. SSS also offers a broad range of workshops that address setting goals, managing various forms of test taking and math anxiety, building self-esteem, developing career plans, and cultivating effective study skills. Students have access to several types of tutors, including professional staff and peers. Some of the latter are Chancellor's Scholars—high-performing students who tutor in math, English, and the sciences. One of the groups targeted by the SSS program is the Bronco Cohort. In one recent year, everyone from the Bronco Cohort returned for the sophomore year, and most (82%) achieved at least a 2.0 grade point average. The combination of practices used in SSS—counseling, tutoring, cultural activities, financial assistance—helps create the conditions for student success at FSU and persistence to graduation.

Fayetteville State believes in "meeting students where they are"—which means developing students' talents, regardless of their academic preparation or background. This belief is not expressed explicitly in the mission or philosophy and value statements, but as one faculty member offered, "The majority of faculty members here understand that this is a part of our mission." We say more later about this important theme in FSU's philosophy.

George Mason University: "The Right Place, The Right Time"

Founded as a branch of the University of Virginia, George Mason University (GMU) granted its first baccalaureate degree in 1968. Now the third largest of the fourteen four-year public colleges and universities in Virginia, GMU's total enrollment is approximately 27,000 across three campuses. Approximately half of the 16,000 undergraduates transferred from nearby community colleges. The university's aspirations are made plain in the opening lines of its mission statement: "George Mason University will be an institution of international academic reputation providing superior education enabling students to develop critical, analytical, and imaginative thinking." According to Alan Merton, George Mason's president: "We are in the right place: The nation's capitol region is the epicenter of the world's political web, its information and communications network, and its new economy. We are ready. . . . In an age that demands originality and imagination . . .George Mason will be . . . innovative, resourceful, and responsive, while drawing on the intellectual and cultural heritage of the classical university."

"The Right Place, The Right Time" slogan is emphasized in a variety of university publications, including admissions and marketing pieces. Other key words—"innovative," "resourceful," "diverse"—are more than assertions. Indeed, they animate Mason's living and lived mission.

The diverse student body plays a significant role in creating an enriching educational environment. Mason reflects the world it intends to prepare students for: more than one-third of undergraduates are students of color and 12% are international students. Twenty percent of Mason's first-time freshmen report that English is not their native language, and 7% state their religious preference is Islam.

> GMU's Technology Across the Curriculum initiative redesigned more than 100 courses to incorporate technology.

This blend of ethnicities, ages, and backgrounds creates, as one junior articulated, a "pleasant culture shock" for new students. According to several student leaders, Mason's diverse student population was a huge influence on their choice of—and satisfaction with—the institution. A faculty member noted it is impossible for Mason students to hide from diversity: "We can talk about diversity because our classes are diverse."

Illustrative of Mason's commitment to innovation is its Technology Across the Curriculum (TAC) program. The College of Arts and Sciences developed ten instructional technology goals with input from faculty, students, technology professionals, and prospective employers. More than 100 courses, reaching about 12,000 students, were redesigned to emphasize collaborative learning using information technology, as well as becoming familiar with legal, ethical, privacy, and security issues. In addition, TAC balances the challenges associated with technology use with appropriate support for both faculty and students through the Student Technology Assistance and Resource Center. The program promotes student-faculty interaction and applied learning by employing technologically savvy students to coach and assist faculty with their technology needs.

One factor in George Mason's ability to innovate is because people there still think of the university as "young." GMU has few established traditions which makes organizational and curricular change less contentious. For example, the university undertook a massive curricular reform initiative in less than two years, something that would take most schools much longer to implement. The university's teaching and research emphases, distinctive academic programs, and commitment to diversity contribute to its entrepreneurial spirit of innovation. A junior faculty member told us, "I feel less constrained as [a] faculty member because I have more opportunities to be interdisciplinary and to encourage students to be so. There's so much more room for intellectual growth."

Gonzaga University: Undergraduate Education in the Jesuit Tradition

Gonzaga University is a comprehensive, Jesuit institution located on a 108-acre campus bordering the Spokane River close to downtown

Spokane, Washington's second largest city. Founded as a school for men in 1887, Gonzaga enrolls approximately 3,800 men and women in 92 undergraduate programs. "Inspired by the vision of Christ at work in the world," Gonzaga's mission is distinctly humanistic, Catholic, and Jesuit, emphasizing the development of creativity, initiative, and intelligence within the framework of Christian reflection and interpretation. Gonzaga bases its educational philosophy on the 450-year-old Ignatian model that aims to educate the whole person—mind, body, and spirit—by integrating science and art, faith and reason, action and contemplation.

The foundation of the academic program is the Core Curriculum in the Arts and Sciences. Students complete eleven courses, including English composition, speech communication, mathematics, English literature, a three-course sequence in religious studies, and a four-course sequence in philosophy. The Core contributes to a shared experience for both students and faculty, which reinforces Gonzaga's belief that education and formation are outgrowths of meaningful student-faculty relationships. Other aspects of the curriculum also reinforce Gonzaga's Catholic and Jesuit mission and roots. For example, students in the Honors Sophomore Colloquium partake in a multimedia study of the history of American Catholicism; students in the Junior Colloquium study the poetry of a Victorian Jesuit poet.

In spring 2003, Gonzaga enrolled more than 450 students in 15 service learning courses that produced about 9,400 hours of service to the community.

Another feature of the Jesuit tradition at Gonzaga is an emphasis on service and civic engagement. Each year, 400 to 600 students provide about 30,000 hours of service to the Spokane community and beyond. Some service activities, such as the Honors Program Freshman Colloquium, which includes a 20-hour service component, are directly linked to the academic program. The epicenter for community service is the Center for Community Action and Service Learning (CCASL) which identifies volunteer opportunities and service learning courses, coordinates service projects, matches volunteers with local agencies, and raises funds to support these and related activities. Students plan and deliver every aspect of the operation, including service-learning programs such as alternative spring break. They report gaining practical experience in leadership and decision making and policymaking, as well as forging meaningful relationships with peers, administrators, professors, and Spokane residents.

Longwood University: A Culture of Involvement

Founded in 1839 in Farmville, Virginia, as a private seminary for women, Longwood became a college in 1860 and a normal school for women in 1884. After a succession of name changes, the school became Longwood College in 1949 and Longwood University in 2002. Coeducational since 1976, two-thirds of its 4,000 students are women, and preparing teachers remains a major curricular emphasis.

During the late 1980s, the Longwood faculty discussed its general education requirements extensively, ultimately revising and expanding them by adding foreign language and capstone courses for seniors. In the late 1990s, the State Council for Higher Education in Virginia (SCHEV) implemented a performance indicator system, which pressed Longwood to pursue additional initiatives, including a system to monitor student and institutional performance. At the same time, Longwood worked diligently to connect out-of-class experiences to the academic program in more educationally purposeful ways. The campus now has about 100 student organizations—a high "student-to-opportunity" ratio compared to similar-sized universities. No classes are held on Tuesdays from 3:45 to 5:00 P.M. so that student organizations can meet and other campus committees can conduct their business. As part of the revised general education program, all seniors must take a writing course that addresses issues in developing citizen leadership. A simple but powerful student development concept—"Preparing Citizen Leaders for the Common Good"—is integrated into the general education program and lends itself to efforts to connect the curriculum and cocurriculum.

> Students are assigned to one of the 40 sections of the required Longwood Seminar according to their chosen major, live together in a residence hall with other students in their Seminar, and also take an introductory course in their chosen major during the same term.

A foundational element of the Preparing Citizen Leaders initiative is the Longwood Seminar, a one-semester, one-credit course required for entering students. The course is not unlike the first-year "orientation to college" courses found at many U.S. colleges and universities. However, the Longwood Seminar is unusually effective because of the high degree of cooperation between academic and student affairs, a working relationship that was two decades in the making. About two-thirds of the instructors are faculty, one-third is student affairs staff. Seminar "peer mentors," students who have completed the Longwood Seminar, receive formal training for their role (which involves tutoring students on academic subjects) and work with the faculty and staff in each of the sections for the Seminar. Students in the same Seminar live in campus housing in close proximity and take an introductory course in their chosen major, increasing the likelihood that students who live and spend lots of time together will have some academic content in common.

The result of all these efforts is a campus climate with a tightly knit social fabric, a desirable condition for learning.

Macalester College: Preparing Citizens of the World

Located in a pleasant urban residential neighborhood in St. Paul, Minnesota, Macalester (known as "Mac") is a private liberal arts college with 1,700 students. Since its founding in 1885, the college has maintained rigorous academic standards leavened with an abiding concern for ethical performance and social justice. Four "pillars" constitute Macalester's mission: academic excellence, multiculturalism, internationalism, and service. The college aims to provide a high-quality liberal arts education while making certain that students engage intellectually, socially, and ethically with pressing issues of the larger community and the world. Few courses have prerequisites. Students are encouraged to challenge one another to perform at high levels.

Macalester's commitment to community service and diversity runs broad and deep. Fewer than 70% of the students are what the college describes as domestic white students; 11% of the students are domestic students of color. All 50 states and 78 foreign countries are represented in the student body. More than half of Mac students study abroad in programs emphasizing global citizenship. Many students choose majors with a social justice orientation or public policy component. Macalester is one of ten Project Pericles® pilot schools, an initiative designed to prepare students for socially responsible citizenship. More than 85% of first-year students and 80% of seniors are involved in service. Among several college-sponsored initiatives to promote diversity are internships in the Twin Cities, an annual conference on

> Macalester College's "Into the Streets" event is part of the required first-year seminar, taking students into local neighborhoods to do community service. Half of all students participate in internships; 90% do a senior capstone project.

race, and participation in the Mellon Mays Undergraduate Fellowship Program. The Lealtad-Suzuki Center provides a range of services, including training and development opportunities for faculty, staff, and students pertaining to multiculturalism, intentional multicultural programming, and multicultural education and consultations (http://www.Macalester.edu/lealtad-suzuki/). Other key Center programs include the Hewlett Pluralism and Unity Program, which engages approximately 30 first-year students in dialogues, field trips, and community outreach to advance their understanding of identity development and diversity. Student collectives (Black Women of the Diaspora, Men of Color, for example) provide opportunities for groups of students to talk about diversity issues within their collective and in intergroup dialogue.

Miami University: "An Involving College"

Miami was established by the Ohio General Assembly in 1809 as a college for men and named for the Miami Indian Tribe of the Miami Valley region of Ohio. The site selected for the college was named Oxford, to symbolically connect the institution to the English model of college. Miami's reputation for student involvement in cocurricular activities began soon after, with the establishment of two literary societies in 1825 and founding chapters of several fraternities by 1855. In 1852, it was also the site of the first college football game in Ohio when Miami played what is now the University of Cincinnati.

Today, Miami enrolls about 15,000 undergraduates and 1,300 graduate students in nearly 100 undergraduate majors and almost 60 graduate programs. Its mission statement begins, as do many other statements, with expansive prose about preserving and transmitting knowledge. But then Miami's statement goes on to focus very specifically on undergraduate education: "to provide an environment conducive to effective and inspired teaching and learning. . . . Miami's primary concern is its students [and] to individualize the educational experience. . . . It educates men and women for responsible and informed citizenship, as well as meaningful employment."

The focus on students and their learning and personal development is supported by a wide variety of academic programs and other challenging opportunities beyond the classroom.

The Miami Plan Core Curriculum introduced in 1990 features a substantial liberal arts foundation for all major areas of study made up of a minimum of 48 (about 38%) of the hours needed for graduation. The Plan comprises three sets of learning experiences: (1) foundation courses in humanities, fine arts, social and natural sciences, and "formal reasoning," including a first-year seminar, (2) a thematic sequence of in-depth study outside the majors (a series of typically three related courses, each of which builds on the knowledge and experiences provided in the former), and (3) a senior capstone experience that requires students to integrate liberal learning with specialized knowledge.

Miami consistently ranks among the top 10 universities in the nation for the number of students studying abroad.

In addition to bringing coherence to the curriculum, the Plan is designed to channel student time and effort toward educationally purposeful out-of-class activities. For example, the Plus One Option/Extra Credit Option allows a student, with the agreement of the professor, to add "one extra credit hour" in any Miami Plan Thematic Sequence course (with the exception of foundation courses in sequences) or Capstone if the student engages in service-learning activities that directly connect with the content and objectives of those courses.

Student involvement is a distinctive element in the campus culture. One student indicated that the most successful and satisfied students at

Miami are those who immerse themselves in the life of the campus. Another student observed that, "From a student perspective, involvement is the Miami way." Many students participate in one or more of the hundreds of student organizations and other formal student activities, including volunteering on and off campus. Recreation and physical activity are particularly important; one brochure indicated that more than 10,000 students are part of 1,800 intramural teams in 45 sports. A variety of leadership opportunities are offered under the comprehensive "Miami Leadership Commitment" program coordinated by the Office of Student Affairs.

The combination of in-class and out-of-class activities creates a cultural press that impels Miami students to devote considerable time and energy to their studies and other worthwhile endeavors.

Sewanee, University of the South: Oxford in Tennessee

Located atop the Cumberland Plateau, between Nashville and Chattanooga, is the University of the South, affectionately known as "Sewanee." The picturesque 10,000-acre campus was once described in *The New York Times* as "a bit of Oxford in America." Indeed, the campus *looks* as though it were a nineteenth-century college, complete with Gothic architecture. Sewanee's approach to undergraduate education is very much in accord with the traditional English model. According to the Sewanee catalog, the institution intends: "To develop the whole person through a liberal arts education of high quality. . . . [The college's] aims include training and personal initiative in social consciousness, in aesthetic perception, in intellectual curiosity and integrity, and in methods of scientific inquiry. It endeavors to achieve these objectives with excellence in the context of a small college with a faculty of character and distinction maintaining close personal contact with a carefully selected group of students."

> Sewanee's 10,000 acres of forested campus, "The Domain," with 65 miles of trails and many streams, waterfalls, and beautiful views, is used for a variety of teaching, research, and recreational purposes.

Enrollment in 2003–2004 was 1,364 students with a student-faculty ratio of ten to one. Moreover, because 90% of the students and their professors live in close proximity, they see one another frequently. As one dean put it, "everyone is your neighbor in a figurative sense." A common practice is "the passing hello"—stopping to speak to those you see out and about, whether you know them or not. Anchoring the academic program is a comprehensive core curriculum that has changed little since its inception. All students take math, science, philosophy or religion, English, history, social sciences, fine arts, foreign languages, and physical education. The Sewanee curriculum also features writing; the core includes two writing-intensive courses and writing across the curriculum, encouraged in part by a restructured teaching load introduced in the late 1980s. Faculty typically give students extensive feedback on their writing and exams, a practice that creates additional opportunities for interaction when students seek their teachers to explain notes written in the margins of papers.

Engagement is a way of life at Sewanee. It is a small, intimate community with a clear sense of purpose, coherent values, and a collegial atmosphere. Students and faculty members share a "moral obligation" to make Sewanee an intense, rigorous academic experience. Students want a traditional collegiate experience and find it on a campus that has few outside distractions, such as the absence of cable TV in student residences. From the first week on campus, almost all students get involved in something. The institution instills in its students a sense of collective responsibility for operating important areas of the campus. Students tutor peers at the Writing Center, plan major events, serve on institutional committees and task forces, and hold approximately 700 leadership roles in clubs and organizations.

Sweet Briar College: Intentionally Residential

Sweet Briar College (SBC) is tucked away in the rolling hills of central Virginia, east of the Blue Ridge Mountains, about twelve miles north of Lynchburg and approximately 50 miles south of Charlottesville. The college aims "to prepare women to be active, responsible members of a world community." The curriculum emphasizes liberal arts and sciences to promote the development of critical and creative abilities, prepare students for graduate and professional school, and encourage graduates to continue to learn long after leaving Sweet Briar. General education requirements focus on oral communication, writing, and quantitative reasoning. Its 600 students also must take three writing-intensive courses, one in the major. The college has had a Phi Beta Kappa chapter since 1949. Almost a quarter (23%) of the class of 2001 immediately enrolled in graduate school.

"Intentionally residential," Sweet Briar's philosophy is that the close proximity of students' and faculty members' living and learning provides a superior educational experience. Students are required to live on campus through the senior year, except for the few who live at home with their families. Nearly half of the faculty also lives on campus. Faculty play multiple roles: instructor, career counselor, mentor, and friend. Its many distinctive social clubs and rituals might be the strongest expression of how Sweet Briar constructs its identity as a women's college. The close-knit campus culture almost compels students, faculty members, and staff to weave their personal lives into the academic and intellectual fabric of the college.

As recently as 2004, SBC reaffirmed its commitment to women's education, a liberal arts focus, and a residential student body as part of the development of its current strategic plan. Its holistic philosophy of education is reflected not only through its emphasis on the liberal arts education for women, but via its bountiful leadership and extracurricular offerings that connect students to the institution and one another.

University of Kansas: Balancing Undergraduate Education with Research

The University of Kansas (KU), established in 1866 in Lawrence, was the first university on the Great Plains. The institutional mission identifies five main areas in which the university strives to excel: instruction, service, research, internationalism, and humanitarian values. Research and teaching are declared to be mutually reinforcing with scholarly inquiry underlying and informing the educational experience at undergraduate, professional, and graduate levels.

Over the past decade, the university has emphasized high-quality undergraduate instruction, the product of a deliberate effort to balance

its research and teaching missions. Longtime faculty members characterized this shift as a "sea-change" from several decades ago. The highest

administrative levels reinforce this change in
philosophy, including the provost, who frequently reminds his colleagues that "good
teaching matters," and effective teaching
complements good scholarship and vice
versa. The renewed focus on teaching also is
manifested in institutional practices and
norms, including the expectation that all
executive-level administrators teach at least

University policy regulations
at Kansas require that all
committees (with the
exception of the personnel
committee) have a mini-
mum of 20% student repre-
sentation.

one class each year. Even the Chancellor teaches, symbolizing to faculty
and students KU's commitment to undergraduate education.

In addition, teaching is underscored in new faculty recruitment and
in promotion and tenure decisions at the department and university levels. This message is reinforced during new faculty orientation and
throughout the early months of the academic year. Mentoring and training for graduate teaching assistants (GTAs) is stipulated in union contracts. The Center for Teaching Excellence (CTE) sponsors a wide variety
of programs and services, including an annual fall "teaching summit"
attracting more than a third of the faculty; a Best Practices Institute
(a two-day experience for 10 new faculty); faculty seminars, in which faculty members meet to discuss readings in the scholarship of teaching;
Faculty Fellows and Teaching Grant programs, which provide grants for
research aimed at improving teaching; and support for GTAs, including
a day-long symposium on teaching for GTAs at the beginning of the
school year. Several major teaching awards publicly reward good teaching
including the prestigious $5,000 Kemper Awards made to 20 faculty
members on the first day of fall classes and the senior class HOPE award
presented to a deserving faculty member during halftime of a football
game.

The regional and campus cultures influence KU's focus on student
success. Due in no small degree to the state's populist heritage, a cooperative ethic is almost palpable on campus, undergirding the widely shared
belief that "students come first" and are important, valued participants in

the life of the university. For example, university regulations require that all policy committees (with the exception of the personnel committee) have a minimum of 20% student representation.

In addition, administrators and faculty members embrace an ethic of "going out of your way." People pull together. There is a very strong sense that "we are all in this together." Faculty are willing to "give up a little from their own area" to benefit the whole. This attitude and a willingness to think broadly about the nature of education work together to create an atmosphere of engagement and involvement among students, faculty, and administrators.

University of Maine at Farmington: Values in Action

Designated as Maine's public liberal arts college, UMF is part of the seven-campus University of Maine system. Nestled in rural, western Maine, only 45 minutes from Canada, UMF offers its 2,000 undergraduates a traditional residential collegiate setting typical of small New England colleges. Founded as a normal school in 1864, the college's original mission centered on teacher training grounded in the liberal arts. The institution has since added other majors, but remains proud of its strong tradition in teacher preparation. The university also remains committed to serving students in its region by being "the affordable alternative to a private liberal arts college."

> UMF's Student Work Initiative created jobs for more than half of its students (1,000) on campus, emphasizing two of the university's priorities: maximizing limited resources and connecting students to campus in meaningful ways.

The current focus of the institution emerged in the late 1980s as a result of a spirited period of introspection. Today, substantial agreement exists as to the university's mission and how it should be implemented. Administrators frequently mention UMF's core values—talent development, collegial relations among students and faculty, and scholarly inquiry characterized by collaboration by students and faculty members on research. A senior administrator noted, "We all value the same thing. The maintenance crew is as concerned about student growth and development as the faculty."

More than 80% of UMF students receive some form of financial aid, averaging about $8,500 a year. Because most UMF students must work to pay college expenses, UMF made a conscious decision to emphasize the dignity of work and increase persistence rates by encouraging student employment on campus. Begun in 1998, the Student Work Initiative is a campus-based work-and-learn program to promote student-faculty and student-staff interaction and connect students to the campus in meaningful ways. Students work in a variety of offices and programs, ranging from student services, laboratories, and field research. Now, more than half of all UMF students (1,000) have jobs on campus. Positions are funded by federal work-study, departmental budgets, and the Student Work Initiative program. Departments depend on student workers and value student input. These experiences provide students opportunities to apply what they are learning to practical, real-life situations; introduce students to the world of professional work; and prepare them for what they can expect as they seek employment after graduation.

University of Michigan: A Tradition of Excellence

The University of Michigan's mission is "to serve the people of Michigan and the world through preeminence in creating, communicating, preserving, and applying knowledge, art, and academic values and in developing leaders and citizens who will challenge the present and enrich the future." The university is marked by an intense, achievement-oriented campus culture. Excellence is its watchword. Many Michigan faculty members have received international recognition for their scholarship. Their accomplishments set high performance expectations for students.

Striving for excellence makes perfect sense for a university that attracts bright, highly motivated, and diverse students. Of its 24,500 undergraduates, 87% graduated in the top 10% of their high school class; almost a quarter graduated in the top 1%. So perhaps it is not surprising that 95% of first-year students return for their sophomore year and 82% graduate within five years. Even so, the university can be a confusing, chaotic, and challenging place, rich and varied in intellectual and social opportunities. Students hear long before they arrive on campus that to survive and thrive at Michigan, they will have to take initiative. One dean described the learning environment at Michigan as "boot camp." Student success, he noted, is "dependent on their will to succeed—to go beyond their limits." For this reason, Michigan goes to extraordinary lengths to support its students, both inside and outside the classroom, to meet its high performance standards. As will be explained later (Chapter Six), the university has invested substantial resources to create innovative, responsive, and effective undergraduate education support programs. These include the Undergraduate Research Opportunity Program (UROP), Sweetland Writing Center, and the first-year seminar program, all of which are described later in more detail.

> Michigan's Undergraduate Research Opportunity Program and Scholars Research Program allow dozens of first- and second-year students to work with a faculty mentor on a research project.

Another distinctive feature of the University of Michigan is its uncompromising position in support of affirmative action. Aligning the university's espoused and enacted missions in this way makes the campus fertile ground for students to live out commitments to social responsibility. Here again, Michigan allocates resources to support its values. Among the examples of highly effective initiatives that support diversity are the Ginsberg Center for Community Service and Learning; Arts of Citizenship Program; Intergroup Relations, Conflict, and Community Program; Michigan Learning Communities (that is, 11 residential living-learning centers and programs); Women in Science and Engineering Residential (WISE) program; and the University Mentorship Program.

Michigan's commitment to excellence also is reflected in its will to continually improve. It has, for example, conducted difficult discussions over the past decade about the types of challenge and support that will best foster student independence and high achievement. Faculty and administrators periodically compare Michigan's programs and practices with those at other universities and identify strategies for making the University of Michigan the best it can be.

University of Texas at El Paso: "Two Languages, Two Cultures, Unlimited Opportunities"

In 1913, the Texas legislature established the University of Texas at El Paso as the State School of Mines and Metallurgy. Its original mission was to foster "the economic development of far west Texas and northern

Mexico through education in fields enabling the region to make maximum use of its geological and mineralogical resources." The university was renamed Texas Western College (TWC) in 1949; in 1967, Texas Western College became the University of Texas at El Paso (UTEP).

Twenty-five years ago, UTEP was on a trajectory to become an elite liberal arts–oriented institution appealing primarily to white students from affluent West Texas families. In those days, people often thought the institution aspired to be a "Harvard-on-the-border." But in the mid-1980s, the changing demographics of the region and the growing proportion of Hispanic students enrolling led to a public affirmation of UTEP being a "Hispanic-majority" institution, a label that was initially enormously unsettling to a number of faculty, leaders in the business community, and others, who feared the university would lose prestige and student quality as a result. As we explain in Chapter Six, institutional leaders pressed forward and accelerated plans to welcome and educate the increased number of Hispanic students predicted for West Texas. Now UTEP is the largest institution in the nation with a majority Mexican American student body.

> UTEP's UNIV 1301, a nationally heralded first-year core curriculum seminar, introduces students to an engaging intellectual topic and requires students to assess their academic strengths and areas where they need to improve their skills.

Two institutional mantras represent UTEP's identity: "talent is everywhere, opportunity is not" and "access and excellence." Central to UTEP's mission is a commitment to making higher education accessible and affordable to the people in El Paso and the surrounding region who are geographically isolated with limited economic and educational opportunities.

To work effectively with large numbers of first-generation college students for whom English was a second or third language, the university had to become learner-centered, providing challenging educational programs along with the appropriate academic and social support to meet students' needs. UNIV 1301 is UTEP's signature intervention designed to facilitate students' transition to college by luring students into discovering the rewards of deep learning. Titled "Seminar in Critical Inquiry," the core curriculum course engages students intellectually in an academic topic of their choice while acquainting students with the UTEP campus. All UNIV 1301 classes are small, making it possible for students to work more frequently with others and to get to know their classmates in a setting that values learning. An instructional team of a faculty member, peer leader, and librarian teach each section, emphasizing active learning techniques including "open forums" and group projects. UNIV 1301 faculty members along with the peer leaders meet with all students in their class one-on-one twice during the fall semester to discuss their academic progress and then are expected to follow up with their students the next semester to inquire about their progress.

UTEP has a coherent mission and identity. It redesigned its policies and programs to nurture and support students when and how they need assistance to achieve their educational aspirations. Equally important, the attitudes, values, and routines that constitute the institutional culture also complement UTEP's commitment to helping students from historically underserved groups succeed.

Ursinus College: It's All About Student Achievement

Ursinus College, located in Collegeville, Pennsylvania, is named after Zacharias Ursinus, a 16th-century reformation scholar. Chartered in 1869, the college had historical connections to the United Church of Christ, though now it is an independent, private institution. The total enrollment in 2002–2003 was 1,310 students.

In the late 1980s, Ursinus reshaped itself to be a college fundamentally committed to the liberal arts. At that time, the college was known as "Urscience," primarily for its preprofessional programs. To pursue this new direction, the college recruited faculty members committed to both teaching and an active program of scholarship. In 1991, the faculty voted to enhance the role and visibility of scholarly productivity and revised promotion and tenure criteria to emphasize

All Ursinus students complete an Independent Learning Experience (ILE), such as an independent research or creative project, internship, study abroad, student teaching, or summer fellow program or comparable summer research program.

scholarship in addition to high-quality instruction. This brought about a wave of innovations, including increased opportunities for student-faculty research, a concentrated focus on student achievement, and a common intellectual experience for first-year students.

Today, the mission of Ursinus College is to prepare students to become "independent, responsible, and thoughtful individuals through a program of liberal education. That education prepares them to live creatively and usefully, and to provide leadership for their society in an interdependent world." The Common Intellectual Experience (CIE) was developed to create a challenging, yet supportive learning environment that helps students move from dependent or guided learning to independent learning. Addressing some daunting questions, such as "What does it mean to be human?," CIE provides new students a shared intellectual experience and cultivates critical thinking skills. Interdisciplinary in orientation, it features effective educational practices, such as learning in community, student-faculty interaction, and academic challenge. The positive impact of these emphases is reflected in its scores on the NSSE survey which have increased across the board as CIE has been fully implemented.

To maintain focus, the college features student achievement as a signature emphasis in its publications and in other venues. The college also adopted a "campaign" approach, which underscores the sense of urgency and importance of an institutional goal, to enhance the intellectual vitality on campus. The campaign metaphor for change values innovation and flexibility, empowers faculty, and celebrates achievement by displaying student artwork and faculty activities in its annual summary of summer research projects. Moreover, as one administrator noted, "student achievement governs all kinds of decisions" at Ursinus.

Wabash College: A Male Model of Excellence

Wabash College, located on 55 wooded acres in Crawfordsville, Indiana, was founded as a college for men in 1832. Today, Wabash conveys its mission in a single sentence: "Wabash College educates men to think critically, act responsibly, lead effectively, and live humanely." Five core values capture the college's identity: (1) a rigorous liberal arts education,

(2) personalized teaching and learning, (3) individual responsibility and trust, (4) a socially, economically, and ethnically diverse student body, and (5) a tradition and philosophy of independence. These five key elements of the Wabash mission are evident in virtually all aspects of the college, such as admissions brochures, freshman orientation activities, policy-making, and planning. As an administrator put it, "We're terribly consistent and clear about a few things. And that has a cumulative impact."

Staying true to its mission as a college for men has not been easy. Being a single-sex institution is the college's "greatest hurdle" in recruiting new students, especially as it is one of only a few colleges for men left in the United States. Nevertheless, Wabash uses its single-sex status to create a powerful setting for learning. For example, a faculty member who teaches women's studies commented, "When I teach women's studies, all the students are men, so we can have an enormous educational impact *because* they're all men." Many students told us, "I was not interested in an all-male college, but the visit sold me. The sense of tradition and the feeling of pride—it just felt right."

> Wabash's code of conduct, the Gentleman's Rule, charges each student to conduct himself, at all times, both on and off the campus, as a gentleman and a responsible citizen.

One of the college's enduring traditions is its student conduct code, the Gentleman's Rule. The Gentleman's Rule, in place for more than 50 years, states, "A Wabash student is expected to conduct himself, at all times, both on and off the campus, as a gentleman and a responsible citizen." And that's it; the entire code of conduct for Wabash students is found in this single sentence. This concise, elegant statement has profound implications for virtually all aspects of campus life. Many interpersonal conflicts are handled through negotiation and interpretation of the Gentleman's Rule, which leads to learning on several different levels. First, interpreting what the rule means in a specific situation is an exercise in active and collaborative learning, such as when fraternity members are challenged to examine and account for indiscretions in relation to their responsibilities to the larger campus community. On an individual level, working through the implications of the Gentleman's Rule brings students into direct (if not always comfortable) contact with faculty and administrators, thus adding another dimension to student-faculty interactions. The ambiguities associated with living by the Gentleman's Rule create an environment reflecting in many ways what students will experience after college, where many rules are neither clearly stated nor invariably enforced. Thus, some of the important lessons Wabash men learn are not from books or classroom discussions, but from being held accountable and taking responsibility for their actions.

Since the college's 1992 decision to remain a men's college, this distinctive aspect of the campus ethos has eclipsed all others. During our two campus visits, most students, faculty, administrators, and alumni professed unswerving allegiance to the mission of exclusively educating men. For example, when we asked seniors the one thing they would not change about Wabash, they were unanimous: "I wouldn't change that it's a men's college." The college has reached consensus about the kind of institution it wants to be and resists efforts aimed at revising its mission or altering its niche in higher education. The Wabash community understands its mission and knows how to live it.

Wheaton College (Massachusetts): Making Coeducation Work

Founded in 1834 as a women's seminary in Norton, Massachusetts, Wheaton became coeducational in 1987 in response to concerns about enrollment and maintaining high-quality liberal arts offerings. Many alumnae, faculty, and students opposed the decision to admit men, but through thoughtful, respectful discussion, the college resolved to "do coeducation differently." This included acknowledging that gender roles and gender socialization affect women *and* men, colleges and their curricula, and college students and their experiences. Therefore, the college's new mission explicitly addresses gender: "Wheaton teaches women and men to live and work as equal partners by linking learning, work, and service in a community that values equally the contribution of men and women."

Wheaton's Research Partnership allows faculty members to use work-study funds to hire student research assistants who, in turn, perform a variety of tasks, including entering data, conducting library searches, reading and discussing articles, collecting data, and refining measurement instruments.

Wheaton became "consciously coeducational" and infused into its programs, policies, and practices many of the developmentally powerful elements of a women's college, such as an emphasis on collaboration, nurturing noncompetitive interactions and a supportive campus environment. These key elements served the campus well as it engaged in a self-described "reflective period" after the admission of men. In effect, Wheaton had to decide what it wanted to be and for whom.

To enhance student learning, the college analyzed its strengths and recommitted itself to providing high-quality experiences for all its students. A new "gender balanced" curriculum emphasizes making connections—across subject matter, among faculty, and between faculty and students. For example, art history courses consider the gendered nature of who produced art, and who were the audiences for art. Moreover, according to faculty and administrators, "Our students just eat this up." In addition, Wheaton aspires to become a center for new scholarship on women, an intentional effort to maintain connections with its history as a women's college. Wheaton further enriches the learning environment by offering many research opportunities for students, such as the Wheaton Research Partnership, which provided work-study funds to faculty members to hire 24 undergraduate research assistants in 2003.

Members of the Wheaton "family"—faculty, students, staff, and graduates—are committed to and value collegial, collaborative relations. Whether regarding a major shift, such as a change in the college's mission or curriculum, or day-to-day communication about the business of the college, Wheaton emphasizes and values the individual's contributions to the whole. The message is clear: everyone is welcome at the table.

Winston-Salem State University: "Enter to Learn, Depart to Serve"

Winston-Salem State University is a public university with a primary mission to offer high-quality educational programs at the baccalaureate level for its predominantly black student population. For decades, WSSU was perceived as the "little college on the hill." In the shadow of nearby institutions such as Wake Forest, Salem College, and North Carolina School of the Arts, WSSU got "lost in the shuffle." Now the university is recognized as a vibrant place and receives accolades from many quarters for the quality of education it provides. For example, the NCAA recently recognized WSSU for significant improvements in graduation rates of student-athletes.

WSSU's Lamb to Ram Pinning Ceremony initiates first-year students into the Ram Family. Following speeches by the Chancellor, Miss WSSU, and other dignitaries, the first-year "Lambs" walk through the Arches for good luck.

Winston-Salem State University's motto, "Enter to learn, depart to serve," is featured prominently on university brochures, recruitment pamphlets, and attractive, eye-catching placards placed on high-rise street posts on and near the campus. The motto represents the university's educational philosophy and expectations—that those who enter through its gates be open to learning and be willing to repay the debt they owe to society for the privileges of freedom and education. Toward that end, WSSU focuses considerable institutional effort to helping students develop leadership skills based on a firm academic and social foundation. All new students and transfer students with fewer than 30 credit hours must enroll in one of three new student adjustment courses: freshman seminar, honors colloquium, or nursing strategies (intended for students who will major in nursing). Freshman seminars at WSSU are similar in structure and program to orientation to college courses at many other institutions. The full-semester, one-credit-hour course focuses on transition, including evaluation of student abilities and development of study skills. Instructors also mentor and advise the 20 or so students in their section. Following their training, they meet every other week to discuss how the course is going and to share ideas. An administrator described the freshman seminar as vital to student success at WSSU: "If we can prepare first-year students, equip them with what they need to know about the university, they'll have a better chance of success."

Woven into the fabric of WSSU is an abiding commitment to care for and support students. At the same time, "rigor" and "challenge" are key concepts in the university's history and its contemporary lexicon. Reinforcing the university's tradition of demanding high academic achievement, Chancellor Dr. Harold L. Martin Sr. recently wrote, "Our faculty take great pride in molding the minds of our students in nationally accredited academic programs so that they are well prepared to assume leadership roles in their fields of study and in their communities."

Wofford College: Continuity of Purpose and Leadership

Chartered in 1851 as a liberal arts college for men, Wofford College is named for Benjamin Wofford, whose $100,000 gift founded the institution in Spartanburg, South Carolina. The first class entered in 1854 and Wofford has operated continuously since then on its original campus. Affiliated with the South Carolina Conference of the United Methodist Church, Wofford was one of 10 colleges from the South, including Duke and Vanderbilt, that met in 1895 to form the Southern Association of Colleges and Schools. During the 40-year presidency of Henry Nelson Snyder, the college grew in size and stature, a trend recognized with the awarding of a Phi Beta Kappa chapter in 1941 (the first chapter at an independent college in South Carolina).

A master plan set in motion in 1987 called for significant new investments in all facets of college life, including new and renovated facilities, endowment for scholarships and professorships, state-of-the-art teaching technologies, and additional support for the campus ministry and volunteer programs. In the past decade, the college introduced interdisciplinary learning communities, adopting an effective pedagogy consistent with its residential liberal arts college roots.

One example of interdisciplinary pedagogy at Wofford is the "Novel Experience." All first-year students are sent a common reading prior to their arrival on campus. Then, students write a short reflective essay about the novel. The college publishes some of the most provocative responses along with photos of the student authors in a glossy, high-quality booklet distributed to all first-year students. Students, faculty, and administrators

Wofford's first-year students read Charles Johnson's *Middle Passage* prior to starting college in fall 2002. After arriving, they wrote a short essay relating their life to that of the main character, Rutherford Calhoun. Eight essays were subsequently published along with photos of the student authors in a glossy booklet distributed to all first-year students.

dine together in local restaurants to discuss the readings. The program acculturates new students to college-level academic norms and expectations and sets the tone for academic excellence and challenge, while connecting faculty, students, and administrators around a meaningful academic experience. As one administrator explained, "Publishing the student essays created the first celebrities in the first-year class." Thus, status at Wofford is obtained by excellent academic performance.

Wofford's mission and philosophy embrace the importance of teaching and fuel student-faculty contact. A faculty member said that he comes to work every day "expecting to be interrupted" by his students and his colleagues. This is not a pejorative statement or complaint. Rather, it is a widely accepted norm and a way Wofford extends the reach of the classroom to learning outside of class. Campus norms encourage students, faculty, and staff to interact as equals, leading most to repeatedly refer to Wofford as a "family." The family metaphor connotes the genuine affection faculty, staff, and administrators have for their students.

Mission-Related Challenges

We began this chapter with the assertion that, despite their great differences, the missions of DEEP schools have two characteristics in common: (1) their educational purposes and aspirations are clearly articulated and widely shared, and (2) the mission informs both complex institutional decisions and daily activities of community members. In addition, the operating philosophies of DEEP institutions—"how we do things here"—are consistent with their missions and form a coherent rationale for institutional policies and practices. The introductions to the 20 DEEP colleges and universities provide a context for understanding the institutions and their practices and, more important, highlight the ways in which their missions, philosophies, cultures, and people are aligned to foster student success.

A caveat is appropriate, however: Do not assume consistency and coherence mean absence of disagreement or contested terrain. Not every person at every DEEP school embraces or endorses without reservation the direction the institution is headed. DEEP colleges are not without controversy about important educational matters. Many, if not most, people on these campuses understand, and agree with, what their school is and wants to be. Strong differences of opinion often exist about how to achieve these aspirations. We turn next to the ways in which DEEP schools deal with these challenges.

MAKING SPACE FOR DIFFERENCE

As with other colleges and universities, DEEP institutions experience tensions and disagreements about institutional aspirations and priorities. Some issues, such as striking an appropriate balance between teaching and research, can quickly galvanize parties into staking out all-too-familiar positions that inhibit or foreclose alternative interpretations or reconciliation efforts. These issues are rarely—if ever—resolved.

To varying degrees, all 20 DEEP colleges and universities face such challenges. To deal with this common, predictable phenomenon of dissenting voices, DEEP schools make space for people to hold different and sometimes conflicting views. In this way, community members can be productive while pursuing goals and aspirations that differ from those of the mainstream.

The most common approach these institutions use to deal with differences of opinion and competing views of institutional priorities is public discussion about institutional aims and values (Tierney, 1993). Faculty leaders and senior administrators often take the lead in such dialogues to keep differences from festering and paralyzing institutional functions. When done well, public conversations strengthen academic values and remind colleagues of their responsibilities to encourage and model reasoned discourse about complicated matters and differences of opinion. Specific issues about which the DEEP colleges make space for dialogue include (1) balancing the priorities and demands of teaching and research, (2) maintaining a clear, shared sense of mission, and (3) developing pluralistic learning environments for students. These issues surface periodically and are considered in more detail in Chapter Thirteen.

MISSION CLARITY: "TELL ME AGAIN— WHAT ARE WE ABOUT?"

Because institutional missions are written and prominently featured, they appear to be fixed in stone. But accepting this proposition is risky. Missions do change, sometimes intentionally (as was seen in the case of UTEP and Wheaton), and sometimes because people stopped paying attention and drifted off course to pursue their individual intellectual interests. DEEP schools are different in this regard. Most are quite vigilant about making certain the institution is doing what it claims to do, and doing it at the highest level of effectiveness possible.

Macalester is a case in point, as community members reinterpret the college's mission in the context of contemporary issues. Perhaps this is because, in part, people realize and cherish the fact that Macalester's mission symbolized by the four pillars of its mission—academic excellence, multiculturalism, internationalism, and service—are *not* empty assertions. To the contrary, they guide thought and action on a daily basis. Students, for example, noted recent campuswide conversations about the relevance of two of the pillars, academic excellence and service. The entire campus was invited to a Saturday afternoon discussion on the values stated in the mission statement. The goal of the discussion was to reaffirm these values—as a community—or change them. Though about 400 people attended the meeting, few were students. A listserv was started as a way to initiate more thoughts from a broader group of campus community members. Snippets of comments from the listserv suggest varied interpretations of the pillars and their importance to Macalester:

Academic excellence. Educational excellence would include academic excellence and rigor as traditionally viewed, but also would stress the development of the whole person and the lives of all people on campus [including] the development of healthy relationships between and among students, faculty, staff, and alumni.

Service. While service to society was generally viewed as a core value, this term was felt to need substantial clarification. Most agreed that valuing service would mean, as one participant put it, "responsibility to myself as well as to the community and society, to give in service." Some suggested alternative terms such as social or civic responsibility. Others thought perhaps service was viewed too narrowly if it refers only to volunteering, when it should include the pursuit of careers that serve society such as teaching or working at the United Nations.

A committee of faculty, staff, and students used the information from the listserv and the Saturday discussion to compose a statement of core values. Macalester's mission statement stayed the same, but the words in the statement became more clearly defined in the minds of students, faculty, and staff. As with other such exchanges, settling matters for once and for all was not the goal. Instead, by sharing perspectives and preferences about what the college should be and aspire to, the Macalester community kept the mission alive and the institution on track to achieve its educational purposes.

Similar intense discussions animated the Gonzaga campus in 2003. The discussions focused on the institution's aspirations, and were prompted in part, by what would appear to be a happy situation: growing enrollments. Some believed Gonzaga should be satisfied with its identity as a regional Catholic university and focus on this niche. Others wanted the institution to develop a national reputation, taking advantage of the recent success and visibility of its men's basketball team. Issues central to the debate were academic quality and the core values of a Gonzaga education in the Jesuit tradition. Faculty, students, administrators, and graduates care deeply about Gonzaga and its ideals. Out of heated discussion and quiet reflection emerged greater understanding of different points of view and renewed commitment to the institution and its students. As one administrator explained, "Despite the tensions and rifts, all the parties care about GU and our students, which is the glue that keeps us together." Because of grappling with these issues, the university has a clearer sense of its mission and purpose.

SUMMARY

All 20 of the DEEP institutions face challenges similar to those of other colleges and universities, challenges that if left unaddressed could derail their commitment to student success. That they have not allowed that to occur is noteworthy, and their strivings offer useful examples for other colleges and universities who wish to focus—or refocus—on effective educational practices throughout the institution. Instead of undermining the institution's progress, the periodic expression of these differences—and the ways in which these differences are aired and addressed—contribute to the clarity of purpose common to DEEP schools and maintain the focus on student learning.

WHAT'S NOTEWORTHY ABOUT A LIVING MISSION AND LIVED EDUCATIONAL PHILOSOPHY

- Some DEEP institutions have deviated little from their original mission, whereas others adopted new or revised missions or expanded their educational purposes. Common to all is a focus on student success consistent with institutional values, traditions, and educational purposes.

- Institutional values really do guide actions at DEEP schools. Not everyone in the institution readily articulates these values using the same words, nor are they necessarily exhorted by all campus groups. However, key institutional leaders frequently remind people what their institution holds to be important.

- DEEP schools go to great lengths to make their missions, values, and aspirations transparent and understandable to their constituents.

- The larger DEEP universities rely on an operating philosophy that values students and their success in attempting to manage in educationally purposeful ways the challenges posed by their size, multiple educational purposes, and organizational complexity.

- DEEP colleges make space for those who have different aspirations and values and wish to express different views. Under the right conditions, public discussion of tensions and disagreements helps sharpen the institution's focus.

- Though the missions, operating philosophies, and organizational and structural characteristics of DEEP schools vary, all have developed complementary policies and practices tailored to the school's mission and students' educational and social needs, interests, and abilities. An essential element of these policies and practices is their steadfast focus on student learning, a topic we address next.

Exhibit 2.1. Answers to Educationally Effective Colleges Quiz.*

1. Alverno College
2. California State University at Monterey Bay
3. The Evergreen State College
4. Fayetteville State University
5. George Mason University
6. Gonzaga University
7. Longwood University
8. Macalester College
9. Miami University
10. Sweet Briar College
11. University of Kansas
12. University of Maine at Farmington
13. University of Michigan
14. Sewanee: The University of the South
15. University of Texas at El Paso
16. Ursinus College
17. Wabash College
18. Wheaton College
19. Winston-Salem State University
20. Wofford College

*It is possible that institutions in addition to those listed here can also be "correct" answers to some questions.

3

An Unshakeable Focus on Student Learning

VIRTUALLY ALL COLLEGES claim to be committed to student learning. However, just as not all espoused missions are enacted, many colleges do not live up to their own exhortations. DEEP schools do, to an impressive degree. An emphasis on holistic student learning runs broad and deep in institutional policies and practices. This is no accident. Community members are selected for their commitment to student success and effective educational practices. More important, most connected with the enterprise—faculty, administrators, staff, and students—are encouraged to be both learner *and* teacher. Four streams of practice characterize the learning environments at DEEP colleges: (1) valuing undergraduate student learning, (2) experimenting with engaging pedagogies, (3) demonstrating a cool passion for talent development, and (4) making time for students.

Most DEEP schools have programs to develop the academic and cocurricular needs of their students; they also have enrichment programs, such as honors offerings, as do hundreds of other schools. The key difference is that the holistic, talent development philosophy of DEEP colleges does not favor one approach or the other. Both are seen as worthy of faculty and staff time and energy, and the performance of students in both groups is celebrated.

VALUING UNDERGRADUATES AND THEIR LEARNING

By definition, small colleges such as Ursinus, Alverno, Wofford, Sewanee, Sweet Briar, and Wabash are supposed to concentrate on undergraduate students and their learning. However, as the experiences of DEEP universities illustrate, this focus is possible for large institutions as well.

Though teaching does not automatically lead to student learning and personal development, approaches to teaching can be more effective at engaging students and enhancing their learning. DEEP institutions recognize this and place a high priority on promoting high-quality teaching. For example, the "sea change" that occurred at Kansas to emphasize undergraduate instruction included assigning experienced, highly skilled teachers to lower division and introductory courses whenever possible. Faculty members in each academic unit serve as "faculty ambassadors" to advocate faculty needs and concerns to the Center for Teaching Excellence and lead discussions on instructional issues with their colleagues. In addition, course enrollments are kept low in a high percentage of undergraduate courses; 80% of undergraduate classes have 30 or fewer students, and 93% have 50 or fewer students. One way Kansas does this is by offering a few huge enrollment classes, which we will describe later in this chapter.

George Mason's Center for Teaching Excellence (CTE) and the Instructional Resource Center (IRC) offer many opportunities for faculty to improve their teaching. The CTE, established in 2001, grew out of Mason's emphasis on experimentation and the critical role faculty development plays in fostering innovations in teaching. As one administrator noted, although GMU "recruits entrepreneurial, risk-taking faculty," the university assumes "if you expect someone to do something, you have to expect to teach them how." Faculty development efforts at George Mason include workshops on topics such as understanding GMU students ("Your students are not you and at Mason, that's even more true") and "survival skills" (for example, learning objectives, evaluation, pedagogy) for faculty new to teaching.

Michigan's priorities for enhancing the quality of undergraduate education are enumerated in the President's Commission Report on the Undergraduate Experience (2002):

1. Make the campus more interconnected, integrated, and permeable.

2. Connect students to the community and the world.

3. Treat the undergraduate career as a life-course journey, both intellectually and socially.

4. Equip undergraduates with good maps and good guides for their journey.

5. Create a student community that is diverse, inclusive, adventurous, and self-reflective.

6. Provide resources and nurture practices that renew the faculty commitment to undergraduate education and enhance faculty-student interaction. [pp. 11-14]

The university demonstrates its commitment to achieving these goals by substantial investment in an array of innovative and responsive programs to enhance student learning. In a recent three-year period, the university committed $3 million to develop new interdisciplinary courses for undergraduate and graduate students. In addition, the provost has a $10 million discretionary fund to support innovative initiatives directed toward improving undergraduate education.

The projects and programs supported by these funds touch a significant proportion of Michigan undergraduates in meaningful ways. Among those that affect large numbers of students are the Undergraduate Research Opportunity Program (UROP); the Sweetland Writing Center; the First-Year Seminar Program; the newly adopted College of Engineering Curriculum 2000; the Ginsberg Center for Community Service and Learning; the Arts of Citizenship Program; the Intergroup Relations, Conflict, and Community Program; the Michigan Learning Communities (11 residential living-learning centers and programs); Women in Science and Engineering Residential (WISE) program; various undergraduate life science initiatives; the University Mentorship Program; the Center for

Research on Learning and Teaching (CRLT); and the Comprehensive Studies Program (CSP).

One manifestation of Miami's commitment to improving undergraduate education is the Faculty Learning Community (FLC), cross-disciplinary faculty groups of 5 or more faculty members (8 to 12 is the recommended size) who take part in year-long programs to examine issues related to the scholarship of teaching and learning (http://www.units. muohio.edu/flc/what.shtml). Each FLC participant identifies a specific course to improve, discusses ways to make improvements, and implements changes in the course during the academic year. Some FLCs are theme-based, focusing on such issues as cooperative learning, ethics across the curriculum, team teaching, humanities disciplines and technology, and small groups to enhance learning. Other cohort-based communities focus on preparing future faculty and addressing needs of junior faculty, mid-career faculty, and department chairs. Other groups explore problem-based learning and teaching portfolios and course assessment strategies. During its 20-year history, more than one-third of the current faculty has participated (about 10 percent in the most recent year); this level of involvement gives broad-based legitimacy to efforts to enhance student learning.

Capital priorities also can demonstrate the value of undergraduate teaching and learning. Steadfast in its commitment to develop a comprehensive approach to improving undergraduate education, the University of Texas at El Paso (UTEP) successfully lobbied for state funds to construct its Undergraduate Learning Center (ULC), a vibrant campus crossroads replete with state-of-the-art technology and multimedia resources. Its learner-centered technology is a magnet for faculty and students alike. The Center for Effective Teaching and Learning (CETaL) offers workshops on instructional techniques, including problem-based learning and techniques for cooperative learning. UTEP's University College was created to assist students in the transition to college. Described by one staff member as a "hybrid of student and academic affairs," it coordinates a host of programs and services (for example, admissions, financial aid, orientation, registrar, academic advising). Specific University College programs include University Studies, which coordinates learning communities (two or three courses intentionally linked for the same cohort of students), and

University 1301: Seminar in Critical Inquiry, a three-hour core curriculum course required of all first-year students.

By focusing human and financial resources on programs and initiatives designed to enhance teaching, DEEP universities have demonstrated their commitment to undergraduate learning, an area that often poses a challenge at other large, research institutions.

EXPERIMENTING WITH ENGAGING PEDAGOGIES

As previously stated, teaching and learning do not go hand in hand in that teaching does not necessarily lead to learning. Indeed, over the past two decades a discernible shift from a focus on teaching to an emphasis on student learning has taken place in many corners. A key element supporting the shift is systematic use of active and collaborative pedagogies. These activities include classroom-based problem solving, peer tutoring, service learning and other community-based projects, internships, and involvement in a variety of educationally purposeful activities outside of class. What all these activities have in common are opportunities for students to practice what they are learning in the classroom, develop leadership skills, and work with people from different backgrounds. Many of these activities are easier to arrange when class sizes are reasonable—20 to 30 students. At the same time, active and collaborative learning activities can be applied successfully in large classes. Baxter Magolda's (1999) work from large classrooms demonstrates how, for example, interactive lectures emphasizing experiential examples and actual data can get students to connect to the course and the content. DEEP schools offer many examples of using engaging pedagogies inside and outside the classroom to foster student learning.

Active and Collaborative Learning

The learning environment at Evergreen State seems to be one long uninterrupted collaborative learning experience. A key vehicle for this experience is "seminaring" (Evergreen shorthand), a learned approach in which students practice bringing to bear multiple points of view on a problem, discuss readings, and engage with their peers in spirited discourse. As one new student told us, "I learn the most in seminar. When I've done all my readings and have thought about my questions and views on the topic, I get a lot out of it." A first-year student suggested that seminars are central to the learning environment and that it is important to learn how to do "seminaring" well. "Seminaring is a science here," he asserted, and faculty and peers help teach newcomers how to do it. One junior explained: "The instructor asks us to talk about the quality of the seminar throughout the course." Faculty members foster students' speaking and listening skills in seminars. "They [faculty members] stressed that it is important for us to feel comfortable talking and emphasized ways to help people feel comfortable talking in seminar." A first-year student mentioned that in one of his programs, "We did retreats, community building . . . we broke barriers in the beginning of the quarter so we would feel more comfortable in seminar." We observed one seminar where students continued the discussion beyond the stated end of the class. Afterward, students told us they did not want to cut short the conversation because some of the most interesting comments are made at the end of class.

"Necessity is the mother of invention" at Fayetteville State University (FSU). "Most faculty seek to involve students because traditional approaches simply don't work" with FSU students. "To be successful, you have to enjoy experimenting with different instructional methods—i.e., discussion boards, games and contests, assigning points, etc." These statements illustrate a willingness to experiment with a variety of innovative pedagogies, most of which reflect active and collaborative learning strategies. Faculty members in the College of Business, for example, require students to evaluate one another's group projects. Following the evaluations, students must list what they have learned from the process. One faculty member summarized the importance of experimentation in the classroom when he stated, "If you don't engage students, you quickly lose them." FSU faculty members understand the needs of their students and recognize the benefit of keeping students actively engaged in learning in and outside the classroom.

Sweet Briar connects students' in-class and out-of-class experiences so that students can put into practice what they are learning in real-life

Students in one Evergreen class decided to give each member 10 beans, with the idea being that a bean be surrendered for each contribution to the discussion as a way of monitoring one another's participation. Once a student's 10 beans were gone, they couldn't contribute any more that day. The day we observed, the class was abuzz with different groups reporting on their discussion. Some talked straight from the assigned readings, others incorporated experiences and information from other classes. One woman, who already offered a number of pithy observations, prefaces her next comment with, "My beans are almost up now." Another who said relatively little offers up some of her beans. Still another less talkative student opens with, "I had better use up some of my beans. . . ." This goes on for more than 90 minutes. Close to the ending time, the faculty member says, "I see people packing up; my sense is that we're done." Two students voice their objection, "No, let's hear from the last group." The last group briefly summarizes their work. The faculty member then asks, "How did we do on our process?" One student tells another, "You seemed quiet today." The student responds, saying that she felt that she talked too much last week and was trying to let others respond today. Another student comments that he "liked the challenge of today's discussion . . . I don't think we needed the beans today." By the end of the class almost everyone has contributed at least once.

situations. Faculty members model how to do this. One English instructor, for example, asked his students to write a poem and set it to music. To model the learning process, he then wrote a poem, set it to music, and performed it with the college chamber orchestra at a spring concert. Another example is the marketing seminar where students design and implement a marketing research strategy for a campus operation. In 2003, the client was the SBC bookstore.

University of Texas at El Paso faculty also understand that many of their students must be taught how to get the most out of active and collaborative learning activities. It starts in UNIV 1301, a course that emphasizes collaboration, teamwork, and active learning. New students receive very direct messages about how to learn effectively. One faculty member tells students: "I want you to learn to be interdependent. You have to meet outside of class. You have to find out each other's schedules." He emphasizes preparation and practice: "You need to use PowerPoint for your presentation and practice at least an hour. In your group presentation you need to be clear about who will say what." He provides criteria for evaluating the group presentation and notes that the group will get one grade. The same instructor uses a scavenger hunt to help students get to know the campus and the services and resources available to them. The activity requires students to meet and talk with faculty and staff across the campus.

Active learning is the norm at Longwood University. A business communications class, for example, engages students with unusual teaching methods: "In one class we used hula hoops to learn a concept; in another we threw balls over a building." Another business school activity is the Lancer Student Investment Fund, where a faculty advisor and local broker advise students who manage $250,000 of the university's portfolio. The activity brings abstract concepts to life, giving students practice by making presentations to the Longwood University Board and Longwood Foundation. Other examples of engaging pedagogy at Longwood include the American literature class that takes field trips related to the twelve novels read in the course, a chemistry professor who gives students red and green cards to indicate if they agree or disagree with questions posed in class, and another faculty member who established a "board of directors" for his class to give him feedback including changes in course assignments to more actively engage students.

Alverno's arrangement of classroom tables and chairs into small work groups allows students to work intensely with peers and their instructors. For example, in a literary criticism class students worked in small groups of four to six to discuss the characteristics of four different literary frameworks while the faculty member circulated to all the groups. Group projects and peer evaluation are intentionally structured into the first two years of the curriculum. "You have to demonstrate your understanding through a group project. You're evaluated by the instructor and your peers as a team and as an individual. Peer evaluation is so much a part of the process here. Sometimes it's formal, sometimes it's informal," explained a senior.

Electronic Technologies and Active Learning

DEEP schools use electronic technologies to engage students with their teachers, peers, and coursework, both in and out of classrooms. Used appropriately, instructional technology can increase the amount of time a student spends on a given subject. For example, a face-to-face course that incorporates the use of a course Web site filled with additional references, resources, or online exercises may encourage a student to spend more time on the course outside of the classroom. This additional contact time helps move course concepts from short-term memory into the more stable long-term memory (Bruning, Schraw, Norby, & Ronning, 2004).

California State University at Monterey Bay (CSUMB) faculty frequently incorporate multimedia to enliven the presentation of new material and to allow students opportunities to practice and apply what they are learning. As at many campuses, course management software such as Blackboard or WebCT is commonly used along with digital technology, making it possible for students to access subject matter in remote locales such as archeological sites.

The University of Maine at Farmington (UMF) implemented several technology initiatives through its EXCEL (Excellence through Connected and Engaged Learning) program, a dual platform, wireless computing and computer lab project that supports technology to improve instruction. EXCEL is intended to raise expectations for student learning, encourage student-faculty interaction, and help create deeper, more meaningful connections among courses and between students and faculty. As one faculty member put it, EXCEL turns "faculty loose to let their creative minds play." Some composition classes use Blackboard so that students can post suggested readings online for other students along with drafts of their written assignments for immediate feedback from the professor and peers. They also participate in online critiques and group editing tasks. Consistent with the institution's philosophy for giving students both financial support and a great deal of responsibility, and expecting them to apply their learning in real-world settings, EXCEL employs students as tutors and technology troubleshooters. Mini-grants for technology applications for elements of courses are available with more than 30 awarded in the first couple of years of the program. The annual EXCELebration provides a showcase for ways technology is used in teaching and learning, including an environmental audit of UMF, "discussion boards" to address common class questions, photo essays on international travel, and course-related Web pages. A student participating in a recent EXCELebration demonstrated a Web page for a comparative politics course, noting, "I learned way more from doing this than if I'd done a research paper."

DEEP institutions are committed to infusing technology into the curriculum to benefit student learning. Moreover, these institutions have devoted time and resources to training faculty and students to ensure the success of the initiatives. For example, Miami hosts an annual Learning, Technology Summer Institute, while George Mason University provides regular training and support to faculty through its STAR (Student Technology Assistance and Resource) Center (described further in Chapter Eleven).

Engaging Students in Large Classes

Effective pedagogies can be adapted to large classes, or courses at the gateway to fields, such as introductory mathematics and science, which typically have higher rates of failing grades or withdrawal than small classes (Gainen, 1995). As mentioned earlier, the University of Kansas (KU) created a few "super-size" undergraduate classes to enable certain departments to continue to offer a reasonable number of smaller classes as enrollment increased. However, instead of retaining a lecture format in the super-size classes, KU adapted various active learning pedagogies. For example, Business 240—Financial Accounting I enrolls about 400 students and meets in a vast auditorium. At the beginning of the class we observed, students divided into small groups and got to work verifying the number of light poles on the KU football field and calculating the annual cost to illuminate the field. As they organized to collect data across campus, students talked about how to calculate depreciation and post revenue. Students told us that such activities were a regular element of the course. In addition, the instructor incorporates some form of technology for most lectures to maintain students' attention on key concepts, requires class attendance, and holds students accountable by giving a quiz almost every week. Because students are never sure when quizzes will be given, or at what point in the class meeting (at the beginning of class, in the middle), they tend to show up for class and stay for the entire session. The instructor also uses short videos and other interactive displays, and moves the video camera around the classroom to make the class feel small. The camera occasionally catches someone who is dozing (an embarrassment that tends to keep almost everyone awake!). One of the graduate teaching assistants affirmed that the video camera and computer technology are vital to the effectiveness of the course: "You can't set up with an overhead in a class this big, and expect to hold students' attention."

Active and collaborative learning are "part of the DNA" of CSUMB: one of its founding principles was to incorporate effective educational practice throughout the curriculum. As the provost put it: "We don't do lectures . . . [we] do active learning, problem solving." CSUMB actively recruits and rewards faculty who buy into this pedagogical approach. For example, "Math Huge" was designed to instruct regular math classes of 60 to 90 students through a collaborative and technologically enriched format.

CSUMB's director of the Center for Teaching, Learning, and Assessment works closely with faculty to make sure they have a clear understanding of the value of active and collaborative learning, as well as command of approaches to execute them effectively. Care is taken to be sure everyone understands that active and collaborative pedagogies when used effectively require considerable knowledge, sensitivity, and skill on the part of the instructor and practice by students. Indeed, students sometimes complain that they do all the work and that instructors do not teach. A CSUMB science professor shared one such story. One of his students told him, "You instructors don't teach us; you make us learn it ourselves." This student went on to get a job based on the skills and knowledge she had developed through her service learning project, and the benefits of her classroom experience became apparent. Looking back on her experience, a CSUMB alum explained, "This place understands that most learning is between students. . . . Not everyone can learn from lectures. I learned the most when I had to work on group projects in and outside of class." Another graduate described the powerful learning experience that can occur when students form learning relationships with their peers. "When I found a partner to study with and got to know my classmates, I had a connection. . . . I found someone else who understood my struggle. . . . Since in groups you just don't talk about homework or the test, you talk about home, and share about yourself. . . . It was a tremendous support for me."

A CSUMB education faculty member commented that some students assume mistakenly that the use of active and collaborative learning is all process and no content. However, when she gave them a study guide for an upcoming test, the students realized that they actually *had* learned the material through their discussions and group projects. Students acknowledged that this approach could be deceptive, because they learn without realizing how much.

Learning in the Company of Peers Outside the Classroom

Engaging pedagogies at DEEP schools are not limited to interactions between students and faculty or to in-class learning. Students are actively engaged in the teaching and learning of their peers. At Wofford, working with classmates on class assignments both in and outside of class is the norm. "Some of my profs insist on group work, in class and out. . . . But I usually study with people anyway, especially for tests," explained a junior. A senior clarified, "Faculty encourage group work, but there is not much assigned." Even so, students study together regularly. Six students in a religion seminar told us they often get together to order pizza, and then watch and talk about the films assigned for the class discussion. Wofford's learning community class schedule, in which students spend most of Tuesday and Thursday in their seven-credit-hour class, allows ample time to take advantage of the power of peers by having students spend large blocks of time together on field trips and overnight experiences. One example is the "Cosmology" learning community (which links physics and humanities courses) that went to the Pisgah Astronomical Research Institute to learn about the satellite-tracking station and make astronomical observations.

At Michigan, expectations for forming study groups to discuss class readings and work collaboratively with classmates outside of class are communicated to new students during orientation. A senior noted, "My study group is also my social group." Granted, it is sometimes challenging for students to create study groups in large classes where they have few occasions to get to know their classmates. To address this concern, Michigan created the Comprehensive Studies Program (CSP), a learning community that provides support services to more than 2,000 undergraduates and offers "enriched classes" that meet an additional hour each week for group study, and the Science Learning Center where study groups and tutors are coordinated for students.

DEMONSTRATING A COOL PASSION FOR TALENT DEVELOPMENT

Undergirding an institutionwide commitment to student learning is a "cool passion" for making the necessary changes in institutional policies and pedagogical practices to help students realize their potential. In *The Modern American College,* Chickering (1981, pp. 782–783), borrowing from Hegel, emphasizes that passion is associated with all significant accomplishments. However, he offers this caveat: "Frenzied, unbridled passion, whether in love or work, seldom serves us well. Indeed, it often harms more than helps. To be inflamed, carried away, by an affection, ideology, or cause is easy, but such a state shrinks from reflective thought, public scrutiny, and tough-minded testing. Maintaining a steady fire that is critical as well as creative is more difficult, especially when it suffers frequent doses of icy logic and frigid resistance. Cool passion seeks a fulfillment by joining the forces of heart and mind, commitment and critical analysis. Such passion pursues its purposes with 'tenuous tenacity.'"

People at DEEP schools demonstrate cool passion through their steady, unwavering enthusiasm for the task at hand. Unlike the quick flaring of hot passion, cool passion's flame of innovation and commitment does not fade over time, but persists—steady, unrelenting.

Talent development refers to the notion that every student can learn under the right conditions. A college or university committed to talent development arranges resources and learning conditions to maximize student potential so that students leave college different in desired ways from how they started. Cool passion and a sincere commitment to talent development are expressed in different ways at different DEEP schools. Given the educational and socioeconomic backgrounds of many of their students, Fayetteville State University, Winston-Salem State University, University of Maine at Farmington, California State University at Monterey Bay, Alverno College, and University of Texas at El Paso are especially instructive examples. We provide specific examples from some of these schools in Chapter Eleven.

Fayetteville State University

As we stated in Chapter Two, talent development at FSU means "meeting students where they are," a frequently uttered refrain on campus. FSU's commitment to work with all students regardless of their academic preparation is long-standing. One faculty member described this commitment simply and eloquently: "This is a part of our mission." Another faculty member commented, "This is what distinguishes us—working with students [with] diverse backgrounds and talents."

Fayetteville State's talent development philosophy is clear from the moment a student arrives at the college. Throughout his tenure as chancellor, Willis McLeod frequently emphasized the importance of focusing on the academic and personal success of first-year students: "If student development is important for colleges and universities generally, it is even more important at Fayetteville State University. . . . Many of our freshmen come from families whose incomes are less than $20,000 per year; a significant portion comes from small towns and rural areas; many are first-generation college students; and they have varied academic preparations for university-level work. . . . If we are committed to helping our students achieve academic success, we must be concerned about their total personal development—academic and personal, intellectual and social." (McLeod, 2003, http://www.uncfsu.edu/chanoff/FYI01.HTM)

Fayetteville State attracts its share of well-prepared students, but more than two-fifths receive low scores on math and reading proficiency exams and need to improve their communication skills. FSU does not apologize for its students, however. Instead, it practices the age-old educational adage, "You have to reach them to teach them." As one faculty member summed it up: "You must teach the students you have, not the ones you wish you had." An administrator described the philosophy this way: "We will meet you where you are, but we will tell you where we want you to go." Another elaborated, "We don't want students to go *through* school, but for school to go *through* them," meaning that the FSU experience should help students develop their talents fully.

To encourage FSU faculty members to discover and understand their students' academic needs and potential, the Center for Teaching and Learning sponsors workshops that introduce ways to assess the abilities of individual students. Many of these workshops devote a portion of time presenting "right up front" the diverse learning needs of FSU students. Alternative assignments are common, such as giving students the option of replacing an exam with a short paper. The net effect of these efforts is a nurturing, yet challenging, campus environment as evidenced by NSSE scores and other data.

California State University at Monterey Bay

A key premise of CSUMB's "assets" philosophy is that students' prior knowledge and experiences should be used to foster learning in college. This pedagogical strategy, coupled with CSUMB's interdisciplinary, problem-based curriculum, helps instill a sense of agency in students. In addition, starting with what students know reinforces the expectation that students are preparing to make a difference in the world and are empowered to effect change. For example, many faculty members design assignments that integrate adult students' work and life experiences into the classroom. In a human communications course on oral history and memory, all students conducted life history interviews and created primary historical documents related to the experience of students who are first in their families to go to college or to aspire to go to college in an effort to shape policies that will make a difference for first-generation college students. When discussing environmental and political problems in local and regional communities, faculty pose the question: "Now what are you going to do about it?" Responding to such questions requires students to apply what might otherwise be abstract knowledge. Widespread use of assessment to gauge student progress and document course outcomes buttress such concrete learning approaches. In some classes, faculty ask students to develop strategies that will help them achieve outcomes, a task that permits students to build on their strengths, not focus on their weaknesses. Over the course of the academic term, the instructor makes certain that students expand their repertoire of approaches to attaining the course goals, thus broadening their set of skills and competencies.

Alverno College

Alverno's approach to student learning is based on extensive and ongoing individual assessment of students by faculty and institutional assessment staff. To graduate, every Alverno student must be proficient in the eight abilities (that is, outcomes) it considers foundational to the liberal arts: communication, analysis, problem solving, values-based decision making, social interaction, global perspective, effective citizenship, and aesthetic engagement. Each ability is conceptualized as a series of developmental levels corresponding to a student's progress across her college career. The student moves from general education (levels one through four) to specialized work in the majors and supporting areas of study (levels five and six). Faculty devise criteria for each level of each ability. The college values students' life experiences by building them into the learning goals criteria that faculty and external assessors use as standards for evaluating and certifying that students have met or exceeded the abilities and the outcomes established for the major. Working with individual students so that they can master the eight abilities requires an enormous amount of time on the part of faculty members and others, which is the next issue we address. For more information on this one-of-a-kind curriculum, see (http://www.alverno.edu/about_alverno/ability_curriculum.html).

MAKING TIME FOR STUDENTS

Maintaining an unwavering focus on student learning is labor-intensive. To foster student success, faculty, staff members, and others must "make time for students," and making time for students demands a lot of time from faculty and staff. There is no substitute for spending time interacting with students, whether face to face or electronically.

At Sweet Briar, not only do students and faculty regularly "stumble upon one another," they interact because of intentional elements that have been put in place to promote their interaction. Faculty members are expected to integrate their research into their teaching ("It's part of the teaching environment; it's just part of what we do") and to involve students in their research. From the beginning, faculty are told that they are expected to be involved with students and their activities outside of class.

As one faculty member noted, "We are here every weekend for something or other." Another faculty member who compared her experiences at Sweet Briar with those at another small liberal arts college confirmed this, saying she was "truly impressed" with the amount of time and attention students get at SBC and the level of commitment Sweet Briar faculty members have to students' success and improvement. And students notice. One commented, "The professors here are absolutely passionate, approachable, and compassionate. When I feel over my head, they take the time to make sure I know it's do-able." Another praised "the warm and encouraging atmosphere" created by SBC faculty: "They do whatever they can to help us learn and are so willing to help us get where we want to go." Because of the amount of feedback faculty give students on papers and assignments, students feel obligated to reciprocate by devoting more time and energy to their studies than they might otherwise. The small size of the full-time student body and the human-scale campus make it easy for students and faculty members to connect outside of class to discuss ideas presented in class, graduate school options, and other matters.

At Wabash, student-faculty relationships frequently evolve into friendships. As one faculty member told us, "We celebrate together and we mourn together." Another said, "You can expect students in your office any time. I've learned that interruptions *are* my work." A colleague observed, "Faculty are here all day long with their doors open." A senior faculty member noted, perhaps only half-jokingly, "The students get our attention because we don't have other lives." Faculty described their relationships with students as "warm, cordial, and informal; we're on a first-name basis." In addition, "Students know faculty are concerned about them, and are invested in their learning and their general well-being." Students concurred. For example, a senior asserted, "It's really tough to get an A or an F. They just won't let you fail, but they ask a lot of you."

Extensive student-faculty interaction also is a cornerstone of the Longwood ethos, dating back to the institution's beginnings as a teacher's college for women. A student is assigned a faculty member who, at the student's request, serves as her or his advisor for her or his entire career at Longwood. Faculty members seem to find time to listen and respond to students even though they teach heavy course loads. Holding office hours is the formal policy at Longwood, as at many other institutions, but students say the usual practice is "open door." That is because most faculty are on campus at least four days a week. One administrator noted, "If you were not in your office with the door open, people would ask if something was wrong with you. Were you sick or ill or needed help?" Students know they can make an appointment whenever they need to and they can call faculty at home on evenings, holidays, and weekends. A student commented, "When you need help here, you go straight to the professor. They want you to succeed and they take the time to make sure you know how." Many of the students we talked with had been in a faculty member's home or had met with a faculty member outside of the classroom for lunch or coffee.

The Wofford story is similar to that of Longwood. Faculty and staff are advisors, instructors, mentors, and friends to students and develop relationships with them that go beyond the classroom. As at other DEEP schools, Wofford selects new faculty with these practices in mind. The introduction to Wofford (in Chapter Two) described the collegial environment that is central to the Wofford culture. As a result, faculty members get to know their students very well, and take a personal interest in their performance and well-being. One student explained, "I arrived in class and one of my teammates was absent so the faculty member sent me to his room to get him."

Faculty at large DEEP schools also make time for students as well, though in many cases students must initiate the contact for extensive and intensive interactions with faculty. For example, the University of Michigan is very clear about student-faculty interaction outside the classroom: the student takes the initiative. As one student put it, Michigan provides "a very good quality of education, *should you pursue it.*" Administrators expressed similar views: "The burden is on the student," so student-faculty interactions are "much more variable beyond the classroom." That said, however, Michigan has several programs designed to foster such interaction. One program is the Undergraduate Research Opportunity Program (UROP) for first-year students, a campuswide initiative involving 900 students and 600 faculty participants each year. The UROP was created to provide research opportunities for students from groups historically underrepresented, but the experience is no longer limited to such students. The networking potential of UROP is powerful. One student with whom we spoke continued to do research with her UROP mentor during her sophomore and junior years and met many of her mentor's colleagues and graduate students working in the laboratory.

Not all faculty members at the University of Kansas interact frequently with undergraduates, but students' expectations for spending time with faculty are defined by those faculty who devote an extensive amount of time to students. Representative of the leaders in this regard is the faculty member who collects student information on class data cards. In addition to standard contact information, students indicate what they are involved with on and off campus. The faculty member occasionally follows up on this information, initiating discussions with students about clubs and organizations from which they might benefit. Another faculty member tells all her students, "It will take me a little while to learn your names but I will remember them for the rest of my life." We heard many stories about faculty members who reached out to students to help, such as the professor who made arrangements to arrive early at class so a student could check out a piece of equipment she needed. Another student described being "adopted" by a faculty member who invited students to her home to study a foreign language. A KU journalism student was surprised when the faculty member teaching her large science class acknowledged her good performance on exams and encouraged her to consider majoring in science. She appreciated the accolade, but also realized that although she was in some large classes, she was not anonymous! Through these and many other small daily gestures, KU faculty members send the message that students matter.

At CSUMB, and many other DEEP schools, students frequently rely on e-mail to obtain feedback on projects and assignments. Students often e-mail papers to faculty before they are due to seek additional feedback. In addition, faculty members frequently use e-mail to initiate contact with students. A student leader indicated that many "profs will e-mail or call if you are not in class." Students at many DEEP schools mentioned they used e-mail to ask their faculty members questions instead of going to office hours.

UTEP students also use e-mail to communicate with faculty. Many professors collect e-mail addresses at the beginning of a course and often send messages throughout the term about opportunities and campus events. Some faculty members arrive on campus as early as 7:00 A.M. to meet with students because they know that the remainder of the day will be very busy. Why? One faculty member offered an explanation: "I was put on the planet to do something meaningful." Another instructor, a UTEP graduate himself, has empathy for the experiences of many UTEP students: "I believe in this institution. I am reminded of where I started, [especially] when I meet parents who bring their children [to UTEP]. I see a lot of what they're experiencing [which is similar to] what I experienced coming here."

FEEDBACK: IMPROVING PERFORMANCE, CONNECTING STUDENTS AND FACULTY

Feedback from faculty to students is timely and frequent at DEEP schools, as demonstrated both by NSSE data and by our interviews with students and faculty members.

Feedback is a centerpiece of the Alverno experience, and emphasizes progress rather than mastery and grades. A student said, "You're constantly getting feedback—constructive criticism, ideas about how to improve." Both strong and weak performances receive feedback about areas of strength and areas for improvement. Thus, feedback is intended to motivate students to do their best and not just meet minimum levels of mastery, more than "clearing hurdles set up by some external person." Students also obtain feedback on external "Assessment Days," which bring students and external assessors together to consider a variety of student activities and projects. External assessors are volunteers from the community trained to assess students' performance. An external assessment might entail a student presentation or what is called "a social interaction" (a simulated activity required of all students); other examples include an "in-basket" exercise, a book discussion, and preparation of a business plan. An external assessment in business, for example, considers whether the student "has learned the frameworks and course materials and can apply them in the context of the discipline." One external assessor told us, "Key things we're looking for are did they acquire the content and do they see relationships among issues." Feedback from the external assessors is provided directly to the student's developmental portfolio, rather than to the student. A faculty member stated that external assessment is "another more formal way to provide students the kind of feedback needed to improve." In addition, "Students take this seriously because the assessors really provide valuable feedback."

At Sewanee, most informal feedback that students receive is right before or after class, and much of it occurs on writing assignments. Some faculty members even read papers that their advisees prepare for other classes. An anthropology professor showed us some examples of the kind of feedback he provides to his students on a three- to five-page written assignment. Each set of carefully worded comments was about a half to a third of a page long. "I put my time into comments that aim to engage the student as a thinker," he said. In addition to constructive criticism, he typically concluded each set of feedback with a note of encouragement:

Don't be discouraged. You simply headed in the wrong direction. It's okay to go outside the book but don't go so far that you ignore it. I know that's easy to do. I've done it more than once.

I hope you don't misunderstand. Your essential point about symbiosis is excellent and your concluding sentence is profoundly true. You've still written a well organized and forcefully argued paper. Its energy and clarity are impressive.

Don't be discouraged. Without realizing it, you've tackled one of the most challenging ideas in the course. Few students will get as far as you've gone in trying to reason out how society works. I'd say this is a truly excellent beginning.

According to this professor, students really appreciate when he tells them, "I know how hard you worked on this," even if they receive a "C" on the assignment.

Most faculty members at Sewanee described the importance of working with individual students and in particular helping students improve their academic work. Across all disciplines, faculty members told us they spent a lot of time evaluating student work. In addition, many faculty members mentioned their practice of meeting with students individually to discuss their assessments. Sewanee stresses writing across the curriculum, and makes writing a central activity in most classes. A first-year student recounted that she met with one of her professors after class that day to discuss a paper that she had to resubmit. During another meeting with student leaders, a junior philosophy major shared a story of her most significant interaction with a faculty member: "I wrote a paper my first year and the grade was really bad. I just could not understand what I did wrong. . . . My teacher sat down with me and helped me revise it. Three meetings later I had a great paper. He did not just tell me what to do and how to correct my paper. He invested in me and my work and helped me revise the paper. The funny thing is now he is my advisor."

Our student tour guide described that most of his interaction with faculty centered on discussing his academic work. He met with his professors regularly to "get lots of feedback." His standard practice was to compose a draft of a writing assignment and then meet with his professors. He admitted that most of this interaction was at his request and he always found his faculty members were willing to assist.

The extent of feedback and quality of interaction between students and faculty at Sewanee exemplifies the value placed on one-on-one work with students to help improve their academic work. Students corroborated Sewanee faculty members' perspective that students frequently interact with faculty members to receive feedback on academic work. Connected to the level of respect faculty have for their students and their work, the observation of one group of students was that faculty do seem to value the work they put into the papers they write, encouraging improvement of student work via one-on-one conferences. A senior, who described the academic work at Sewanee as very challenging, told us: "You can get really discouraged. The work is hard." However, a sophomore quickly added that faculty are available for support: "Today I talked with two of my professors and corresponded with another via e-mail about my assignments."

Because approximately two-thirds of the CSUMB students live off-campus, it is sometimes a challenge for students to meet with faculty to get prompt feedback on assignments. Faculty members in English and history departments frequently require that students upload rough drafts, sometimes multiple drafts, onto Blackboard prior to the submission of the final paper. By receiving extensive feedback, students produce more polished final submissions. A sophomore told us she learned so much from her English professor because "she was so challenging. . . . She would proof my papers and give me lots of feedback and then I had to go back and make a lot of changes." Another student said that this professor motivated him to do his best work because she routinely returned papers with useful suggestions. In addition, she displayed and mentioned the good work of students for others to emulate.

Faculty members at Sweet Briar engage students in a cycle of continuous feedback and improvement, pointing to examples in which faculty members write one or more pages of notes describing very clearly what students need to improve on certain products and in certain courses. Students also talked about the quality of feedback, indicating that it is not unusual to get one or more pages of typed comments that point out how the work can be improved. Often the feedback is very direct but typically delivered in a matter-of-fact way that reinforces the high expectations faculty members have for student performance. In one class we observed the faculty member—using an adapted Socratic method—telling students that their answers to questions were "not right."

Nowhere is feedback more extensive than at Evergreen. Because letter grades are not used, students and faculty spend considerable time reviewing student performance. In addition, students reciprocate, providing feedback to faculty on their teaching and the overall quality of the program. All feedback is provided in writing, which allows room for rich descriptions of students' thoughts on the learning process. At the conclusion of a class, or program, students submit a self-evaluation in which they reflect on their work and describe significant learning experiences. The student also prepares a written evaluation of the faculty member. Typically, students and faculty exchange and discuss these evaluations along with faculty members' evaluation of the student at the end of the program. The student's evaluation of the faculty member then goes to the dean after the student and instructor have discussed it.

SUMMARY

As the examples in this section and those described later (Chapter Nine) demonstrate, DEEP schools take students and their learning seriously. This is evident in how much time faculty and staff spend with students focused on educational purposeful activities. Using engaging pedagogies inside and outside the classroom is commonplace, not marginalized as is the case at many schools. They also harness the power of peers to make learning more interesting, relevant, and socially rewarding.

WHAT'S NOTEWORTHY ABOUT FOCUSING ON STUDENT LEARNING

- Student learning and personal development at DEEP schools is a priority. Though this might seem to be a simplistic and hardly revolutionary statement, DEEP schools are special precisely because their commitment to this priority is authentic and they pursue it with a high degree of effectiveness.

- DEEP colleges recruit and retain faculty and staff who are committed to student learning and take the time and measures necessary to foster that learning. Faculty and staff members elsewhere surely work as hard as their counterparts at DEEP schools, but not always with the same intensity of focus on student learning and growth.

- Faculty and staff members at DEEP colleges make a lot of time for students. They recognize that there is no substitute for human contact, whether face-to-face or via e-mail.

- DEEP colleges recognize and accommodate, to the best of their ability, multiple styles of learning. Because many students prefer concrete, practical applications, DEEP colleges respond with active and collaborative learning approaches that provide opportunities for students to apply what they are learning to their lives outside the classroom.

- Faculty and administrators at DEEP colleges challenge students to raise their aspirations, and provide timely and apt feedback and support designed to meet their students' needs.

- DEEP schools work with the students they have, in contrast to the all-too-common fixation on trying to recruit the best and the brightest. This is a very important message: institutions and students can succeed despite the odds. Powerful learning environments and significant learning outcomes can be achieved no matter what the institution's resources or students' preparation.

4

Environments Adapted for Educational Enrichment

T HE INSTITUTIONS in Project DEEP differ considerably in geographic location, architecture, and physical facilities. Winston-Salem State University is situated in the Piedmont Triad, one of the most heavily populated and rapidly growing Metropolitan Statistical Areas between Washington, D.C., and Atlanta. In stark contrast, the University of Maine at Farmington sits comfortably in rural, western Maine. California State University at Monterey Bay is on the other coast on what was once a military base. UTEP effectively straddles two countries: 10% of its students commute daily from Juarez, Mexico. Macalester College is a residential liberal arts college in the traditional sense but is situated in a pleasant residential neighborhood in a large urban area. Some campuses are expansive, spanning thousands of acres, whereas others are compact. Some have high-rise student residences and academic buildings with classrooms that seat 1,000. At others, no structure is more than three stories, few if any classrooms seat more than 25, and small student houses dot the campus.

Despite these widely different settings, students, faculty, and administrators at every one of the 20 DEEP schools believe their location and campus setting are advantages in terms of student learning. Indeed, the students we talked with across all the institutions were enthusiastic about their school, routinely volunteering that their college was "special," that "there is no other place like it." For example, students at the University of Maine at

Farmington thought that their rural Maine campus offered opportunities for learning and cocurricular leadership that did not exist anyplace else. Macalester faculty and staff pointed to their proximity to the Twin Cities as offering exceptional opportunities for educational enrichment.

To a large extent DEEP schools make themselves "special" because they are "place conscious" (Gruenwald, 2003). In a deeply emotional way, the "place" of the institution transcends the physical setting or location of the college. Physical properties, such as Jayhawk Boulevard at the University of Kansas and the coherent brick architecture at Miami and WSSU, landscaping, and campus design mix with memories of activities and events to build loyalty and connection among students and campus members as a whole. UTEP students described their school's unique Bhutanese architecture as truly "special." As one faculty member put it: "There is a sense of place here," which is due in no small part to the unusual architecture that defines the campus. The physical plant draws from the style of the monasteries of the Kingdom of Bhutan. Though the university's backdrop—the Franklin Mountains—is not quite like Bhutan's Himalayas, still UTEP is the "only university, not only in the United States but in the western hemisphere—and perhaps the world—with Bhutanese architecture."

As a result, a campus becomes much more than a specific location or set of arranged physical spaces as buildings, green spaces, walkways, and more take on a range of emotional overtones. Some spaces begin to symbolize institutional ideals and enduring values through remembrances of

Excerpted from a job ad for a faculty position: "Maine has been ranked by the Children's Right Council as the best state in the nation in which to raise a child; it is also noted for its snow, black flies, and April mud season."

What might a prospective applicant for a position at the University of Maine at Farmington think after reading this? "How much snow *do* they get?" "How big *are* those black flies?" "What exactly *is* a 'mud season'?" These questions notwithstanding, the ad communicates some important things about the institution. First, this is a school with a sense of humor. Self-deprecating wit aside, the university does not apologize for what or where it is. Equally important, UMF plainly states what potential faculty and staff are getting into should they take a job there, black flies and all.

Student Success in College

the rituals and ceremonies performed there year after year. Walking through a particular building or passing by a favorite spot reminds one of what was and could have been in recalling the events and activities that once occurred in these places. The physical and emotional become inextricably intertwined to form an almost palpable "sense of place," one that has profound if not always clearly understood meaning to many members of the campus community.

DEEP schools not only embrace where they are located, but they also have fashioned learning settings on and off campus to achieve their educational purposes. They have created spaces that enhance and complement their commitment to student engagement and success. Because they understand the importance of "place" in education, these institutions recognize the potential learning opportunities in their setting, and the ways that students, institution, and community can interact for mutual benefit. DEEP institutions forge partnerships with their community, linking people and resources to address issues that affect the quality of life on and off the campus. And they alter the physical environment on campus to create spaces and settings where teaching and learning can flourish.

This chapter highlights some of the natural, constructed, and psychological environments designed or adapted by DEEP schools to attain their educational missions and promote student success.

USING THE SETTING FOR TEACHING AND LEARNING

The following sections detail how DEEP institutions purposefully employ the natural resources of the campus, gathering places, campus residences, and community connections to enhance teaching and learning both in and out of the classroom.

Natural Resources

Several DEEP institutions are ensconced in unusually rich natural environments, which they use to full advantage. For example, Sewanee's vast, isolated mountaintop is an impressive educational resource. With its

10,000 wooded acres, 65 miles of trails, streams, waterfalls, and majestic views, "the Domain" (as it is known on campus) is a laboratory for teaching, research, and recreation, especially in environmental studies, forestry, and geology. A 65-foot-high tree canopy walkway connects students to, and provides a unique perspective from which to study, the forest ecosystem. In addition, many students majoring in forestry and geology use the Domain for their senior capstone project, investigating environmental challenges facing the college. Faculty in psychology use the Domain to teach their students about animal behavior, and religion faculty structure inquiry projects to examine cultural influences on the landscape. The Domain also provides opportunities for active learning outside the classroom through PRE, the first-year orientation program, and the Outing Program, which coordinates recreational trips such as hiking and boating. Because only one professional staff member runs each of these programs, student assistance is necessary. For example, in the 2002–2003 PRE orientation program, 78 sophomores, juniors, and seniors volunteered to lead 178 first-year students through rock climbing, caving, hiking, and ropes course activities. Six students coordinate the Outing Program's mentoring and apprenticeship system during the school year. The Program uses a mentoring ladder, through which students receive increased responsibility as they improve their skills and learn from more experienced peers, in the Domain to develop student leadership. In addition, because the college manages all of the natural resources on its property, students have many opportunities to help with and learn from carrying out these important tasks.

Evergreen State enjoys a similar symbiotic relationship with its natural surroundings. Near the campus are a densely wooded preserve and the Puget Sound shoreline, which, taken together, offer unparalleled opportunities for students to study plants, ecosystems, and marine life. The campus farm pursues small-scale organic agriculture as a sustainable source of food for the campus, providing internships and other learning experiences for students along the way. Students, faculty, administrators, and staff are proud that the farm provides the dining hall with fresh produce so that it can feature a "made with organic" menu. Students manage the farm and also market fresh produce to the campus community.

Farmington is a small town in Western Maine, a long distance from an urban area, transportation hubs, and major entertainment venues. But rather than lamenting the absence of diversions such as professional sports teams, night clubs, and so on, UMF faculty, staff, and students make good use of their location, finding various ways to entertain themselves. When the weather is warm, people enjoy the woods and other natural resources. In the winter they downhill or cross country ski. However, when inclement weather forces residents indoors, the student center becomes the hub of campus entertainment. An estimated 300 students attended the 2003 Halloween dance—about 15% of the student body. Other activities are available on campus, in faculty members' homes, the residence halls, and anywhere the admittedly "outdoorsy" students and faculty of the university gather.

Beautiful physical spaces certainly help to create a sense of place. The Wofford campus is essentially an arboretum through which students move on the way to class. They can't help but experience the rich sense of place created through the collection of ordinary and extraordinary trees. The University of Kansas has gone to great lengths to preserve the sense of history and tradition in Jayhawk Boulevard. Student guides talked about the thrill of walking down the boulevard that reeked of history and tradition.

Gathering Places

DEEP schools design and, when appropriate, alter physical facilities to promote student engagement. The richly appointed, well-lit Acorn Lounge in Wofford's Milliken Science Center is a favorite place for students to study. The open spaces designed into the center feature moveable tables and chairs near faculty offices, as well as comfortable seating near a café to facilitate student-faculty interaction, group study, and collaborative work.

Ursinus College redesigned space and added large tables, chairs, and laminated whiteboards to create "interaction areas" near faculty offices and classrooms. The chemistry department chair referred to the spaces as a "visual image of achievement and aspiration," in that the space and the artifacts inspire an intensity of focus on learning. Students use the areas for quiet study and small group work. Students at Wofford and Ursinus reported that people really "pile" into these rooms and finding one available is difficult.

Macalester College's Ruth Stricker Dayton Campus Center opened in 2001. Both students and faculty members describe it as an inviting, convenient place to meet. Its strategic central location, high-quality food, and intentional balance of attractive, well-designed curricular–cocurricular, group–individual, and office–public spaces make it the focal point of Macalester student life outside the classroom. The availability of ample, comfortable, large chairs in an open and airy second floor encourages students to use this space for reading and studying. Outdoor gathering areas surround the building. The center also provides seminar rooms and office space for student organizations. In keeping with the college's emphasis on internationalism, the center's Cafe Mac offers cuisine from the four hemispheres and a "grab-n-go grill." Classroom dialogues easily spill into dinner conversations with faculty, and campus organizations make use of "cubbies" to conduct their business. These qualities—central location, ample multipurpose space, "amazing food," and the opportunity for student-faculty interaction—explain why Macalester's Campus Center is a vibrant campus gathering space.

Winston-Salem State University's architecture is a mix of old low-rise buildings and newer brick structures connected by clear pathways and nicely landscaped flowerbeds. A low brick wall borders the south side of campus, and attractively designed arches signal the entrance to the campus from Martin Luther King Jr. Drive. Many students told us that the physical appearance of the campus was a "major selling point" in their decision to attend WSSU. An inviting structure, the Cleon F. Thompson Jr. Student Services Center—a large, modern brick building with tall windows offering a good view of the entire campus from the hill—is the gathering place for students and guests of the university. The Thompson Center houses many essential student services, including registration, financial aid, career planning, and student activities. Centrally located, the center is a " one-stop shop" for student services and has several spaces that students frequently populate, including an open atrium and such facilities as a commuter and TV lounge, food court, post office, bookstore, Student Government Association (SGA) office, student dining hall, meditation room, and other meeting spaces.

At Evergreen State, the Longhouse Education and Cultural Center hosts large community gatherings. Its modular design includes moveable walls that, when configured for all-campus events, make the Longhouse the largest gathering space on campus. More important, the Longhouse is emblematic of the institution's commitment to promoting multicultural study and understanding. The structure incorporates Northwest Indigenous Nations' architectural concepts and design, and communicates Native American traditions of hospitality. Longhouse performances, ceremonies, and artists bring members of the Evergreen and Olympia communities together with local and regional Native American communities.

Since its opening in 1996, the George W. Johnson Center at George Mason University is "a unique facility designed to encourage learning [and] emphasize the integration of curricular and extracurricular activities among and within the diverse communities that compose George Mason" (http://coyote.gmu.edu/map). Located in the center of the campus and designed to integrate academics with student life, the Johnson Center is a focal point for universitywide learning. The four-story structure is both figuratively and literally the heart of the campus, with students passing in and out of its doors throughout the day and into the evening. As one student put it, the Johnson Center "is the hub of student life—the place to be." It has the look of an international bazaar; bright flags hang from pillars, and students in native dress—North American to North African—eat, study, or just "hang" together. The feeling is energetic, cosmopolitan, and communal. The Johnson Center is also home to a library; food court; movie theater; learning labs; retail outlets; coffee and jazz café; computer labs; myriad academic and support services for students and faculty; Undergraduate Admissions; centers for research on women, global education, and African American Studies; the Student Technology Assistance and Resource (STAR) Center; the Center for Teaching Excellence; and facilities (including lockers) for commuter students. Space for individual and small group study is plentiful.

At Michigan, the "diag," a confluence of many diagonal walkways, provides a central gathering place full of enriching educational opportunities. This intersection, particularly near the "M" insignia located in front of Hatcher Graduate Library, helps make visible students' passion for social issues, some of which are controversial. In this physical space, it is common for students to receive leaflets and other printed material, participate in discussions and listen to speeches, and look at signboards all related to various causes, programs, and events. During our visit, leaflets were being distributed announcing "National Take Affirmative Action Day," a program cosponsored by the University of Michigan's Chapter of the National Association for the Advancement of Colored People and the United States Student Association.

Gonzaga's Unity House is "a place to come to talk about diversity, a place to hang out, a safe and comfortable home for all students." In keeping with that purpose, Unity House does not feel institutional. It looks and feels like a home, not an administrative office. In fact, the university purchased the house on the edge of campus and did not renovate it. As a result, students sit at the dining room table to dine and converse. Or they can watch television or read (possibly books or periodicals from Unity House's small library) in the cozy living room. Staff members refer to the house as a safe haven, which is a fitting descriptor based on time there. The director encourages professors, students, and Spokane community members to schedule classes and meetings in Unity House; many accept this invitation. It is a home base for campus and Spokane organizations such as the NAACP, PIER (Program for International Education and Relief), the Black Student Union, and the Native American Student Association.

As with many other institutions, DEEP schools have spaces where students and faculty members gather informally over a meal. The coffee bars and excellent food available at Macalester, Wheaton, Sewanee, Wofford, and Wabash encourage diners to linger long after meal's end. Evergreen, Wofford, Wheaton, and Longwood also have faculty dining rooms where colleagues met frequently to discuss students' academic progress and related issues. At Wheaton, for example, we were told the faculty lunch room "sustains our self-aware collegiality. If you want to get something discussed, take it to the lunch room."

DEEP schools also have designed common spaces to foster academic engagement. At Ursinus, small-group meeting spaces for students were placed near faculty offices with this intent in mind. George Mason's Johnson Center, mentioned earlier, is an entire building devoted to providing student academic services, such as tutoring, career counseling, and so forth amid a food court, the library, and several other offices. UTEP created space in its state-of-the-art Science and Engineering building for individuals and groups to study and meet, to host workshops and symposia, and to afford a comfortable place for students to relax and visit informally with other students and faculty.

Campus Residences

As with many other institutions, DEEP schools use campus residences to augment, complement, and enrich students' academic experience. One reason DEEP campus residences seem to work as well as they do is that the curriculum and other aspects of the academic program are well designed and engaging. As a result, residence life staff are not expected to bear all of the responsibility for enriching the out-of-class experiences of students in residence.

The University of Kansas houses about 5,500 students in its residence halls, scholarship halls, and apartment complexes. Some of the residence halls offer special communities, including an honors program residence, creative arts hall, and a leadership and volunteerism program. Among the special theme communities is Lewis Hall, where residents commit to engage in leadership, community service, and diversity experiences. About 500 students elect to live in "schol" (short for scholarship) halls that emphasize cooperative living; everyone shares cooking and household responsibilities in exchange for reduced costs for room and board. To continue living in a schol hall, students must complete at least 28 credit hours during the academic year and earn a minimum 2.5 grade point average. In addition, each hall awards at least one scholarship based on academic achievement, citizenship, or leadership.

Although some of the programs discussed here benefited from well-planned and built residence halls, this was not essential to the success of the programs. DEEP schools often make do with the physical space available and rely on a coherent operational philosophy that complements the institution's educational mission. Older, smaller residence halls often were the preferred places to live on DEEP campuses because of the environment created through the mix of students. Traditional classroom spaces become rich learning environments through the adoption of a faculty-agreed-upon, coherent pedagogy. Even inadequate studio space is fondly referred to because the educational environment created transcends the scarce physical space.

The sheer size of the University of Michigan—a large, decentralized public research university with more than 24,000 undergraduates and 13,500 graduate students—can seem overwhelming. However, even large institutions can reduce their psychological size. One way Michigan does this is through living-learning centers and the residential college (RC). These residential units foster an environment that encourages collaboration among students and faculty and facilitates active learning via small classes and a variety of cocurricular activities. Additional residential programs such as the Women in Science and Engineering residential program (WISE) and the Undergraduate Research Opportunity Program (UROP) in Residence also provide a supportive environment in which students work with peers on projects of common interest. Students in the Michigan Community Scholars Program (MCSP) in Couzens Residence Hall told us most of their "bonding" comes from their common interest in civic engagement. Relationships form early, as students live together and take at least one MCSP course together each semester, which are typically small classes focused on a civic engagement theme. Tutors are available to work with MCSP participants. It is but one of many initiatives Michigan provides. Most of these niche programs touch directly a relatively small number of students. But, taken together, they involve literally thousands of students yearly.

As with many other institutions, many of Longwood's diversity-awareness initiatives take place in the residence halls. Resident assistants (RAs) help raise awareness and encourage student participation in the many events sponsored by the Office on Multicultural Affairs. Indeed, the work of Longwood RAs is integral to attaining the university's educational mission, and RAs receive helpful training and advice to carry out this role. As with all the other student affairs programs, residence hall programming is organized around the developmental goals that complement and support the Longwood mission.

Miami University is an excellent example of how residence halls can play a central role in the undergraduate experience. New students are required to live in first-year residence halls and the residence hall director becomes well-acquainted with students by providing academic advising and other services. In addition, a substantial proportion of upper-class students continue to live on campus because campus housing is convenient, well maintained, and educationally enriching. All residence halls are considered living-learning communities. Fourteen of the 15 options for living-learning communities offer specific themes focused on a particular area of interest, such as "Celebrate the Arts," "International Living and Learning," and "Leadership, Excellence, and Community." Most of these living-learning communities offer courses relevant to the theme. Some communities require participation in one or more courses, whereas others offer optional courses or noncredit programs.

Many Macalester students see the residence halls as a retreat from what is an intense academic experience. Compared with many other colleges, educational programming is less prominent in the residence halls. However, the amount and frequency of offerings seem to be appropriate, given the culture and academic mission. At Gonzaga, residence hall programs complement and enrich what is already available on campus, particularly in the area of service to the community. Gonzaga students have a serious commitment to service, and numerous volunteer programs are organized on a campuswide basis. The residence halls build on this commitment and offer additional service opportunities for students.

Finally, at the DEEP schools that are essentially commuter institutions, such as Alverno and UTEP, the influence of campus residences on the quality of the undergraduate experience is more limited. Nonetheless, they are replete with many of the same high-quality programs found at residential schools, such as the learning communities and peer education opportunities offered at UTEP and George Mason.

Community Connections

DEEP institutions constantly scan their surrounding communities, looking for educational opportunities to benefit their students as well as the community. Instead of the commonly strained relations between "town and gown," DEEP schools strive to cultivate mutually beneficial connections with their surrounding communities. For example, when the town of Farmington, Maine, needed more opportunities for indoor recreation, more tutors for area children, and a larger public library, UMF became a partner in addressing these community needs. The campus recreation center at UMF now is the primary indoor recreation site for the community. Increased demand for fitness classes and other instructor-led activities created additional jobs for students and increased the interaction between students and community members. The institution and town collaborated to raise funds to expand the library, which the university and community share. By working together to plan and acquire the necessary resources, this university-community partnership has enriched the educational environment for students and community members.

George Mason takes advantage of the wealth of intellectual, social, and political resources of nearby Washington, D.C., to enhance students' educational experiences with internships, service learning experiences, and cultural events. Mason also forged connections with the business community to augment classroom experiences. For example, each school has its own advisory committee of businesspeople from the region, which helps infuse community needs and issues into the curriculum. To expand and further capitalize on local resources, Mason created the Century Club, a nonprofit organization comprising business, professional, and government organizations dedicated to fostering collaboration between George Mason and organizations in the metropolitan area. Century Club members, in cooperation with Mason faculty and students, volunteer time and professional expertise to direct and support educational programs associated with the university. These programs include job and internship fairs, résumé and interviewing workshops, and networking opportunities. The result is a synergistic partnership between the Century Club members and Mason and between Mason and its surrounding communities.

Wheaton College uses its proximity to Providence, Rhode Island, and Boston, Massachusetts, to place students in a variety of out-of-class learning venues. Students choose from over 100 internship, service learning, and research sites in the Boston and Providence area to gain practical experience and apply what they are learning in the classroom. Wheaton's Filene Center for Work and Learning coordinates student internships and service learning experiences. As one administrator put it, the Filene Center "seeks to engage students in their learning out of class, and is an institutionalization of the premise that what you experience in the classroom has meaning in the world and vice versa."

In a similar way, the Macalester College community enthusiastically embraces its urban location as an educational asset. Many community service opportunities are available, thus allowing the college to live its core values in meaningful work with its neighbors. Macalester's East Side Community Outreach Research Projects are one example of a service opportunity addressing community needs. Collaborating with the University of Minnesota's Center for Urban Affairs and Metropolitan State University, Macalester students and faculty work on interdisciplinary teams to conduct research projects requested by local nonprofit, governmental, or neighborhood organizations in the economically depressed neighborhoods of East St. Paul. In addition, through the Off-Campus Student Employment Program, students are able to meet their financial aid work-study obligations by working at a nonprofit organization in the community.

The University of Texas at El Paso demonstrates its commitment to serving populations in the El Paso community that have been denied access to education. For example, UTEP supports six community health clinics in partnership with Texas Tech University. The "Mothers and Daughters" program is part of a long-standing relationship between UTEP's College of Education and area public school districts. Established in 1986, the program engages sixth-grade girls in formal and informal activities designed to inspire them to seek college degrees. Based on the success of the program, UTEP created a "Fathers and Sons" program for the same purposes in 1997. In addition, a College of Education faculty member teaches her "Service Learning for Future Teachers" course in a downtown El Paso library.

Winston-Salem State University exposes its students to a diverse array of active learning opportunities off campus and in the region. For example, Opera@WSSU, which began in 1995 with a small group of interested students and faculty, sponsors trips to the local opera. Before students attend the opera, they receive instructions about how to dress and conduct themselves at the event to ensure that all students, whether seasoned opera attendees or not, have a positive experience. Another example of getting students "out and off of the campus" at WSSU is the Community Service/Service Learning Program (CS/SLP), which coordinates student involvement in all community service activities, including volunteer and community service as well as service learning experiences.

Service learning also is one of the vehicles that connects the CSUMB curriculum to the Monterey community. All CSUMB students must complete two service learning experiences, one at the lower division of the curriculum and one at the upper division. This requirement explicitly reinforces the expectation that CSUMB students will act on what they know. "We're exposed to the knowledge, then we have to figure out what it means to us, and then we're expected to do something with it," a student explained. CSUMB's service learning program is described in more detail in Chapters Nine and Eleven.

Alverno College realizes the educational advantages of its location by including Milwaukee community members in the college's educational program. As discussed in Chapter Three, each year Alverno involves approximately 400 community volunteers as "external assessors" of students' educational development. A local business owner might, for example, be asked to assess the quality of an Alverno student's business plan. External assessors participate in extensive training to prepare for their task, and they describe their experience as assessors as a powerful learning opportunity. To involve community members in this way, Alverno recruits widely through personal referrals and open calls for participants.

Turning Obstacles into Opportunities

Although some DEEP institutions would admit that at times their location or physical facilities present challenges, they strive to address these issues and turn them into positive educational opportunities. Creating a sense of community on campus and among students and faculty is a persistent challenge at commuter institutions such as George Mason. Mason, however, has developed an array of structures and opportunities to bring community members together to connect with one another and the university. Programs such as International Week and Celebrations of Scholarship along with other events sponsored by the Center for Teaching Excellence affirm shared values and experiences and honor community achievements. Also, as one GMU administrator noted, "We're very careful about writing thank-you notes here."

Wabash College's setting offers a challenge of another sort: Crawfordsville, Indiana, is not an ethnically diverse city. Yet through much of its history, the college has enrolled a diverse student body. About 20% of the current student population are students of color. These are two of many reasons Wabash College developed the Malcolm X Institute (MXI). Its purpose is to promote educational, cultural, and social programs of concern to the citizens of Wabash and Crawfordsville communities, particularly black citizens. In November 2002, the MXI moved into a new home on the Wabash campus, an 8,500 square–foot facility. The building is consistent with the college's uniformly Georgian architectural style, but also captures the symbolism and spatial arrangements found in a traditional African village. The facility features lecture and reception areas, study space, classrooms, student offices, and the Jasmine Robinson Computer Laboratory. MXI sponsors the KQ&K Mentoring Program—named for the students who founded the program in 1989—an initiative that offers after-school tutoring twice each week to local school children; an academic support network for Wabash students (for example, study tables, test files, library resources on the Black Experience, a computer lab); and community programs (for example, Kwanzaa celebration, DJ parties, Comedy Night, speakers, trips to other campuses). Each semester, the MXI also publishes a journal, the *X-Position*. MXI hosted a conference, "Negotiating Success: Workshops for Black Men in the Liberal Arts," in April 2003 that brought together black and bi-racial male students and faculty from colleges around the country to discuss issues affecting black men in a liberal arts college setting.

Summary

The physical characteristics of DEEP schools and their surroundings vary widely. What they all do well, however, is use their settings to educational advantage by creating engaging spaces for learning. They maximize the educational potential of their natural and physical resources on campus and in the local region. In addition, campus facilities, including residence halls and gathering spaces, are in tune with the academic mission of the campus. In the next section we describe the important concept of maintaining human scale environments to promote student success.

CREATING HUMAN SCALE LEARNING ENVIRONMENTS

Through buildings, signs, and the landscape of the campus, the physical environment communicates messages that influence students' feelings of well-being, belonging, and identity. The psychological environment includes the availability of personal space, sources of support and challenge, an absence of anonymity, and the presence of multiple subcommunities of students. Personal spaces, such as wooded areas, courtyards, and nooks, offer places for students to reflect on what they are learning in and out of the classroom. Students are more likely to flourish in small settings where they are known and valued as individuals than in settings in which they feel anonymous. By providing small residences and classes, maintaining effective communication networks, and widely disseminating information in a timely manner, even large colleges and universities can encourage their members to get to know one another. DEEP colleges offer some excellent examples.

Although Miami University encompasses more than 1,900 acres, it was designed to feel small. One can traverse the campus on foot in any direction in about 15 minutes. The campus is organized in quadrangles that enclose, and are separated by, green space. Buildings are set back from the street, creating the sense that they are apart from the hustle of campus traffic. The feeling of smallness also is attributed to the use of Georgian architectural style for almost all university buildings. Few buildings are more than three stories. No single building dominates the campus. The 36 residence halls that house some 7,000 students are both physically and psychologically manageable. Most of the academic advisors of first-year students, all of whom are required to live in campus housing, also live in the same building as their advisees. As a consequence, as one administrator told us, Miami is a campus, not a group of buildings in close proximity to one another. As one staff member observed, "We have a mindset here that we're not as big as we are." The psychological size of Miami "creates an intimacy of connections you would expect at a much smaller school."

Residence halls at the University of Michigan also help connect and create smaller campus communities to ameliorate the potentially overwhelming physical and psychological size of the campus. For example, Michigan offers a variety of opportunities for students to participate in small, theme-oriented classes, or learning communities. The courses are generally limited to first-year students and participants in various residential programs. Courses such as these blur the lines between in-class and out-of-class. Michigan further enhances the learning community experience by placing faculty offices in the residential college, allowing more frequent student-faculty contacts in the hallways, as well as at meals or in evening discussion groups. Student respondents who were participants in the university's learning communities spoke positively about their small class experiences in the honors program and the residential college.

UTEP has created a similar human scale structure in its learning communities, in which cohorts of students take several courses together. Seeing the same students across different courses can facilitate peer relationships and reduce students' feelings of anonymity. UTEP's learning communities are described more fully in Chapter Nine.

In addition to building in academic and social support through learning communities, UTEP has designed in other environmental qualities that make the campus seem smaller than it actually is. As described earlier, the Bhutanese architecture of the buildings, which features low-rise buildings painted in earthy tones, reflects a graphic institutional identity and communicates warmth. New and renovated buildings are well designed to encourage human interaction, such as the Undergraduate Learning Center (ULC) which is replete with state-of-the-art technology and multimedia resources. The level of sophistication and technology attracts many faculty members who wish to teach in the center. Its impressive atrium space, with its Bhutanese tapestry and details, is a hub of student interaction, especially between classes. The campus union offers numerous places, including Starbucks, where students can sit and meet with peers, faculty, or staff. Another place for informal student contact is Miner Village, a new apartment-style campus residence; students are quite pleased with its family-like environment. Athletic and recreational facilities, along with outdoor spaces, are well suited for interaction among students, faculty, and staff, too.

WHAT'S NOTEWORTHY ABOUT ADAPTING ENVIRONMENTS FOR EDUCATIONAL ADVANTAGE

- Although geographic location and physical topography of a college are fixed, DEEP schools do not apologize for where, who, or what they are. Instead, they adapt their surrounding and campus environments in creative and educationally purposeful ways. In effect, they make wherever they are "a good place for a college!"

- DEEP schools connect to the local community in ways that benefit students, the institution, and the surrounding community. Such efforts take time, unwavering commitment, and goodwill to bring to fruition.

- DEEP schools are "place conscious." They create learning environments from natural and constructed settings, and design curricular offerings and pedagogical approaches that induce people to form strong attachments to the "place."

- DEEP schools harness the educational potential of their campus residence halls by matching the environment to the intellectual mission of the institution.

- Buildings, classrooms, and other physical structures are adapted to "human scale." Living units, classrooms, and meeting spaces are kept small to the extent possible.

- Interior and exterior spaces are adapted to reduce the psychological size of the campus and to encourage participation in campus life.

5

Clear Pathways to Student Success

AT THE 1994 Student Learning Imperative teleconference at
Bowling Green State University, K. Patricia Cross compared college to a
jigsaw puzzle (King, 1999). Students, Cross said, start college with a bag
in which they put puzzle pieces they collect during the course of their time
in college. Into the bag goes a puzzle piece for every activity, starting with
fall orientation, advising sessions, classes, cultural events, dorm meetings,
and so forth. For many students the jumble of pieces does not create a
coherent, sensible picture. That is a problem because students who cannot discern meaning from their college activities often report academic
difficulty or social isolation, and are at risk of leaving school. Unlike a
jigsaw puzzle that has a picture on the box top, college often comes without directions; many students are unlikely to know they are constructing
a picture, nor do they have strategies for making that picture meaningful
for the present or useful for identifying future learning opportunities. This
is particularly true for students who are the first in their families to attend
college. Understanding the importance of coherence in learning to student success, DEEP institutions have created pathways clearly marked to
show students what to expect and what success looks and feels like. In
short, they create structures and practices that help students bring meaning to their college experiences.

Some schools, such as Fayetteville State, UTEP, UMF, and Winston-
Salem, attract large numbers of students who, because of inadequate

academic preparation and lack of knowledge about college, need explicit directions to use institutional resources and support services profitably. To be sure students take advantage of these resources, these colleges require students to take part in activities, such as summer advising, orientation, and fall welcome week, and follow up with advising and other events that mark student progress over the course of the first year. At other schools—Sweet Briar, Wabash, Wheaton, and Wofford—peers and faculty members routinely go out of their way to point students in the right direction. Most use some combination of required activities and social support to guide their students.

Toward this end, DEEP schools do two things very well. First, they teach students what the institution values, what successful students do in their context, and how to take advantage of institutional resources for their learning. We refer to this as acculturation. Second, they make available what students need *when* they need it, and have responsive systems in place to support teaching, learning, and student success. We call this alignment—making certain that resources match the institution's mission and educational purposes and students' abilities and needs.

According to some faculty members there, CSUMB's required senior capstone is comparable to master's degree–level work. One alumna graphically described it as "your challenge and your nightmare." Another called it her "defining academic experience as an undergraduate." How do undergraduate students get through it? The university begins to prepare students for this culminating activity from the beginning. First-year students learn about the capstone project in the first-year seminar. In the required Junior ProSeminar, librarians work with students to help them develop research questions. One faculty member includes a "capstone light" assignment in her ProSeminar, asking students, "If you were to do your capstone right now, what would it look like?" Then students do something similar in the course on a much smaller scale. The capstone project itself is divided into two semesters of work. Many students use the first semester to brainstorm with their peers and the faculty member directing the project to flesh out the topic and approach. The second semester is dedicated to completing the project. Writing tutors are on hand to help.

ACCULTURATION

DEEP colleges are thick with expectations about college life. They recognize that people rarely exceed their own expectations without being challenged. For this reason, these institutions have high expectations of everyone—students, faculty, administrators, and others. They begin preparing students to meet these expectations long before the students arrive on campus. Students get warm, positive messages of welcome and support from admissions personnel and advisors along with suggestions—or, in some cases, instructions—for how to find resources when they need them. After newcomers arrive on campus, they take part in a host of orientation and other socialization activities, some of which continue through the early weeks and months of the academic year. At some institutions, these events occur throughout the entire first year. To keep students from slipping through the cracks, institutional policies and processes provide both academic and social challenges and support, inside and outside the classroom. And they challenge students to stretch their aspirations and perform beyond their preconceived limits.

"You Don't Go to Wofford, You Join It"

The Wofford admissions view book and catalogue send powerful messages to prospective community members about what "joining" Wofford means, what students can expect of the college, and what the college expects of its students. As soon as newcomers arrive, they are accepted and treated as full members of the Wofford family. And by all accounts, students respond positively, as illustrated by Wofford's 89% first-to-second-year persistence rate. Most students, whether they were fourth-generation Wofford "legacies" or the first in their family to go to college, told us that upon arriving they felt the college was a place where they would fit in and "matter." Indeed, just as the admissions view book promises, students and faculty reported they develop meaningful relationships that extend well beyond the classroom, a "tradition of putting the emphasis on the individual student [that] goes back 150 years." Thus, Wofford demonstrates that using official institutional publications to welcome students can be effective, as long as what students experience after arriving is consistent with what the institution claims.

Gonzaga: Faith, Service, Ethics, Justice, Leadership

The Gonzaga Experience Live, or GEL, program is a powerful recruitment tool for Gonzaga, as about 70% of the students who participate in GEL enroll at Gonzaga. The GEL weekend, a spring event for prospective students, includes tours of the campus and Spokane, academic sessions, meals, a club and organization fair, evening social activities, and a night in a residence hall with a current student. An admissions staff member told us that GEL is intended to appeal to students with a "social justice bent who want a sense of community." Discussions during the GEL weekend frequently focus on questions about how to live a moral life—what is good, how one should live. Thus, Gonzaga signals the importance of such questions long before students arrive on campus. The centerpiece of *Your Total Self,* an attractive publication that targets prospective students, is a series of individual student profiles, including one about a student pursuing medical research and her relationship with her Gonzaga faculty mentor, and a journal entry from another student documenting his semester-long collaboration with peers on a mechanical engineering project. This and other Gonzaga publications express two consistent messages: (1) at GU students have many different opportunities to pursue their academic goals in the context of a Jesuit community, and (2) Gonzaga is a place where students form deep, enduring relationships with their teachers and other students.

Wabash College: "Boys Will Be Boys. Men Go to Wabash"

From their initial contacts with the college, prospective students are told that a Wabash education is difficult but, as the admissions materials say, "It's worth it." When asked why he chose to attend Wabash, a senior said, "For me it was the academic tradition. You know, 'It's not going to be easy, but it's worth it.' I liked the work ethic." Another said he was attracted by "the camaraderie of going through something tough together." These expectations seem to prepare students for striving to meet academic challenges. A faculty member commented, "They come assuming it will be hard." Another said, "They're prepared to read and write more than they've ever done." In fact, "students complain when a teacher does not give them enough work." Looking back on his four years, a senior told us, "You have to invest a lot of energy in a Wabash education, not just tests and scores. You have to work hard to do well in every aspect, but then you feel good." A classmate commented, "I came here to be challenged. And it's very gratifying when you're done."

WHAT NEW STUDENTS NEED TO KNOW

Most DEEP schools have programs that focus on first-year students and attempt to shape first-year experiences in educationally purposeful ways. They use formal orientation activities to make certain their students do not get lost in the shuffle or struggle needlessly. In addition, many informal processes and mechanisms communicate to new students, faculty, and staff what is valued and how things are done. In this section we offer a few examples of how DEEP schools organize their resources to respond to student learning needs and concerns during the critical first year of college. Others are described in Part Three.

Winston-Salem State University has First Year College (FYC), the centerpiece of its effort to cultivate a supportive campus environment. Most FYC offices and programs are housed in one building near the center of campus, thus conveniently locating most sources of academic support for new students under one roof. As described in Chapter Two, all new students and transfer students with fewer than 30 credit hours must enroll in one of three new-student adjustment courses. A twist that distinguishes WSSU's seminar from those offered at other institutions is that certain sections are designated for students interested in specific majors. Faculty members teaching these sections also serve as students' academic advisors and "mentors" for the first academic year. Student services professionals teach sections for undecided students. The FYC instructors receive preservice training and meet every other week to discuss how the course is going and to share ideas.

CSUMB introduces new students (including transfers) to academic programs and university life through the Freshman-Year Experience Seminar. Students at CSUMB design an Individualized Learning Plan (ILP) to achieve the Seminar's five learning outcomes:

1. Indicated awareness of both personal contributions to the CSUMB Vision and the vision's contribution to one's own academic and personal development

2. Demonstrated college-level oral and written communication skills

3. Demonstrated skills in gathering and assessing information in a multicultural context

4. Applied understanding of CSUMB University Learning Requirements (ULRs) to develop an Individualized Learning Plan (ILP)

5. Demonstrated collaborative learning skills, and understanding of the importance of collective work

Following the first year, students update their ILP to respond to their changing educational and professional goals. The ILP is reviewed in a junior year common learning experience, the major-specific ProSeminar 300.

To prepare newcomers for a rigorous academic program and help graduating seniors make meaning of their college experiences, Sewanee features a "bookend experiences model." The First Year Program (FYP) is anchored by a small, intensive seminar course designed to foster communities of learning and introduce new students to college-level work. An innovative "pre-orientation" program called PRE involves over 60% of the entering class in a variety of outdoor programs that help students get to know one another in a setting that requires cooperation and introduces them to the rich opportunities of the Domain. The other bookend—the Senior Year Experience—includes a required capstone project and comprehensive examinations in the major. More will be said about both later in Part Three.

Contributing to Evergreen's road map to success are its "Expectations of an Evergreen Graduate" that set forth what students should incorporate and strive to attain as part of the individualized academic plan required of all students:

1. Articulate and assume responsibility for your own work

2. Participate collaboratively and responsibly in our diverse society

3. Communicate creatively and effectively

4. Demonstrate integrative, independent, and critical thinking

5. Apply qualitative, quantitative, and creative modes of inquiry appropriately to practical and theoretical problems across disciplines

6. Demonstrate depth, breadth, and synthesis of learning and the ability to reflect on the personal and social significance of that learning (*Advising Handbook,* 2001–2002, p. 10)

The expectations flow from the five foci for teaching and learning noted in Chapter Two (interdisciplinary learning, learning across significant differences, personal engagement with learning, linking theory to practice, and collaborative learning). Along with the five foci, the expectations are posted in highly visible places on campus, including main buildings and outdoor kiosks, so new and seasoned community members keep them in mind.

At Ursinus, all first-year students live in Freshman Centers contiguous to campus, an intentional strategy to create community among first-year students. Another purpose of the first-year housing is to deepen conversations among classmates about ideas encountered in the Common Intellectual Experience, the two-semester interdisciplinary course that introduces students to the intellectual life of the college. The Freshman Centers focus attention on transition issues specific to first-year students. Staff members provide additional structure to out-of-class living environments to support and encourage students to move from dependence to independence, which is a cornerstone of the college's educational philosophy.

Applicants to the University of Michigan receive a compact disc describing university experiences, including opportunities for research with faculty and other kinds of student-faculty interactions. Current students travel to area high schools to discuss the Undergraduate Research Opportunity Program. They also describe the "Michigan Way" as an expectation that students will take much of the initiative in contacting faculty members. The importance of student initiative is emphasized again during the three-day first-year orientation that occurs prior to the beginning of fall classes. Students meet with their academic advisors, learn about the University Mentorship Program (described below), and hear presentations by faculty described as particularly interested in working with new students.

AFFIRMING DIVERSITY

Formal programs that support students from groups historically underserved in higher education and affirm institutional commitments to diversity are powerful tools to bring students successfully into the institution. The University of Michigan and Wheaton College sponsor POSSE (Pathways to Student Success and Excellence) programs on their campuses. One of the program's goals is to increase the retention and graduation rates of academically and economically disadvantaged undergraduate students by using approaches that encourage collaboration within the institution. Participants learn about the importance of meeting with their instructors during office hours to be sure they are performing satisfactorily and are given study tips and advice about how to use tutoring services effectively. In addition, each student is assigned a counselor who makes sure the student does not "just feel like a number." Although at Michigan POSSE is viewed as a "transitional program" geared toward first- and second-year students, many participants maintain contact with their POSSE peers and continue to rely heavily on their counselors for advice, friendship, and perspectives even as juniors and seniors. As one Michigan student stated, "POSSE taught me how to survive the University of Michigan." Another commented, "POSSE taught me how to go and talk to professors . . . how to ask for help . . . go to the writing center."

Several other DEEP schools offer summer transition programs to support entering students who might need extra assistance adjusting to college. The Bridge Program at Ursinus College brings students to campus three weeks before the start of the semester to help them "bridge the gap between high school and college." Created with external funding about 14 years ago, the Bridge Program started with about 15 students; in 2002, 44 participated. During the last two weeks of July and the first week of August, Bridge Program students take an intensive sociology or literature course as a way to acclimate to Ursinus's academic demands and campus culture. The four-unit course continues in the fall semester, when Bridge students enroll in three other courses to fill their academic program. The program also aims to help students develop a close working relationship with their faculty advisor, a relationship that also extends into the fall semester. Faculty advisors monitor students' progress in courses and meet with students on a weekly basis. The program seems to be successful by any measure, but particularly noteworthy is that the percentage of Bridge students graduating from Ursinus is comparable to that of other students.

Creating Higher Expectations for Educational Readiness (CHEER) is Fayetteville State's summer transition program, which is intended to help students acquire the academic skills and social confidence they need to succeed in college. CHEER students engage in activities to improve reading, writing, and study skills, and earn three hours of credit for Math 121 (Introduction to Algebra). Participation in the program, which is free, enables students to receive a scholarship of $220 for tuition and books associated with the mathematics course.

Acculturation experiences at DEEP schools also acknowledge and affirm diverse styles of learning. George Mason, Alverno, and Fayetteville State demonstrate in multiple ways the value of taking different approaches to student learning. As mentioned earlier, Fayetteville State faculty and staff recognize, but do not lament, that their students are not as well prepared for college as they would like. They get on with the task: "We work with the students we have, not those we wish we had." As one administrator explained, "We may be open admission, but we are not open graduation." The point is clear to FSU students long before they arrive on campus: If you choose to join us, be prepared to work harder than ever. Moreover, know this: "Failure is not an option!"

Socializing New Faculty

DEEP colleges also teach new faculty about their new setting and what they can do to help students succeed. University of Maine at Farmington, for example, dedicates considerable time and energy to ensure that the faculty member–institution fit is right and that potential colleagues have a good understanding of the local culture. One such strategy is a two- to three-day campus interview that occasionally includes staying at the home of a UMF faculty member. The provost looks for individuals who seek the rural New England lifestyle, value collegial relationships with colleagues and students, and are committed to the liberal arts. As we said in Chapter Four, recruitment ads draw attention to the black flies endemic to rural Maine, as well as an emphasis on working extensively and intensively with undergraduate students.

Ursinus has about 110 full-time faculty members, 40 of whom were hired between 1998 and 2003. To smooth the transition to Ursinus for each new cohort, the vice president for academic affairs brings together all new faculty members once a week to meet in the "Faculty Colloquium." Senior faculty members discuss teaching and pedagogical approaches that seem to be effective with Ursinus students. Participants swap teaching tips and approaches. Another goal of the colloquium is for newcomers to better understand the cross-disciplinary culture of Ursinus. This in turn supports the goals of the Common Intellectual Experience (CIE) course taught by faculty from all disciplines.

Longwood values meaningful student-faculty relationships, a point emphasized in new faculty recruitment. As one academic administrator put it: "If the applicant wants a research-based career without undergraduates, this is not the place for them." A faculty member told us, "In the hiring process we ask about interest in teaching and caring for students. We want the right kind of people coming here." Noteworthy, too, is the fact that Longwood students have a direct, integral role in new faculty recruitment and hiring processes. Student participation and input are readily acknowledged by administrators and senior faculty as invaluable in assessing an applicant's commitment to working with students.

California State University at Monterey Bay goes to noteworthy lengths to inform new faculty members of its students' needs. Student-centeredness is emphasized when faculty members are recruited and again during the four-day faculty orientation program for which all new full-time and part-time faculty are compensated. During orientation faculty are challenged to answer the question, "What will teaching and advising look like if we are carrying out our vision?" The highlight of the program is a half-day trip to the surrounding community so that faculty can see firsthand where many of their students live and identify potential service learning sites. After the trip faculty members are asked to reflect on what this excursion meant to them and their focus on supporting students. The university's student-centered ethos is reinforced again on the first day of school at an all-faculty assembly during which every faculty member signs an enlarged copy of the CSUMB Vision Statement as a symbolic rededication to the university's values.

Because all University of Kansas decision-making committees—including search and screen committees—have 20% student representation, new faculty begin to interact with students and come to know their interests and needs during the recruitment process. In addition, new faculty orientation pairs a senior faculty mentor with a new faculty member to foster understanding of the campus culture, including an emphasis on undergraduate student learning.

Connecting Students to Each Other and Their College

Done well, rituals and traditions can bond students to one another and to the institution. Feelings of belonging help students connect with their peers and the institution, relationships that, in turn, are associated with persistence and satisfaction. Such events also can teach institutional values, including the value placed on academic achievement.

The University of Kansas uses "Hawk Week" to acquaint students with KU traditions. One of the week's popular events is "Traditions Night," where more than 3,000 students gather in the football stadium to rehearse the Rock Chalk Chant, listen to stories about the Jayhawk, and learn the "I'm a Jayhawk" school song. Intended to represent the historic struggles of Kansas settlers, the Jayhawk, a mythical bird that serves as the campus mascot, remains a powerful, enduring symbol of impassioned people committed to keeping Kansas a Free State. Other stories and rituals are meant to instill and deepen new students' commitment to graduating from KU. Admissions tour guides tell visiting prospective students that KU students do not dare walk through the campanile until they've earned the right to walk through at commencement. Another Traditions Night ritual is to recognize achievement by asking students who are second- and third-generation Jayhawks to stand. In addition, a torch is passed from a senior to a representative of the first-year class (representatives usually are fourth- or fifth-generation Jayhawks).

At Wofford, "there is a right way, there is a wrong way, and there is the Wofford way." The campus chaplain only half in jest described the "Wofford Way" slogan as "a mystical thing": "If the plumbing does not work—it is the Wofford Way, if we beat the Citadel in football—it is the Wofford Way." The "Wofford Way" also describes students hanging out at the Acorn Café, using the Great Oaks Hall for "casual study" and socializing, and going to the library or the Olin Building for "serious study." Wofford orientation leaders present skits that depict these and other Wofford "dos and don'ts" to incoming students. Often featured in the performance are Wofford rituals such as rubbing the misspelled word "benificence" [sic] on the plaque commissioned by the founder for good luck on tests; faculty-signed Bibles distributed at graduation; and a local neighbor's opening reception and welcome into the neighborhood.

At WSSU, new students are challenged to do what is necessary for academic success during the "Lamb to Ram" pinning ceremony, a formal induction event held during orientation week. This program inspires confidence, builds a sense of membership in the community, and helps new students picture themselves as successful WSSU students. The Ram Ambassadors, and the student government Lamb to Ram program, initiate students into the "Ram family," and communicate what it means to be a member. It is a time, several students further explained, when one becomes an official college student because "you have the pin to prove it." As part of the "Ram family," parents, guardians, and other members of students' families are expected to hold and communicate high expectations for their students' success and be involved in their students' lives at WSSU. In addition to pinning the "Lambs," other highlights of the event include speeches by the chancellor, Miss WSSU, and other college dignitaries, and walking through the Arches for good luck. The Arches physically symbolize a gateway to institutional loyalty and pride and represent WSSU's "Enter to learn, depart to serve" motto. They are an architectural artifact linking present students to the past, and ushering them into future leadership. According to campus folklore, the more frequently students walk through the Arches, the greater the likelihood they will graduate.

Sewanee emphasizes intellectual challenge in admissions publications and during campus visits. Once students matriculate, these messages are reinforced in the outdoor preorientation activity, new student orientation, and the First Year Program. The First Year Program also helps students learn the numerous Sewanee terms of endearment, such as "the Domain" and "the Mountain," as well as campus rituals. One such ritual is "getting a Sewanee angel": students touch the roof of their vehicle as they leave the gates of the Domain to invite a guardian angel to protect them away from the campus. Angels are "released" by touching the roof again when returning to the Domain. These practices may seem old fashioned, even hokey, at first blush to outsiders. Yet in the context of Sewanee, they reinforce the academic ethos, communicate the core values of the institution, and integrate newcomers into the college's culture.

At Sweet Briar College, we heard repeatedly that only members of the Sweet Briar community can fully appreciate the appeal and value of what might appear to be nonsensical, frivolous activities and pastimes. The explanatory refrain was, "It's a Sweet Briar thing. . . . You wouldn't understand." Indeed, scores of terms of endearment, traditions, and other cultural properties work together to socialize newcomers and bond Sweet Briar women to the college and to one another. For example, faculty and staff welcome new students with glow sticks during a culminating ceremony on the last evening of orientation. Much of the campus culture and "how we do things at Sweet Briar" is transmitted from the intentional pairing of first-year students with juniors, a practice typical of women's colleges. Juniors help first-year students understand Sweet Briar's events and traditions and even serve as first-year class officers until the new students elect their own representatives in the fall. The two classes remain sister classes throughout students' careers at Sweet Briar.

Fall Founders Day features an organized march to the top of the hill where Daisy Williams—whose mother provided the endowment to found Sweet Briar—and the rest of her family are buried. The procession is led by a bagpiper and seniors, who wear their academic robes for the first time. These robes are decorated with buttons, patches, and secret pockets reflecting generations of Sweet Briar students' experiences; each new owner adds her own adornments and wears the robe during her senior year. Faculty members also wear academic regalia. Senior students and the college chaplain lead a brief ceremony of remembrance at the top of the hill and lay daisies on Daisy's grave. A community picnic on the campus green follows the event.

To communicate expectations for graduation, departing seniors present their decorated academic robes to juniors. At the spring Junior Banquet, juniors receive gold class rings that feature the college seal in a gemstone that is the official color of the students' graduating class. The class color, motto, and symbol identify the various classes (four different sets of mottos, colors, and symbols are constant and rotate every four years). In addition to lending a sense of continuity and perspective, these traditions and others like them bond students to one another and to their alma mater. Moreover, they give students something to look forward to—a sense that they, too, can achieve something of significance as did those who have gone before.

Like its mission, Wabash's code of conduct—the Gentleman's Rule— is unique and simply stated: "The College expects each student to conduct himself, at all times, both on and off the campus, as a gentleman and a responsible citizen." As we noted in Chapter Two, no other rule exists to govern student behavior at Wabash. It is at the core of becoming a "Wabash man." According to the 2002–2003 Wabash *Academic Bulletin,* "This simple, yet all-encompassing rule allows the Wabash student exceptional personal freedom and requires of him commensurate personal responsibility, which together we believe are essential parts of his education and development." One administrator told us the Gentleman's Rule "is at the center of our culture and deeply embedded in the ethos of the campus." In fact, the Rule is a direct reflection of the core values of the college: "We focus here on values instead of rules. We say to young men, 'we trust you,' and they know we mean it."

Wabash believes its Gentleman's Rule "is the essence of the liberal arts" in that students are expected to critically examine situations and make thoughtful, well-informed decisions. As one administrator told us, "students struggle with the tension between freedom and responsibility and with the absence of clearly defined limits [and] sometimes they screw up." Indeed, the college views students making mistakes as an important part of their learning. The Gentleman's Rule is also a focal point for socializing students to the Wabash culture. New students hear about it long before they matriculate. After they arrive, returning students tell newcomers what is acceptable and what is not. Equally important, students hold each other accountable. Students talked about the Gentleman's Rule with affection and respect. A senior said, "You're constantly asking yourself, 'Are you acting like a gentleman?' It gives you the freedom to make mistakes and learn from them. You're accountable to your peers and you learn to trust each other." An administrator added, "We talk about it all the time, but we have a hard time explaining it. It's a little mysterious." As one student put it, "You can only understand it by being here."

Summary

DEEP institutions communicate preferred ways of doing things and bond students to one another and the institution. They do not leave newcomers alone to discover what it takes to be successful. Even before enrolling, prospective students are provided clear messages about the college's mission, values, and expectations. Bridge programs are available for students who might need extra assistance in adapting to college, but all incoming students participate in structured experiences that welcome them to community membership and provide them with the information they need to be effective students.

ALIGNMENT

Showing new students what they can and must do to succeed in college is necessary but not sufficient to ensure success. Also important is an infrastructure of support, including safety nets, reward systems, and ongoing assessment. At DEEP colleges, resources and structures for student success are aligned with the educational mission, curricular offerings, and student abilities and aspirations. Specific policies and practices for student success at DEEP schools are performance standards, redesigning of programs to meet student needs, early warning systems, advising, and reward systems.

Performance Standards

DEEP schools set standards for achievement at levels consistent with their students' academic preparation that also stretch them to go beyond what they think they can accomplish. If standards are set too high, beyond the reach of students' current ability to perform, many will struggle, become frustrated, and perform poorly; some will leave school. If standards are too low, students will not perform up to their potential. In both cases, human capital is wasted. Thus, absolute levels of academic, personal, and social challenge vary from one school to the next and even within institutions, depending on student characteristics (for example, precollege preparation, family circumstances, major field) as well as institutional mission and context.

As with other aspects of the academic program, faculty members are key to setting and maintaining performance standards, especially faculty whom students consider to be "tough, demanding, but interesting." Students described one WSSU faculty member as "intimidating." But they also view him as a "great teacher" because he sets high expectations for students: "He wants you to be prepared for life, so he correlates real life to the class material. You have to think." For example, seniors in the Department of Business Administration and Economics at Winston-Salem State University complete a capstone class using real-life case examples.

Along with setting high standards, DEEP institutions use various methods to assess students' academic performance. Some institutions require students to complete rigorous written or oral comprehensive examinations. For example, Wabash students take comprehensive examinations in January of their senior year. A two-day written exam is followed by an hour-long oral exam presented to a committee (faculty in the student's major and minor fields of study and an at-large representative). "Comps" require students to (1) organize and synthesize information to address broad questions relevant to their discipline, and (2) demonstrate competence in the major area of study. A faculty member asserted, "It's the 50-minute oral that's really scary. They have to talk about their field and put it in a broader context than they've had to in their courses." Another noted, "It's interesting to see how they can pull things together." Comprehensive exams are another example of the competitive Wabash student culture. Other schools require the completion of a major paper, such as a senior thesis, or a portfolio that can be later used when applying for jobs or graduate school. We describe several of these in Chapter Eight.

Another way DEEP schools align student performance with institutional expectations is through feedback. Earlier in this section we described Evergreen's emphasis on providing students feedback on their performance. Recall that Evergreen does not assign letter grades, but student performance is evaluated rigorously through individual conferences between students and faculty and written narratives. At the conclusion of a Program, for example, students submit a self-evaluation in which they are encouraged to reflect on their work and describe significant learning experiences. The student also prepares a written evaluation of the faculty member. The faculty narrative evaluation describes the subject areas studied, details the student's accomplishments, and assigns the number of credits earned. Typically, students and faculty exchange and discuss these evaluations during the end of the program evaluation conference. Chapter Three offers more examples of the important ways that faculty at DEEP schools demonstrate their focus on improving student learning through feedback. Additional tools that schools are using to measure academic performance are discussed further in Chapter Eight.

Redesigning Programs to Meet Student Needs

From surveys such as NSSE, UCLA's Cooperative Institutional Research Program (CIRP), and locally developed instruments, DEEP schools know a lot about their students, who they are, and what they need to perform well. Programs and practices are invented, tweaked, revised, or discarded, depending on what data say about students and their experiences. Additional important information comes from ongoing contacts with students—listening to their needs, learning about their successes, and understanding how their success occurs. Every DEEP college has a story to tell: first about the importance of systematically coming to know their students and then using that knowledge to foster success.

Information from NSSE and other sources about how students were spending their time prompted Miami University's first-year experience "Choice Matters" initiative, an effort to channel student behavior toward desirable activities. The goal for students is to use their time wisely and reflect systematically on what they learn from their experiences inside and outside the classroom. A variety of linked programs promote the initiative, including (1) Miami Plan Foundation courses taught by full-time faculty, (2) optional first-year seminars, (3) community living options that emphasize leadership and service, and (4) cultural, intellectual, and arts events. Overall, this and other initiatives to positively affect first-year student experience are part of an intentional effort to align Miami's infrastructure and programs with its values, and their impact is subject to systematic evaluation.

Michigan has done six major studies of undergraduates' experiences since the late 1980s. The first, for the Planning Committee on the Undergraduate Experience, established integrated undergraduate education programs, including the First-Year Seminar Program, the Undergraduate Research Opportunity Program (UROP), and the Sweetland Writing Center. The most recent report was "The Second Chapter of Change: Renewing Undergraduate Education at the University of Michigan," by the President's Commission on the Undergraduate Experience (2002). All of the reports provide candid appraisals of the state of undergraduate education at the university and offer innovative and responsive strategies for improving undergraduates' experiences. Michigan has implemented many of those strategies in one form or another to provide students with guides for navigating the university's bountiful opportunities for learning and for linking classroom and out-of-class experiences.

As described in Chapter Two, many first-generation college students at the University of Maine at Farmington have jobs. Up until several years ago, most UMF students who worked did so off campus, a practice research shows is linked to high rates of attrition. After documenting this behavior and recognizing its negative effects, the university increased the number of meaningful work-study jobs on campus. The program began in 1998 with an $86,000 allocation from the UMF president; in 2003, the Student Work Initiative fund had almost doubled to $168,000. Campus jobs were created with two goals in mind: (1) to provide students with meaningful learning experiences through employment, and (2) to increase persistence and graduation rates. Now about 50 percent of UMF students work on campus; the rate of student persistence to graduation has improved from 51% to 56% and continues to climb.

Early Warning Systems

Several DEEP schools use versions of "early warning systems" to identify and support students at academic risk. George Mason monitors students' performance to ensure they do not slip through the cracks. In the midterm progress report, part of its early warning system, faculty members, who receive reports for their advisees, and the Academic Advising office, which receives grades for undeclared students, contact students with low grades. In addition, the University 100 orientation course uses a series of assessments as student performance indicators. Students can access their assessment records online, as well as faculty evaluations, as they register for class.

Fayetteville State's early-alert system depends on an intricate network of individuals, including faculty, mentors, academic support units, and University College and Career Center staff, to identify and assist students in academic difficulty. Faculty members teaching 100-level courses are paired with University College staff, whereas those teaching courses at the 200-level and above work with colleagues at the Advisement and Career Services Center to intervene when needed. Within the first two weeks of the semester, all faculty teaching freshman-level courses receive a roster indicating the mentor (usually the instructor of the First Year Seminar course) for each first-year student. The faculty use this information to contact the mentor and the University College to alert them about students experiencing difficulty. Mentors, in turn, contact students and determine whether additional referrals are needed. The Advisement and Career Services Center communicates with students about strategies to address their difficulties and offers workshops that coincide with progress letters sent to at-risk students.

At Winston-Salem State University, staff members in the Center for Student Success monitor the academic progress of all first-year and second-year students by reviewing daily class attendance, academic performance after the fourth week of classes, midterm exam grades, and final exam grades. The center sends individual "progress reports" for each student to faculty teaching in the core curriculum. Faculty are asked to comment on the reasons for students' difficulty, choosing from among 16 possible affective and behavioral concerns. These concerns include poor class attendance, apparent loneliness, lack of class participation, poor reading skills, failure to appear for appointments, and disruptive classroom behavior. "When I receive a report back from faculty, it puts my services into play," explained an administrator in the center. Center staff contact students in difficulty by phone and e-mail and encourage them to come to the center for help. An administrator in the center explained, "I also burn a lot of shoe leather" in tracking students down in their residence hall or after class. When the center receives a report on a student, or when a student earns a D or F, the student is placed on a monitoring list. Each semester, anywhere from 400 to 700 students are on the list.

At least a half dozen DEEP schools have federally funded TRIO programs, designed to expand access to higher education and provide early intervention to prepare and assist students from historically underrepresented groups. Fayetteville State's Student Support Services (SSS) provides highly structured academic development programs, including personal and group counseling, cocurricular programs, and peer tutors. Involvement in SSS is demanding: students are required to participate in 20 hours of tutoring per week.

Advising

National studies of student satisfaction indicate that advising is the area of their educational experience with which students are the least satisfied (Low, 2000; Noel-Levitz Inc., 2003). DEEP schools organize faculty and staff resources in different ways to address this important aspect of students' academic lives. For example, recall that Longwood assigns a faculty advisor who may work with the student in that role throughout the student's undergraduate program. Some schools embed the advising function in the first-year experience. Macalester, Wofford, and Sewanee connect students to their advisor via the first-year seminar course in which the faculty member serves as students' academic advisor until students declare their major and are assigned a departmental advisor. Wheaton created an advising team composed of the faculty member, peer mentor, librarian, and administrator assigned to instruct in the first-year seminar.

Miami University emphasizes the importance of advising by assigning new students to first-year residence halls with a live-in academic advisor. The first-year advisor serves as the academic advisor and as the residence hall director to students living in the first-year residence hall (ranging in size from 75 to 360 students), although in a few academic programs (Schools of Fine Arts and Engineering and Applied Science, Teacher Education) another advisor is assigned to first-year students. After classes begin, 90% of first-year students invited to schedule an appointment with their first-year advisor show up for this 30-minute conference. Faculty members serve as advisors to all upper division students in their majors, a practice that has disappeared at many large institutions. This advising model ensures that new students have access to a specialist in the advising needs and issues of first-year students, who gets to know them personally through other interactions in the residence hall. The advisor also connects students to faculty in their academic department for advising to ensure that students come into contact with an individual faculty member on a regular basis.

Kansas established the Freshman-Sophomore Advising Center (FSAC) in response to lower-than-desired levels of student satisfaction with academic advising. Its "Graduate in Four" advising notebook, distributed at orientation, is designed to provide students with information about how to make the most of their undergraduate years and what they need to do to complete their degree program in a timely manner. In the welcome letter at the front of the notebook, the university encourages students to "plan out-of-classroom activities such as organizations and internships that develop your skills and experiences, broaden you as a person, and enhance your opportunities for employment or graduate or professional school." The notebook then includes a section for each of the four undergraduate years along with a "checklist" that students can use to help determine whether they are making appropriate choices. The notebooks also help students monitor whether they are, in fact, making progress toward the completion of their degree. Although students seem to use the information in the notebooks for reference, they had not yet adopted the intended practice of bringing their notebooks with them to advising appointments. KU is working to determine the different ways to encourage greater use of the notebooks such as extending their application to other departments, including career services.

Reward Systems

Effective programs and practices cannot be sustained unless the contributions of the people who implement them are recognized. One reason DEEP schools seem to work well is the presence of reward systems congruent with their enacted missions and priorities. At all colleges and universities, tensions about rewards—who is rewarded for what and how—are inevitable; DEEP schools are not immune from such tensions. Yet when conflicts over rewards arise, DEEP colleges handle them as they handle other institutional dilemmas: in the context of institutional mission, values, and resources. This is especially challenging at large, complex institutions with multiple missions that emphasize research along with teaching and service.

Some DEEP schools recognize faculty commitment to teaching undergraduates with financial awards. At KU, each year, 50 to 60 faculty members selected by their students are honored at the Teacher Appreciation Banquet sponsored by the Center for Teaching Excellence (CTE). The university sponsors several teaching awards that carry campuswide respect and prestige, and some carry substantial monetary awards. KU's CTE also supports faculty affiliated with learning communities by providing the faculty members with $500 to fund in-class projects and cocurricular enrichment activities.

George Mason honors teaching by identifying and recruiting outstanding senior faculty members. Twenty years ago GMU established the Robinson Scholars program to attract from other institutions distinguished professors in the liberal arts and sciences who are committed to undergraduate education. Currently, GMU employs 11 Robinson scholars from a wide range of disciplines who teach everything from 100-level and freshman seminar courses through advanced courses.

As part of its systematic efforts to focus on and improve undergraduate education (described more fully in Chapter Six), the University of Michigan established a series of named professorships, the Thurnau Professors, to honor faculty with extraordinary achievements in undergraduate education.

WHAT'S NOTEWORTHY ABOUT CREATING CLEAR PATHWAYS TO STUDENT SUCCESS

- DEEP colleges clearly mark routes to student success. Some guideposts, such as required first-year seminars, advising sessions, periodically updating programs of study, and capstone courses, are tied directly to the academic program. Others take the form of convocations that celebrate educational attainment, passing along gowns that represent continuity of experience, or walking through arches to heighten one's commitment to graduating.

- Institutional publications accurately describe what students say they experience.

- Most DEEP schools do not prescribe overly restrictive pathways to success. At the same time, each institution is unmistakably intentional about telling students about the resources and services available to help them succeed. Some institutions are more intrusive than others in this regard; some require specific activities of some or all of their students, others have few, if any, such requirements.

- DEEP schools tailor their efforts to meet the needs of their students. Each institution sets standards according to what is reasonable for its students' experiences and aspirations and provides the support—remedial, supplemental, or enrichment—students need to meet these standards.

6

An Improvement-Oriented Ethos

DEEP SCHOOLS seem to be in a perpetual learning mode—monitoring where they are, what they are doing, where they want to go, and how to maintain momentum toward positive change. Supporting this orientation toward improvement is a "can-do" ethic that permeates the campuses—a system of values and beliefs that reflect the institutions' willingness to take on matters of substance consistent with their priorities and commitment to student success. They channel limited resources toward mission-related initiatives to promote student success. Difficult budget situations are no excuse to suspend or retard improvement efforts.

To varying degrees, DEEP schools are emblematic of the learning organizations described by Peter Senge (1990) and the firms studied by Jim Collins (2001) that catapulted them from being simply one of many good organizations to being great. They are oriented toward cultivating curiosity and a willingness to experiment. Their motivation for doing "better" is generally internal, while at the same time they are open and willing to look beyond their campus boundaries to other institutions for ideas and inspiration for improvement.

To illustrate how institutions can intentionally modify their policies, practices, and cultural properties to support student success, we briefly summarize the different approaches taken by a subset of DEEP colleges and universities. Then we examine several salient elements of the improvement-oriented ethos that characterized these six schools as well as the other DEEP institutions.

REALIZING THE VISION: THE UNIVERSITY OF TEXAS AT EL PASO

When current UTEP President Diana Natalicio first arrived at the institution as a visiting faculty member, it was a very different place from what it is today, as we described in Chapter Two. As she moved through the faculty ranks and then into academic administration, she became much more aware of the changing demographics of El Paso and what those could and should mean for UTEP. As vice president for academic affairs, she began to envision a different university, one that could play a national leadership role in demonstrating how it could use changing demographics as an educational advantage, both for students and the institution. In 1998, upon becoming president, she began to articulate an inclusive, forward-looking vision that proclaimed UTEP's pride in being a Hispanic majority university, a characterization that prompted grave concern on the part of many faculty members who feared that public use of such a label would be viewed with disapproval by their colleagues elsewhere. Natalicio responded by accelerating the adoption of the university's new mission.

One critical event in converting faculty apprehension into mild curiosity about the changing mission was UTEP's successful application for a National Science Foundation (NSF) Research Improvement in a Minority Institution (RIMI) grant. Natalicio presented UTEP as an emerging "minority majority institution" in numerous trips to Washington, D.C., where NSF staff had little knowledge about the institution even though they were searching for universities to work with to improve science and mathematics training of underserved populations. According to Natalicio, the grant "turned the heads of a lot of faculty in science and engineering. All of a sudden, here was this guy with a million dollar lab and this big, beautiful electron microprobe" (Kuh, 2004). It also helped that the faculty member who received the grant was willing to talk with different groups about what he was doing in the lab and about the minority students working with him. This generated additional faculty interest in the evolving vision and what a revised mission could look like in practice.

While competing successfully for other external grants, Natalicio and her colleagues turned their attention to UTEP's disappointing persistence and graduation rates. Even though the majority of students was first generation and spoke English as a second language, it was simply unacceptable to Natalicio that in the early 1990s only about 63% of first-year students returned for the second year of undergraduate study.

UTEP created the Entering Student Program (ESP), a comprehensive campuswide collaborative effort to address the needs of first-year students through integrated enrollment, orientation, and advising programs, as well as content-based programs, including UNIV 1301 (described in Chapter Two), a student leadership institute, and accessible, high-quality tutoring. Many of the elements of this program were modeled after components put in place for science, mathematics, engineering, and technology (SMET) students through the NSF-funded Model Institutions for Excellence (MIE) grant awarded to UTEP in 1995. An ambitious number of learning communities were also developed, again modeled after the cluster courses (English composition, mathematics, and critical inquiry) created for SMET majors as part of the MIE grant. First piloted in 2000, UTEP's learning communities are organized around UNIV 1301 and have expanded to include a broader set of interdisciplinary offerings (see Chapter Nine).

In addition to closely monitoring persistence and graduation rates, UTEP is systematically assessing the quality of its various University Colleges and related student success initiatives. Every UNIV 1301 seminar is evaluated at the end of the term by students, faculty, and peer leaders. Student progress indicators such as satisfaction and GPA are incorporated as part of the review of various programs, along with qualitative data to better understand student perspectives that can help interpret the quantitative indicators. UTEP's current priority is "throughput": identifying what the institution can do to help students succeed and graduate. For example, various groups are looking at how to help students pay for college. Cash flow is a real-time financial problem, such as having enough money to pay for textbooks at the beginning of the semester. So,

UTEP is expanding its emergency book loan fund. In part, the through-put initiative was inspired by *Moneyball,* Michael Lewis's (2003) book about the Oakland Athletics baseball team, which challenges the folk wisdom of how to win major league baseball games. Instead of relying on common lore of baseball announcers, managers, and scouts, the Oakland team uses sophisticated statistical analyses to identify the factors that are important to winning baseball games. UTEP is using a similar "thinking outside the box" approach to analyzing what matters to student success (Kuh, 2004).

The combination of President Natalicio's visionary leadership and of the hard work of countless faculty and staff members has literally transformed UTEP into a high-performing university committed to student success that serves a highly diverse student body. The campus is now nationally recognized for its student-centric philosophy, effective use of active and collaborative learning techniques, and its innovative first-year student programs. Also, the first-to-second-year persistence rate in 2002 was about 72%, almost a 9% increase since the mid 1990s.

MAKING STUDENT SUCCESS A PRIORITY: FAYETTEVILLE STATE UNIVERSITY

Fayetteville State's tradition of promoting student access and success moved to a new level under the leadership of former FSU Chancellor Willis McLeod (1995–2003). As with UTEP, the impetus for his interest was concern about first-to-second-year retention rates that were well below peer institutions (65% compared to 77%), and a commitment to maintain high standards for academic work. McLeod's position paper, "Linking Retention and Academic Performance: The Freshman Year Initiative" (McLeod, 2003, http://www.uncfsu.edu/chanoff/FYI01.HTM), challenged FSU faculty and staff members to make student development the focus of everything they do. He persuasively and cogently articulated the importance of FSU's nurturing and supportive ethos: "At Fayetteville State University, 'total personal development' certainly includes academics, and our students' intellectual development, but it also includes their psychological, social, and cultural development as well. Students need our assistance in understanding what they can reasonably expect of FSU, and what is expected of them as university students. Most importantly, we must instill in students a 'no-fail' attitude. By this, I mean that we need to help students develop the self-confidence and commitment to excellence that will help them see that success is within their reach, and that failure is not an option."

To advance the agenda, McLeod cited research showing the importance of developing the whole student, such as *The Student Learning Imperative* (American College Personnel Association, 1994) and Chickering and Gamson's (1987) "Seven Principles for Good Practice in Undergraduate Education." He also passionately and persuasively argued for the need for new initiatives by pointing to characteristics and performance of FSU students, drawing on locally produced information and national student survey results. A staff development program was instituted to increase staff awareness of their importance to student success.

Beginning in 1995, FSU launched a comprehensive set of initiatives targeted to its first-year students, including University College (described in Chapter Twelve) and mentoring programs to increase student-faculty contact, outreach efforts such as University Day, which annually provides a "taste" of the college experience to about 2,500 middle school students, and other efforts to forge ties between the community and the university. In addition, an extension grade policy was established to allow students who need help to get access to the university's academic support activities. Anticipating enrollment growth due to both improved persistence rates and projected enrollment growth in the state universities of North Carolina, the Rudolph Jones Student Center was expanded and a new fine arts and classroom building were added along with several more residence halls. Other campus residences were refurbished.

Chancellor McLeod's initiatives further strengthened the institution's commitment to promote student success. FSU's cohesive culture rooted in a talent development philosophy and its many traditions that bond students to one another and the university help to generate a strong sense of loyalty to the institution and in large part accounts for FSU's improving persistence and graduation rates. The impact of these efforts was recognized by the Southern Association of Colleges and Schools (SACS), which fully reaccredited the university with commendations in three areas: outstanding interaction between the university and its nearby communities; cultural outreach in the fine arts; and creating a positive environment for teaching and learning.

INVESTING IN UNDERGRADUATE EDUCATION: THE UNIVERSITY OF MICHIGAN

The impetus for Michigan's enhancements dates back to 1986 when then provost and later president James J. Duderstadt and his colleagues established a Blue Ribbon Task Force within the College of Literature, Science and Arts (LS&A) made up of some of the university's most distinguished faculty members to assess the quality of undergraduate education. Other committees were subsequently formed to focus on specific areas. The initial efforts focused on some of the larger undergraduate programs in LS&A and in engineering and business administration. For example, the College of Engineering took advantage of grants and changing Accreditation Board for Engineering and Technology (ABET) requirements to extend active and collaborative learning experiences. Engineering faculty called on personnel from the Center for Research on Learning and Teaching to help them modify their pedagogy to employ activities to promote team building and group problem solving.

Senior administrators knew that to achieve the broad-based action that would make a marked difference, a comprehensive institutionwide effort was needed. To energize and sustain the improvement agenda, Michigan earmarked about $1 million a year for about 10 years to its Undergraduate Initiatives Fund. Many initiatives were based on students, faculty, and staff. The first round of awards went to a mix of initiatives proposed by academic units, individual faculty members, students, and staff. The major foci were:

- Promoting critical thinking and writing skills;
- Creating a new spirit of liberal learning;

- Encouraging acceptance of pluralism and diversity; and

- Promoting improved faculty-student interactions.

For example, science and mathematics instruction in the first two undergraduate years was systemically revised. The arts (theater, dance, music) were better integrated in the undergraduate curriculum. For instance, "The Arts Alive" First-Year Seminar (FYS) was created to introduce students to art, architecture, and the performing arts in Ann Arbor. Other efforts focused on improving the training of graduate student teaching assistants and counseling services as well as enhancing sensitivity to pluralism university wide. Student proposals were funded as well, ranging from undergraduate colloquia to faculty fellow programs in the residence halls, online counseling and information services, a campus computer network, and an alternative career center.

The second phase of Michigan's comprehensive effort was to work directly with the schools and colleges in order to focus on:

- Emphasizing the unique nature of undergraduate education in the research university;

- Linking the graduate school disciplines and professions;

- Enriching the intellectual life of undergraduate students; and

- Featuring the role of the sciences in a liberal education.

In addition, the university established a set of named professorships, the Thurnau Professors, to honor faculty with extraordinary achievements in undergraduate education. A series of physical plant improvements were undertaken to improve the quality of instructional space on campus, including renovating the undergraduate library and constructing the Angell-Haven Center, a centrally located facility with more than 400 computer workstations accessible to students 24 hours a day. Every classroom on the central campus was renovated. Student services were restructured to integrate them more effectively into the academic life of the university. Another commission was charged with studying ways to more effectively link academic programming into the residence hall environment. In addition, following in the successful tradition of the residential college and other living-learning programs created in the 1960s, several more million dollars a year were designated to renovate or build major new facilities specifically for undergraduate programs, including the Media Union (an educational building open 24 hours a day, seven days a week, to the entire university community), and the Michigan Community Scholars Program housed in Couzens Hall.

Michigan channeled well over $10 million into its Undergraduate Initiatives campaign between 1986 and 1996. The university is an exemplar for research universities that aspire to take undergraduate education seriously. Its academic leaders persuasively championed improvements, sought proposals from faculty, students, and staff, and then financially invested in worthy innovations, a noteworthy feat given other competing worthwhile requests.

FOSTERING INSTITUTIONAL RENEWAL: UNIVERSITY OF MAINE AT FARMINGTON

UMF is a campus where "people listen." This atmosphere of trust, optimism, and support and space to innovate is due largely to the tone set by senior leaders, especially Dr. Theodora J. Kalikow. President since 1994, Theo (as she is known to everyone), has earned the trust of faculty, staff members, and community leaders because she is intelligent, puts people first, champions an inclusive decision-making approach, and is a tireless advocate of UMF's distinctive mission—being Maine's public liberal arts college. One person described her as a "citizen of the campus"—approachable, inspirational, leading as much by example as exhortation. For example, she makes a point of helping new students move into their dormitories at the beginning of the school year. The rest of the UMF senior leadership team exudes many of the same characteristics.

UMF's quaint setting can be deceiving. The campus is alive with a steady stream of innovative ideas and initiatives. These efforts are not driven by pursuit of prestige, but by an authentic commitment to improve the quality of the student experience. For UMF, this means strengthening its liberal arts offerings and enhancing students' professional preparation.

The institution pursues its ongoing improvement agenda in an incremental, evolutionary way. Because Kalikow believes good ideas are generally the result of collaboration, she models collaboration by soliciting and acting on suggestions from all corners of the campus and being more or less assertive. "Some things," she told us, "you make happen—some things you let happen. The trick is knowing which one to do when."

Though resources are in short supply, somehow UMF finds a few dollars to help the most promising ideas take root. For example, she drew on the president's discretionary fund to create about two dozen $600 "mini-grants" to support the development of student learning outcomes assessment at the course level. As one administrator put it, "The mini-grants may not be much, but they communicate support to help the faculty make positive change."

Students are equal partners and take their responsibilities seriously. Most come from small towns and are accustomed to interacting with different members of their home communities, be it protecting the natural beauty of the state, reading to children, or working on community projects. Students are urged to continue this pattern of involvement at UMF by participating in decision-making groups, including faculty selection committees.

One example of UMF's inclusive decision-making process is its successful Excellence through Connected and Engaged Learning (EXCEL) program, that was described more fully in Chapter Three. In 1997, the general consensus was that UMF had fallen behind in implementing instructional technologies. The decision to do something about it came from a campuswide "technology fishbowl" dialogue, not an announcement by the administration. Enthusiastically endorsed by the president, faculty and staff designed the EXCEL program. Because they owned it, faculty and staff members have a real stake in having it flourish.

UMF's evolution into a student success-oriented campus is not a function of grand strategic initiatives. Rather, it is the product of a campus culture where "people and their success" really do matter. Their notable programmatic initiatives work as well as they do *because* people at UMF work well together toward mutually determined desired ends. The result is an engaged community of learners that capitalizes on its size and location, and gets the most out of its limited resources and talented students, faculty, and staff.

CHAMPIONING LEARNING COMMUNITIES: WOFFORD COLLEGE

Wofford President Benjamin "Bernie" Dunlap issued the following challenge at a faculty retreat in 2001: "If you had the assurance of sufficient time and institutional support to teach the sort of course you've always dreamed of, what would you do?" Faculty enthusiastically responded to the president's charge, vetting ideas in meetings and retreats and studying best practices locally and elsewhere. The result was a groundswell of faculty activity called Integrated Learning and an institutional commitment to become a national model for liberal arts education incorporating learning communities, new interim courses, course-linked field experiences, and interdisciplinary courses.

Wofford College's interest in integrated learning dates back to a large humanities grant it received in the 1970s. One of the major outcomes of that initiative was the interdisciplinary humanities seminar, which then became a General Education (GE) requirement for first-year students. Two decades later, a small group of faculty members from different disciplines team taught a course on Christopher Columbus to mark the 500th anniversary of his historic voyage to the New World. Designing and teaching the course generated rich dialogue and occasional heated debate within and beyond the group. Out of this came the recognition that several of the more prominent threads in Wofford's cultural tapestry are collegial relations, collaboration, and cross-disciplinary interaction. It is not uncommon, for example, for a poet and an economist to chat informally about their disciplines over a meal in the faculty dining room. Thus, it is predictable, perhaps, that as learning communities reemerged nationally as a promising practice, Wofford would create its own variant.

For example, interdisciplinary courses that are linked to create a learning community include such combinations as "Human Physiology and Statistics"; "Genetics and Development" with "Chemistry" and "Science and Religion"; and "English, French, and Spanish Theatre and Society." A Landscape and Art field experience class includes outside speakers and field trips to landscape sites. Teams of faculty from different disciplines teach these courses. One pairing of English and psychology classes resulted in a learning community called "Scientific and Literary Perspectives on

Madness: Reality's Dark Dream." Students explored works of literature and the psychological makeup of the authors, and related key themes from the readings to a variety of issues, including the history of the clinical and social treatment of madness.

The primary impetus to develop learning communities was not to improve student persistence as it is at many schools, inasmuch as Wofford's first-to-second-year rate is about 90%. Rather, the faculty saw learning communities to be a vehicle to involve students more meaningfully in general education offerings. One energetic science faculty member revised her introductory science course to address her concern that students were not integrating their educational experiences. "Science was a box that got closed at the end of the class," she explained. She involved students in the revision of the course, by tapping into their creative ideas about science, and having them study innovative K–12 science initiatives and national science standards. The process by which the course was transformed served as a model for creating additional interdisciplinary offerings that became the foundation for other learning communities.

Building on the successful interdisciplinary humanities courses and a well-received first-year learning community pilot, a nine-person faculty team from the sciences and humanities obtained a $200,000 Course, Curriculum, and Laboratory Improvement (CCLI) grant from the National Science Foundation. The grant provided the resources needed to take the innovative integrated learning community idea to scale.

All the conditions were in place for learning communities (LCs) to take root at Wofford, though it's not as simple as it first appears. For example, several major grants that benefited Wofford were funded only after being revised and resubmitted, including the CCLI grant mentioned above. Equally important, it's one thing to launch innovations and quite another to sustain them, something Wofford understands well.

First, as previously mentioned, senior administrators are very supportive of efforts to improve the quality of the student experience. Wofford's president often refers to the LCs as examples of teaching and learning excellence at faculty meetings and when speaking to alumni and friends of the college.

Second, faculty members were enthusiastic about and supported the concept, which is not surprising because cross-disciplinary collaboration is part of the Wofford culture. Even so, it is unusual for a college faculty to come to general agreement on curricular matters in such a short period of time.

Finally, financial support and other mechanisms enabled faculty members to take full advantage of the promise offered by the innovation. The number of learning communities has been increased, thanks to additional funding from a Mellon Foundation grant, the President's Discretionary Fund, and trustee-earmarked funds in the college's operating budget. The academic dean also released funds to help offset the costs of the reduction in faculty load and to support associated faculty development activities. Faculty members teaching in LCs receive a one-course reduction during the semester they teach in the LC, two weeks of summer financial support to participate in the faculty development workshops, and the opportunity to participate in a second summer faculty development workshop. According to faculty, the course-load reduction was a critical element to the success of the program as was a series of well-conceived seven-week summer workshops during which the 82 full-time teaching faculty formed teams to design and develop their learning community.

The LC initiative has had a broad, positive impact on Wofford students and faculty, energizing the entire campus. More than 30 new courses and programs came on line in one academic year alone, involving more than half the faculty. Campus conversations have shifted toward how to get students to more effectively integrate what they are learning. Several faculty members from disciplines other than humanities and science have developed LCs. For example, "Did You See That?!? The Senses, the Mind, and Our Perception of Reality" brings together faculty from the humanities and psychology. In addition, "learning community" is now part of the Wofford lexicon. First-year students identify themselves by the LC they are in as often as they claim affiliation with a Greek organization. And the identity sticks. For example, when a junior or senior says, "I'm one of the *Water People*," most people on campus know he or she was a member of the Nature and Culture of Water LC.

CREATING A CAMPUSWIDE INTELLECTUAL COMMUNITY: URSINUS COLLEGE

The two-semester required Common Intellectual Experience (CIE) for first-year students was a faculty-driven innovation. Introduced in 1999, it is the centerpiece of the college's commitment to strengthen its traditional liberal arts focus. Its precursor was the Liberal Studies Seminar (LSS), which dates back to the late 1970s. The content of the LSS courses was determined by the individual faculty members teaching them. Over time, faculty determined that the rigor of the LSS offerings varied too much. More important, LSS courses lacked integrating themes that would lead to common conversations beyond the classroom between students and faculty.

The idea for the CIE originated during faculty discussions about preparing for the College's Middle States accreditation visit in 1999. Instead of using Middle States traditional model, the college opted to pursue an alternative approach and give special attention to two areas of institutional performance that it was especially interested in strengthening: teaching and learning and students in community. Championed by an influential politics professor, the CIE initiative was developed by the faculty, enabling them to come to grips with what is essential in the liberal arts.

Teaching in CIE was supported in the initial years by small stipends for participating faculty. Today, only those who are teaching in the CIE program for the first time receive small stipends to prepare the course. Annually, about a quarter of the faculty is involved in the course, and so far about half the faculty has been involved in CIE. CIE instructors meet weekly to discuss upcoming readings and assignments, teaching strategies, and related issues. As a result, they learn a lot from one another about teaching and pedagogy. Moreover, working collaboratively helps forge meaningful intellectual and social connections that are as strong as those they have with colleagues in their home discipline. Thus, the usual disciplinary silos that exist even on small college campuses are less of an obstacle when it comes to dealing with other campuswide initiatives.

The course is required, so its common content (described in Chapter Two) helps to create a campuswide intellectual community. It also acculturates new faculty to the central role of the liberal arts at Ursinus. Junior faculty members quickly get the sense that teaching in CIE at some point is important if one is to be tenured. The seminar is taught each term by faculty from various disciplines, who model for students an openness to learning by moving out of their own discipline and collaborating with one another to create a common syllabus. In addition, many CIE instructors are the academic advisor for the students in their section. Thus, they have regular, ongoing contact with their advisees, and a good sense of their academic performance, and of their adjustment to college life.

CIE benefited from the full support of the Ursinus president and vice president for academic affairs. To further cement the importance of CIE and other collaborative interdisciplinary efforts into the culture, the vice president for academic affairs meets with all new faculty members once a week in a colloquium (described in Chapters Five and Seven). Thus, both formal and informal mechanisms are used to introduce and teach new faculty about the college's values and its emphasis on cross-disciplinary learning.

POSITIVE RESTLESSNESS

The other DEEP colleges and universities are similar to the six just profiled in that they are continually looking for ways to improve. DEEP schools do not necessarily desire to be *like* any other institution; they simply want to be the best *they* can be. Never quite satisfied with their performance, they continually revisit and rework policies and practices to get better. They are restless in a positive way. In this sense, "restlessness" does not equate to an organization out of focus, as Tierney (1999) used the term. Rather, we mean to imply an acculturated wariness that what and how we are doing now can well be improved, now or later, if we *stay focused* on the quality of our work and its impact on students and institutional performance.

A faculty member at Evergreen captured this sense of positive restlessness well: "We talk about what needs to be fixed all the time. This is very much a part of our culture." The most obvious example is that much of Evergreen's academic program is organic, reinvented on an annual basis.

Fieldnotes: It's 9:00 A.M. and we're about to begin our first meeting of the day. This is our second visit to Macalester and we're seeking feedback about the college's interim report we sent a few weeks ago. Sitting in the provost's comfortable meeting area, our pens are poised to record what we need to do to enhance the next draft of this report. The provost pulls out his own legal pad and pen and sits across from us expectantly. Turning the tables, he says: "This was a fine report. Now would you tell us how we can do things better here at Macalester?"

As a team finds and readies itself to teach a core or coordinated program—even for a second time—the content and, often, the basic approach change. Other changes to the Evergreen curriculum typically are recommended by Disappearing Task Forces (DTF), groups established to complete a specific task that disband when done. The general education DTF used the annual Association of American Colleges and Universities summer institute to recommend a plan to revise general education requirements using three guidelines: (1) the general education enrichment must fit within the existing curricular structure; (2) two learning resource centers were needed, one to focus on writing and the second on quantitative reasoning skills; (3) advising must be improved although doing so would require reallocation of resources.

Faculty involved in Fayetteville State University's Teaching and Learning Center described a strong institutional emphasis on improving teaching and, as one sociology faculty member put it, are "conscious of the need to understand students and to engage them actively in the classroom." Another faculty member explained that "part of the institutional culture here is to address poor teaching." One faculty member told us he is "shameless about using games and contests. It works. I give them challenges and rewards. . . . I give the first student to respond 10 extra points, the next person 9 points, and so on." Knowing as much as they do about their students, many FSU faculty members recognize they "need to be more creative to keep students interested."

The Faculty Learning Communities at Miami University bring faculty members together to discuss ways to improve teaching. Each participant identifies a specific course to improve, discusses ways to make improvements, and implements changes in the course during the academic year. Theme-based learning communities focus on such issues as cooperative learning, ethics across the curriculum, team teaching, humanities disciplines and technology, and small groups to enhance learning. Other groups explore problem-based learning and teaching portfolios. Another group focuses on strategies for assessing student learning in Miami Plan (the common core) courses. Among the current learning communities, for example, is a group that will design a course to fulfill the university's new U.S. cultures requirement and another group, supported by a National Endowment for the Humanities (NEH) grant, to revise the American studies curriculum. This faculty-directed initiative has given broad legitimacy to efforts to improve student learning, including curricular revisions. These communities reflect Miami's ongoing commitment to accountability and using information to improve teaching.

Similar to Miami's faculty teaching communities, Alverno regularly hosts discussions to assess teaching and learning and to improve instructional practice. Faculty and staff members regularly discuss ways to make teaching more effective. But faculty, students, and staff do not simply reflect and move on. Assessment, collaborative problem solving, and improvement occur as part of a systematic, ongoing process that shapes virtually every aspect of the institution's functioning.

CSUMB's founders intended to create an innovative, learner-centered educational program. Today the university features interdisciplinary academic programs, active and collaborative learning, and service learning integrated into the curriculum. In addition, the institutional culture is, as one senior administrator declared, "highly self-critical. We shoot for the stars and strive for continuous improvement." According to another administrator, "We hold ourselves to a higher standard because we're supposed to be trying new things." The institution's commitment to innovation, transparency, and accountability reflects this self-critical stance. As an administrator explained, "In the early years we were happy to hear ourselves talk about our success. But over the years we've had to produce evidence for our assertion." By recruiting faculty and staff members who are willing to experiment, the campus is more inclined to innovate without facing significant resistance.

George Mason's inclination to innovate also is due in part to its relative youth. Its perceived status as "underdog" in the Virginia higher education system drives improvement as well. As one staff member told us, "Because this is a young institution, there's a strong dynamic sense. There's a sense of growth, openness to trying new things and doing interesting things." Another said, "What's so great is there's no predefined way of doing things, of how this place moves—but forward." Continuous innovation is part of the culture of GMU, an espoused value since its founding. "Students pick up on this quickly—'you can do anything'—we practically hit them over the head with it." An academic dean told us, "This is a young institution that recruits entrepreneurial, risk-taking faculty and lets them grow," resulting in "an unusual sense of destiny and vision." A student echoed this theme: "Sometimes people forget how new we are. But we're big on improvement here, and this place is so responsive. You can make things happen very fast." A faculty member added, "We're entrepreneurial: the attitude is 'let's do it and see what happens.'" If the outcomes are not as desired, "we find the best compromise and move forward."

Even schools that have modest resources seem to be able to find and implement good ideas. For example, resources at the University of Maine at Farmington are stretched thin. Nevertheless, its "can-do" ethos and values-based policymaking decision making are levers for improvement. Due in part to the regional culture and institutional leadership, UMF's financial shortcomings seem to strengthen, not threaten, its sense of community. A senior administrator told us, "We do a lot with a little, but where you put your money speaks volumes." UMF directs small amounts of discretionary dollars to projects and opportunities with potential to enhance teaching and learning and student-faculty relations. Faculty, for example, are invited to "almost a free lunch" twice a month to talk about teaching and learning.

As with UMF, resources at Gonzaga University are limited. But as one senior administrator asserted, "We have a can-do attitude . . . we figure out how to get things done." In addition to being involved in community service, Gonzaga students also contribute in many significant ways to the quality of life on campus. As one administrator stated: "the university needs students to operate." Another described Gonzaga as a "nonprofit organization . . . its success depends on volunteers." Although this is a financial necessity, administrators also recognize the potential for these experiences to be educationally empowering. "These experiences result in significant leadership opportunities for students," explained a student life staff member. Another administrator added that this practice yields strong student ownership of university programming and services.

Some DEEP institutions are in a position to use discretionary funds to support innovation. At Miami University, faculty members told us, "the university puts its money where its mouth is." Small amounts of money are available to support activities consistent with the mission, such as obtaining books or other materials for visits to other campuses to learn more about programs and practices that might be adaptable to Miami. As one faculty member reported, this is how the Summer Scholars program for undergraduates got started: "You can get an idea and you can get support. The attitude is, 'What do you need, and how can we help you?' I really appreciate that."

CURRICULUM DEVELOPMENT

As the Michigan, Wofford, and Ursinus cases illustrate, curricular innovation is ongoing at DEEP institutions. In some instances, changes in the academic program were born of necessity. For example, the shift from a women's college to coeducation at Longwood and Wheaton required nontrivial curricular adjustments. However, at other DEEP schools, improvements resulted from awareness of emerging promising practices and the desire to maintain or enhance educational excellence. Other DEEP colleges, such as the University of Texas at El Paso and Wofford, successfully competed for grants and other external funding to support curriculum changes and related innovations.

In 1998, the Wheaton College provost asked the faculty, staff, and students to find a way to "break out of the mold of the old curriculum." A faculty member stated the focus of this effort: "What are we going to do about the good old Gen Ed checklist?" This set in motion a collaborative planning process to develop a curriculum that would invest students in their learning. The process was as important as the result, instilling a sense of "full, shared ownership" of the curriculum, through "respectful, thoughtful, and open-minded listening." One faculty member told us, "It transformed my relationships with my colleagues."

Connections and *infusion* emerged as cornerstone concepts for the new curriculum. *Connections* means courses should be connected or linked to provide a more creative and rigorous curriculum with greater breadth. *Infusion* provides a rationale and a mechanism for the faculty to introduce concepts important to the college's mission into the course structure. The new curriculum places gender and diversity at the core of the academic program by integrating race, ethnicity, gender, and sexuality into existing courses.

George Mason reformed its general education curriculum in little more than a year—a rare feat for most institutions, but one that is consistent with Mason's innovative ethos. One of the principals in the process described the new curriculum as "more structured and more integrated" than its predecessor, reflecting "a more conscious attempt to provide an intellectual sequence and connections across disciplines, a seamlessness across academic areas." The process was, according to a senior faculty member, "a massive logistical undertaking by a faculty of good will. . . . People really do think outside the box and have the room to do it." Infusing diversity into the curriculum was driven by the same spirit. In the early 1980s, the campus began to promote innovations such as African American studies, a Latin American studies minor, the Women's Center, and the Center for Conflict Resolution. In addition, a campuswide committee examined ways to create synergy across the efforts and to transform the curriculum and alter teaching practices. To model this work, Mason established the National Coalition Building Institute (NCBI) to provide venues for students to talk about sensitive topics, such as race relations. Every year for more than a decade, 1,200 to 1,500 students participate in the institute-sponsored dialogue series, and NCBI-trained staff are widely credited as instrumental for "making diversity work" at Mason.

DATA-INFORMED DECISION MAKING

Improvement-oriented institutions rely on systematic information to make good decisions, and DEEP schools are no exception, as illustrated earlier in the Fayetteville State, Michigan, and UTEP examples. In the words of the University of Kansas provost, "Data drive most of the things we do." Its Office of Institutional Research and Planning collects a wide array of data about student learning and undergraduate education to ensure that quality information is available for policy formation and decision making. For example, results from KU's General Education Assessment, Student Perceptions Survey, Senior Survey, and National Survey of Student Engagement (NSSE) are regularly reported to academic and student life administrators. More important, these data are used to change advising practices, curriculum requirements, and administrative structures. The General Education Assessment Interviews, conducted by faculty to assess the impact of general education courses, provide an annual opportunity for faculty to "sit across" from 120 graduating seniors and learn how to improve the experiences of students in their major fields. Three-person teams (one faculty member from each student's major and two faculty members from outside the major area) conduct these interviews; more than a third of the faculty has participated. Results of this assessment, including major-specific results, are available to academic units.

Longwood and George Mason operate under a number of state-mandated assessment and efficiency requirements that reinforce a data-driven approach to decision making. In 1986, Virginia required all state-supported colleges and universities to assess the educational outcomes of their programs. In 1994, under a "restructuring" initiative, all state-supported institutions were called upon to minimize administrative and instructional costs, ensure the effectiveness of academic offerings, and address the legislature's funding priorities, including enrollment increases. In 2000–2001, the State Council for Higher Education in Virginia implemented a performance indicator system focused on institutional effectiveness. Under recent Council mandates, Longwood must assess competencies formally in writing, oral communication, fundamental mathematical skills, scientific literacy, and the basic use of computers for all of its graduates. To their credit, the Longwood faculty took the initiative to consider the goals of assessment and accountability on their own terms. Extensive faculty discussions during the late 1980s led to a revision in 1990 of the general education requirements, including expansion of the requirements, and the addition of foreign language and capstone courses for seniors. During the early 1990s, discussions about course goals continued, each program considered and evaluated in turn. More recent discussions have led to refinements of the curriculum, more specific outcomes for each goal, and new general education requirements. Longwood evaluates the effectiveness of these changes by using multiple measures, including surveys, academic progress statistics, curriculum evaluations, and competency testing via nationally normed, discipline-specific achievement tests.

One response by the George Mason University faculty to the State Council's call for accountability was the systematic use of student feedback and other information to continually revise courses to meet students' needs. Every semester faculty in the New Century College develop a portfolio assessment for each course. At the end of the term faculty meet with an administrator to discuss changes in the course the next term. School of Nursing faculty use student focus groups to solicit feedback to improve course offerings and pedagogy. Other academic departments meet with the leaders of student organizations to obtain feedback on courses and plan revisions to support student learning. Such efforts are essential, according to one faculty member, because "you wonder if your assumptions of learning are correct because the student body constantly changes and comes from different backgrounds than do many of the faculty."

Faculty at Miami talked of "a sense of momentum" focused on improvement, an environment created and supported by continuous assessment. Groups such as the Liberal Education Council, Multicultural Council, and Committee for the Enhancement of Learning and Teaching review programs regularly and recommend ways to strengthen them. When results of these program reviews are widely discussed, many recommendations that follow from them are implemented. Particularly relevant is the work of the Committee on Student Assessment and Expectations which conducted extensive conversations with key Miami administrators, faculty, and students about benchmarking relevant aspects of the curriculum to nine other institutions and analyzed Miami grading trends along with national reports on promoting and assessing students' learning. The Committee's report to the provost and the community identified essential conditions for learning, teaching, and assessment. Another ambitious benchmarking exercise calls for each department and program to evaluate its own practices, make comparisons to six strong departments at other universities, and implement the best practices found elsewhere. By 2003, more than 100 plans for improvement already have been developed as a result of the benchmarking exercise, and many more recommendations are expected. The Office of Liberal Education recently added a new staff member to coordinate these assessment efforts and conduct faculty development workshops to assist faculty to do authentic assessment. In another recently instituted initiative, a group of 10 faculty members from across the university have been named Assessment Fellows and will develop strategies for assessing and documenting student learning outcomes related to critical thinking.

As mentioned previously, Alverno College is well known for its systemic approach to assessing student abilities and incorporating self assessment in teaching and learning processes. Moreover, a spirit of self-assessment permeates the campus, because the college believes a student's learning includes self-awareness: her ability to judge what she has achieved, how she achieved it, why she did what she did, and what she might yet do to improve. Applying this belief to the college and its practices, Alverno's institutional learning includes self-awareness in its ability to judge what it has achieved, how it achieved it, why it did what it did, and what it might do to improve. The college continues to try out new, promising approaches to improve student learning as evidenced by its new Diagnostic Digital Portfolio, an Internet-based system that allows students to document and monitor their academic progress online throughout their college career.

A culture of assessment also pervades California State University at Monterey Bay. The new Western Association of Schools and Colleges accreditation standards motivated assessment at CSUMB, but now continuous assessment is ingrained: "We are always looking for evidence."

To generate data related to areas of performance that CSUMB values, the institution has an extensive and comprehensive assessment program, coordinated by the Center for Teaching, Learning, and Assessment and the Office of Institutional Assessment and Research. Assessments provide feedback and other evaluative data about the impact of various initiatives. Multiple measures assess student satisfaction and learning, and results are used in decision-making processes. Continuous assessment studies are conducted to learn how to become more effective in providing a challenging and productive learning environment for the diverse students enrolled at CSUMB.

SUMMARY

DEEP colleges followed many different roads to fashioning policies, practices, and a campus climate supporting student success. The brief case descriptions presented earlier tend to understate the amount of time and energy DEEP faculty, staff, and others invested to develop and implement their respective programs and practices. Yet, they are instructive because they illustrate how often ordinary people can do extraordinary things. For example, the impetus for change had different origins. Sometimes an external entity or event stirred a school to action, at other times it was the review of local information that prompted movement.

Some schools converted challenges into opportunities by stimulating experimentation. For example, the changing demographics of El Paso impelled UTEP to rethink and redefine its mission. Alternatively, innovation at Ursinus and the University of Michigan was inspired by a high level of confidence in institutional mission. These schools were confident enough about who they are and where they want to go to experiment with promising approaches. Some of these efforts could be considered "top down," in that they were inspired and led by senior-level administrators with faculty participation, such as UTEP, Michigan, Fayetteville State, and Miami University. Others were "bottom up," in that they originated from the faculty and were subsequently endorsed and supported by administrators, such as Wofford and Ursinus. In all instances, the initiatives were successfully implemented and institutionalized because they garnered significant interest and support by large numbers of students, faculty members, and staff. Equally important, though champions for change came from all levels and corners of the institution, in almost every instance innovations took root because of the encouragement and contributions of others.

WHAT'S NOTEWORTHY ABOUT INNOVATING AND IMPROVING

- DEEP schools are confident enough of what they are and of their values and aspirations to question whether their performance matches their potential. Never quite satisfied with their level of performance, they continually revisit and rework policies and practices to improve.

- DEEP schools are inclined toward innovation. They are not afraid to experiment and invest in promising ideas, even though human and fiscal resources are stretched thin.

- Curricular innovation at many DEEP schools is driven by faculty members with a desire to provide a responsive, challenging undergraduate curriculum.

- Most DEEP schools systematically collect information about various aspects of student performance and use it to inform policy and decision making.

- Efforts to improve and innovate are grounded in DEEP institutions' missions and values. They seek to be best at what they do with the students they have.

7

Shared Responsibility for Educational Quality and Student Success

FACULTY, STAFF, and students at DEEP institutions enjoy mutual respect and share an affinity for their school's mission and culture. Effective partnerships among those who have the most contact with students—faculty and student affairs professionals—fuel the collaborative spirit and positive attitude characterizing these campuses. Every institution has one or more key administrative or senior faculty leaders who regularly speak about institutional aspirations and the importance of supporting learning-centered priorities. Through their actions and words, senior administrators and faculty model preferred ways of interacting, making decisions, and responding to challenges. Equally important, every day, individuals make small gestures that create and sustain a caring community for students.

DEEP schools also expect and empower students to take responsibility for their academic work and social life and that of their peers. Many students on every DEEP campus went out of their way to get other students involved in their productive activities.

The commitment to building shared responsibility for student success begins with leadership. Although presidents and provosts are certainly important, leadership at DEEP schools is also distributed among other administrators, faculty members, and student affairs staff. Students, too, play an important role in influencing the tone of campus life. Another key aspect of the shared models of leadership enacted at DEEP schools is that they carefully choose newcomers, bringing into the community people whose values and aspirations are compatible with the institution's mission, philosophy, and educational purposes. At the same time, they are committed to diversifying their membership to create more inclusive and supportive communities.

LEADERSHIP

It is not surprising that high-performing colleges and universities have effective leaders. At DEEP schools, those who share leadership responsibilities hold positions in different places and different levels of the organization. Sometimes presidents set the tone and direction for student success initiatives, sometimes the provost or dean of students guides actions. Faculty also are instrumental in keeping the institution on course with its mission and philosophy. Student affairs staff members often take the lead in creating educationally enriching experiences for students. Collaboration among campus leaders moves the institution forward.

Senior Leadership

Jim Collins and his research team (2001) studied firms that became exemplary performers in their respective industries. Like the CEOs of Collins's "Good to Great" firms, the presidents and provosts of these 20 colleges and universities did not follow a common career path or have the same personality style. Some came from other institutions to assume their positions. Others were "home-grown," in that they spent years at their institutions, working in various academic and administrative roles before assuming senior leadership positions. The one thing the presidents have in common is all held academic positions prior to their appointments. None came directly from positions outside higher education, although a few, such as CSUMB's Peter Smith (former Vermont state senator, lieutenant governor, and a member of the U.S. Congress) have been in public service. Another element they have in common is relying on other senior administrators and faculty to share responsibility for institutional leadership.

In Chapter Six we described how the senior leadership at Fayetteville State University, University of Maine at Farmington, and Wofford College and some other DEEP schools championed efforts to enhance student success. Another such leader is Longwood University president Patti Cormier. Self-described as having strong reform impulses, Cormier is credited for inspiring the community to develop its "Citizen Leader for the Common Good" focus which is central to the university's mission and strategic plan. Cormier herself is a visible, persuasive representative of "citizen leader" values, volunteering in the local community and on civic boards. Sparked by a desire for Longwood to be among the leading institutions of its type, she initiated a sustained change agenda to ensure that classroom experiences "challenge the theoretical against the practical." Cormier successfully encouraged academic and student affairs staff to collaboratively develop programs complementing Longwood's mission, traditions, and values. For example, several structural links bridge the usual organizational boundaries between academics and student affairs. The vice president of student affairs reports directly to the provost and serves on the tenure committee. This ensures that students' out-of-class experiences are represented by student affairs during meetings of the academic deans, which in turn has resulted in a higher degree of faculty involvement in student affairs programs.

In the past two decades key administrative leaders at the University of Michigan, including presidents, provosts, and academic deans, committed themselves publicly to enhance undergraduate experiences. Former president Lee Bollinger, in his introduction to the Report of the President's Commission on the Undergraduate Experience, summarized the "Michigan Way," seeking excellence in everything the university undertakes, including undergraduate education: "[It is] my belief that the very health of a university, broadly speaking, is connected to how it cares for its students, and perhaps especially its undergraduate students because of their special vulnerability to being neglected . . . even the character and quality of the research emanating from the institution will depend upon the degree to which we feel a desire to nurture, educationally, students into the life of the mind."

UTEP's evolution into a Hispanic-serving institution was inevitable, perhaps, given the changing demographics of its region. But that it embraced this mission with such enthusiasm and commitment is in large part due to two decades of visionary leadership by President Diana Natalicio and the hard work of hundreds of faculty and staff. UTEP's educational philosophy, too, bears Natalicio's stamp. This shift in mission and philosophy brought with it a host of challenges. Institutional policies and programs were redesigned to nurture and support historically underserved students to achieve their educational aspirations. Equally important, the attitudes, values, and routines that contribute to the institutional culture also had to be reshaped to reflect a commitment to helping students succeed at UTEP. The UTEP senior leadership team including the president, provost, academic deans, and student affairs administrators are on the "same page" in their philosophy about undergraduate education, which is captured in two mantras: "Talent is everywhere, opportunity is not" and "access and excellence." Moreover, the values undergirding these principles are consistently used to guide policy and decision making. New faculty members are recruited with these principles in mind and hear them repeatedly during faculty orientation. Some deans ask newcomers to talk about what these beliefs mean to them and how they will affect their teaching and work with students.

A partial explanation for why Kansas has been able to establish and maintain programs and practices associated with higher-than-predicted student engagement and graduation rates is, in the words of one senior faculty member, because "the culture is respectful of administrators." Many at KU attribute this collaborative, student success-oriented culture to the steady, focused administrative leadership and support, particularly from the current provost, who a faculty member described as "extraordinary." As one associate dean put it: "I don't know anyone who doesn't trust the provost," which says volumes about a person's standing in the context of a large, complex campus such as KU. The provost, a senior faculty member in business, has spent more than 20 years at the campus, first as a faculty member, then moving through the administrative ranks as a department chair and into central administration. Most people view him as the architect and major force behind the successful effort to change the faculty ethos about teaching, because the faculty "knows that he will listen and that he understands the culture." Like other key leaders at DEEP colleges, the KU provost's influence is based on his sensitivity to the norms and enduring values of the university and a wellspring of goodwill that has been cultivated over many years.

The Wheaton College provost shepherded its systemic curriculum revision by encouraging the faculty to think about what was true, good, and special about Wheaton. The process gained a very strong foothold with the faculty early on and grew, in large part, because the provost's approach was grounded in Wheaton's collegial culture. In her words, "our faculty is collegial to the nth degree. [As we began the change process], I reminded them how collegial they are and they recognized their specialness." This was interpreted by the faculty, we were told, as the provost trusting the faculty to make well-informed decisions. In the end faculty members were enthusiastic and committed to the changes they proposed. As one senior faculty member noted: "Happy workers do good work."

Distributed Leadership

In addition to people in key formal leadership roles, DEEP schools have people in many corners of the institution who through their commitment to the institutional mission, concern for students, and professional competence help establish and sustain the conditions that foster student success. Shared leadership among administrators, students, faculty, and staff can be most effective when mutual goals are well defined and student success is at the center of work.

The goal of enriching the first-year experience motivated committed faculty members at Sewanee: University of the South to develop the First Year Program (FYP). Faculty indicated that they were encouraged by support from the dean of the college, who dedicated resources for innovative curricular programming, including guest speakers and off-campus trips. Student affairs staff refined the programmatic aspects of the FYP, including the link between the resident assistant (RA) and the course, introducing the program to new students at orientation, and supporting experiential activities. The Common Intellectual Experience (CIE) at Ursinus grew out of discussions with faculty and administrators about how to strengthen the liberal arts mission aided by gentle, steadfast leadership by the dean of the college. Student affairs staff contributed to the effort by creating first-year living units and connecting cocurricular programming to CIE readings and goals.

Evergreen's Disappearing Task Forces (DTF) make it possible for all members of the Evergreen community to participate in the governance of their college. Committees deal with issues in an open and participatory way. No classes are held at designated times on Monday and Wednesday afternoons so that projects and Disappearing Task Forces can do their business. Also, faculty members rotate into the library and perform many regular librarian tasks, such as working the reference desk, helping build and maintain the library collection in their areas as well as other areas, and conducting workshops for programs and others around the campus. Reciprocally, members of the library staff rotate into the classroom to understand more fully the challenges and responsibilities of their teaching colleagues. Library staff also help instruct students in how to access information and other information literacy skills.

Owing to its founding ideals and values, the college's academic and management structures and operating philosophy are unusual compared with most state-supported colleges and universities. Evergreen is also marked by a collaborative ethic; an unusual, functional kind of egalitarianism; and a special level of caring and community. As one person put it,

91–3. That was the outcome of the vote to adopt Wheaton College's new curriculum. How did this near-unanimous vote come about? Collegiality, conversation, and collaboration. The entire campus was invited to participate in the deliberations about the proposed curricular reforms. The provost asked the Educational Policy Committee (EPC) to shepherd the process, which gained a very strong early foothold with the faculty. Soon, 18 faculty "study groups" involving between 5 to 50 members examined issues of interest to various constituents via open forums, e-mail, and Blackboard. The two student representatives to EPC hosted forums to solicit student input. In addition, eight teams of three faculty members each traveled to peer institutions that had recently conducted curricular reviews and to schools with innovative curricular practices. All this and more resulted in Wheaton faculty taking substantial ownership of the college's educational program and the quality of the student experience.

"there is a conviction that we are providing a powerful learning environment," which is manifested as a love for academic work that permeates the place.

FACULTY AND STAFF DIVERSITY

DEEP schools use formal and informal processes to recruit new faculty and staff members with values, educational philosophies, and pedagogical skills that match up well with student needs and learning styles and the institutional mission. But seeking a "good fit" can reinforce the status quo in ways that may inadvertently become obstacles to student success, especially if aspects of the institutional culture are off-putting to some students. For this reason, DEEP schools have intentionally set out to diversify their faculty and staff ranks. Some of the smaller and less diverse among the DEEP institutions have particularly recognized the need to hire more faculty of color to help recruit and serve as role models and mentors for underrepresented students.

In the words of one administrator, "the lack of faculty of color at Wheaton was unsupportable." The college recently passed a unanimous resolution to hire more faculty of color, hiring six during one hiring cycle, and another seven in 2003. All new faculty members participate in a mentor support group. The director of the Multicultural Center reaches out to support faculty of color. The provost insisted that junior faculty and faculty of color have a strong voice in the curricular review process: "It's *their* curriculum and we wanted to make sure that they felt empowered." In addition, early each academic year, the provost hosts a dinner meeting for all new faculty members. After explaining how important it is for them to listen and learn from one another and offering to help them in any way she can, she leaves to allow them to speak freely. Wheaton's commitment to diversity was underscored by appointing an African American as president in 2004.

At Ursinus, about 10% of the faculty is African American. In addition to posting faculty positions in the *Chronicle of Higher Education* and in *Black Issues in Higher Education,* the Campus Planning and Priorities Committee contacts institutions with strong records of producing doctoral students of color to identify graduates who might fill the positions.

To socialize each new faculty cohort and smooth their transition into the Ursinus community, Vice President for Academic Affairs and Dean of the College Judith Levy meets with all new faculty once a week in the "Faculty Colloquium." Both formal and informal mechanisms are used to introduce and teach new faculty about Ursinus College values. Senior faculty members are invited to present to the colloquium, share what they do, and discuss various teaching and pedagogical approaches that seem to be effective with Ursinus students. Another goal is for newcomers to understand the cross-disciplinary context and culture that Ursinus wishes to cultivate and sustain. This in turn serves to support the goals of the Common Intellectual Experience course that faculty from all disciplines teach, efforts that are important for promoting faculty satisfaction and increasing the likelihood that faculty will remain at the college.

In an effort to change what was described as its "good old boy" culture, Wofford increased the number of female faculty over the past ten years. In addition, Wofford aspires to add two faculty of color annually for the foreseeable future. In fall 2004, Wofford began an exchange program with a Historically Black College or University (HBCU) which will send one Wofford faculty member to teach at the HBCU and one member of that school's faculty to teach at Wofford next year.

STUDENT AFFAIRS: A KEY PARTNER IN PROMOTING STUDENT SUCCESS

For decades, many colleges and universities have delegated student retention programs and other student success initiatives to student affairs staff. This practice can become a problem if it absolves other institutional units of responsibility for student success. As at many other colleges and universities, DEEP institutions' student affairs staff members are responsible for establishing the campus conditions that affirm students and for providing the programs and services to meet their academic and social needs outside the classroom. At DEEP colleges, however, student affairs staff are not expected to do this alone, but in full partnership with academic affairs and other institutional support structures. Moreover, a high degree of respect and collaboration exists on these campuses, so faculty, academic administrators, and student affairs staff work together effectively. Cocurricular programs are designed to complement, and not compete with or undercut, student achievement. For example, on many campuses new student orientation and fall welcome week emphasize activities that are primarily social in nature, rather than intellectual or academic. At most DEEP colleges, the intellectual and academic content of summer orientation and fall welcome weeks far exceeds the amount of time devoted to social events. Thus, student life staff set an appropriate tone and expectations for college life.

At Miami, the First-Year Experience and Choice Matters initiatives are the product of what one administrator described as "an amazing collaboration" between the academic and student affairs divisions and their leaders. One faculty member observed, "It demonstrates a fundamental commitment to undergraduates, and an appreciation for the broad spectrum of their learning experiences." We frequently heard the terms "collaboration" and "partnerships" during our visits to the campus. This appears to be due to no small degree to a shared vision held by senior academic and student affairs administrators of what Miami can and should be in terms of the undergraduate experience. Miami also is advantaged because the student life staff believe their fundamental mission is the intellectual mission of the university, and student life programs and policies emphasize intellectual growth and challenge. As a result, collaboration with academic affairs is a high priority and a guiding operating principle.

The Evergreen student affairs staff administer the usual variety of functions and services, including admissions, counseling, health services, student organization advising, orientation, and residence life. At the same time, there is at Evergreen—unlike many other institutions—widespread faculty and administrative acceptance and appreciation of the work of student affairs. This can be attributed, in part, to the college's unwavering focus on educating the whole student. Personal issues that can get in the way of learning are not ignored by Evergreen faculty members and left for student affairs to address. In fact, Evergreen faculty members often behave in ways that resemble student affairs professionals, offering support and advice on personal issues as well as academic matters. For their part, student affairs staff contribute in integral ways to "teaching across significant differences," one of five priorities emphasized in the college's mission. These contributions include promoting multiculturalism through the Longhouse Education and Cultural Center. In addition, student affairs staff work with faculty members who teach in the "Core" (the Coordinated Studies Programs intended for first-year students) as a process observer, teaching students how to monitor their own behavior and that of their peers to make good use of seminar opportunities.

Longwood has benefited from three decades of effective leadership in student affairs, culminating in an unusually high degree of integration of students' academic and cocurricular experiences. For example, student affairs staff are key contributors to summer orientation and the first-year Longwood seminar. Undergraduate residence hall assistants are selected in part for their understanding of the university's educational mission, and receive training and supervision to work with and advise students. As at Evergreen, Longwood's faculty and student affairs staff are recruited for the fit between their educational values and those of the university. That is, many Longwood faculty members are as willing to nurture and support students as are student affairs professionals.

At Alverno, student services staff members describe themselves as "partners in learning in developing a community of learners," having identified desired cocurricular outcomes that complement the college's Eight Abilities outcomes. According to one staff member, "We see ourselves as an extension of the classroom," helping students translate their learning into different settings and reflecting on their experiences outside the classroom. The 2002 Student Services annual report devotes three single-spaced pages to documenting partnerships between student services and other Alverno offices, programs, and local agencies.

After Ursinus approved its revised general education curriculum and related requirements, the student affairs staff considered how they might contribute to the new curricular goals and develop stronger connections with the academic program. One priority was improving residence hall environments for study and academic collaboration. Now residence life staff receive "academic warning" slips for students experiencing academic problems. The staff compare this information with feedback from RAs to identify issues associated with the students' difficulties. As one person told us, "RAs serve as extra ears." Sometimes advisors communicate directly with RAs to learn more about a student's out-of-class life and understand factors that might contribute to a student's poor academic performance. Communication also goes the other direction: faculty advisors are notified if students are subject to significant disciplinary action. The goal of all these interactions is to provide redundant "safety nets" for students at risk.

Who gets credit for student success is less important at DEEP institutions than helping students succeed. At the University of Texas at El Paso the vice president for student affairs eloquently captured the importance of maintaining an unwavering focus on student success as the goal after some student advising programs were moved from student affairs to the University College: "I gave up designs about territory long ago. Yes, one might look at this move as a loss for student affairs, but now we are better partners working to support students." The vice president's collaborative mindset was central to ensuring an effective program.

FOSTERING STUDENT AGENCY

In different ways, DEEP colleges induce students to assume responsibility for their own learning. In some instances, academic programs are organized to demand substantial student commitment and accountability; in others, campus governance structures and processes require student participation and leadership. The cocurriculum at some institutions empowers students to enhance the quality of their education. And some colleges rely on student workers to provide a wide range of student services. Almost always, norms of both institutional and student cultures also impel student engagement.

Students Teaching Students

At Wofford, students teach other students in a variety of settings: tutoring, such as in the Writing Lab; formal student presentations in seminars and community events; and students assisting other students informally outside class hours. Student preceptors work as partners with the faculty and one another in the first-year humanities-science learning communities. Though preceptors can earn either academic credit or a modest stipend, more important to most is what they learned: "It's changed my perspective about teaching and faculty. . . . For the first time I can tell if a professor is really prepared . . . now I am better at identifying where other professors are headed in class discussions and I can be more involved," explained one of the preceptors. Another preceptor put it this way: "It's allowed me to be metacognitive about how I am as a student, and who I am in the classroom." A third preceptor laughed as he recalled his experiences: "I told one student who was doing poorly in the class, 'I saw you out last night, and you're not prioritizing.'" The very presence of preceptors makes both students and faculty try even harder to do their best.

Evergreen State College requires students to take charge of their learning by selecting programs and courses that meet their educational goals and by contributing to the development of program themes. Faculty list curricular proposals on the specified bulletin boards in the library building; students add their own ideas and comment on those suggested by faculty. Students also freely advise deans and faculty about the overall shape, scope, and content of the curriculum. In addition, students sometimes work directly with individual faculty members to develop program proposals or independent learning contracts. Equally important, students hold one another accountable for learning. One student explained, "Those [students] who don't work hard affect the group. Students who try to skate by are visible. In a book seminar, for example, you are exposed." A faculty member highlighted the importance of student voices: "The learning of the group depends on the whole. Each individual depends on these elements that don't come from the faculty" but from other students. One student told us, "You realize that you're as much the teacher as anyone else in the room." A senior concluded: "You have to know what you're talking about if you want to teach someone."

Shared Responsibility for Campus Governance
As with other DEEP schools, UMF encourages students to participate in various aspects of campus life. In fact, student involvement in committees and campus decision making is an explicit campus goal. There are two reasons for this. First, students learn about decision making and university issues through their participation. Second, being involved in meaningful

ways with faculty members and peers helps connect students to the campus, thus increasing student satisfaction and the likelihood of persistence to graduation. A student leader told us, "They ask for us any time a committee is formed. And they ask for our feedback and really listen." Another student provided an example: "The committee I was on was selecting an architect. I didn't like the designs of one of the firms and we spent two hours talking about my concerns." Another student concurred: "One of my teachers said, 'There's no teachers here—we're all students.' They see us as equals. My vote counted just as much as the faculty's." Yet another stated, "They know this is our school and they want to know how we want the university to be run." A senior administrator agreed: "Students have a different mindset and they know it's important to tap into that." And opportunities to take responsibility are plentiful: "It's not just the same people doing everything. They want new perspectives. . . ." In return for their efforts, students learn a good deal about how the university works and the resources available to students.

At Wheaton, students described themselves as "empowered people making important decisions." As we inferred earlier, students sit on a variety of college committees: Student-Trustee Liaison Committee, the Educational Policy Committee, the Budget Advisory Committee, search committees, and task forces. Students played an especially important role in creating and implementing a major curriculum revision spearheaded by the Educational Policy Committee. We observed this committee in action and the students were actively engaged, articulately discussing curricular details and the importance of developing student awareness of the impending changes. These students, along with other members of the student government's Student Educational Council, were responsible for planning and conducting a two-week long "academic challenge." The challenge introduced the new curriculum to the student body, illustrated connections among the various parts of the curriculum, and generated enthusiasm for its implementation. The challenge included new curriculum trivia, and culminated with a parody of the popular *Survivor* television show, where the MVP of each team competed for a trip to the Bahamas.

When the president of Gonzaga's views about how to manage enrollment growth differed from those of faculty and students, students joined with faculty to make certain their view of the institution's ideals were considered. In December 2002, for example, students and faculty held a demonstration to call for the hiring of additional full-time faculty and a decrease in the use of adjunct instructors. Deep concern for academic quality and the core values of the university's Jesuit tradition fueled intense interest in doing what was best for all. Emerging from these heated and healthy debates were strategic alliances between faculty members and students and between academic affairs and student life professionals, along with a strengthened commitment to the institution's goals and values.

Shared governance is a point of pride at KU and is, arguably, a major reason that collaboration and cooperation flourish there. For example, a faculty member is always the president of the 50-member University Council. The vice president—always a student—runs meetings when the faculty chair is absent. A similar arrangement is in place for the University Senate. Grassroots issues—including those raised by students—can lead to policy changes. Recent examples of this are the tuition enhancement plan supported by student leaders and a course repeat policy. KU extensively uses students as Writing Center tutors, about 60% of whom are undergrads. The credit-bearing "Tutoring and Teaching Writing" course has legitimized peer tutoring as a vehicle for sharing responsibility for student learning.

THE POWER OF ONE

In the first chapter we noted that although many schools have individuals who do remarkable things with and for small numbers of students, our primary focus in this study was both broad and deep. At 20 colleges and universities, we sought to discover and understand policies and practices that touch substantial numbers of students and could be adapted elsewhere. At the same time, every DEEP school has individuals who stand out because they add a special dimension to students' experiences. Their presence makes people around them better and they energize all with whom they interact—students, faculty, staff, and others. To represent and pay tribute to these noteworthy individuals, we feature Miss Rita.

Miss Rita runs the Acorn Café, a small coffee shop located in the Wofford College Milliken Science Center. She seems to know everyone on campus—by name! As we observed her for one 45-minute stretch, she had a personal greeting for almost everyone—encouraging some, cajoling others, and freely dispensing her own flavor of advice about students' academic performance and social life. She directed one student who reported that he had performed poorly on a recent test to "go and see the faculty member. . . . [He's a] good person [and] he'll be glad to speak with you." Of another student she asked, "Going to the next home game?" referring to the football team. When the student was unsure, Miss Rita quickly and sternly reminded her that it was important to be there "because the boys need our support." And she further advised the student to "wear black," one of the two school colors. Miss Rita explained to us that it is important to let the students know she cares for them, so she takes time to "give them a little love when they stop by."

After telling this story at a professional meeting, a colleague told us about his daughter who, during her commencement weekend, insisted that her parents meet two people. One was the president, the other was Miss Rita who, she explained when making introductions, "lifted my spirits every day" and was one of the very special people at Wofford.

Miss Rita represents the thousands of staff members at colleges and universities across the country who are in the company of students for countless hours. Their interest, concern, and nurturing attitude are essential to a supportive campus culture committed to student success. Wofford and the other 19 DEEP schools would be much different places without such people.

WHAT'S NOTEWORTHY ABOUT SHARING RESPONSIBILITY FOR EDUCATIONAL QUALITY

- No single unit or office can, on its own, enhance the overall quality of large numbers of students with widely differing needs and characteristics. The dedication and efforts of everyone on campus are needed.

- Leaders at DEEP schools clearly and consistently articulate core operating values and principles that flow from their school's missions and philosophy, select associates who are predisposed to make these principles their own, repeat them early and often, and—most important—use them consistently for key decisions as well as for guiding day-to-day activities.

- Senior administrators and faculty members "model the way." Presidents, provosts, and student affairs staff teach occasionally, and speak regularly about institutional aspirations and learning-centered priorities.

- Supportive educators are virtually everywhere at a DEEP college—teaching faculty, residence life staff, groundskeepers, and presidents.

- DEEP schools, like other highly effective organizations, choose community members carefully. At the same time, they are committed to diversifying their membership to create a climate where people from different backgrounds can survive and thrive.

- The collaborative spirit and positive attitude that characterize DEEP campuses are evident in the quality of working relationships enjoyed by academic and student affairs which operate on many other campuses as functional silos, a situation that is all too common in higher education.

- Through a variety of mechanisms, DEEP campuses expect students to exercise considerable responsibility for their own affairs and hold them accountable for doing so.

- DEEP campuses benefit from large numbers of caring, supportive individuals who perform countless daily acts of kindness and thoughtfulness that make students feel wanted and important.

PART III

Effective Practices Used at DEEP Colleges and Universities

In this section we use the five clusters of effective educational practice featured in the National Survey of Student Engagement (NSSE) to illustrate, examine, and explain what DEEP schools do to engage students at high levels in educationally purposeful activities. Commonly known as benchmarks, the NSSE clusters are broad conceptual categories that represent important student behaviors and institutional factors that previous research indicates are related to desired outcomes of college (Astin, 1993; Chickering & Gamson, 1987; Chickering & Reisser, 1993; Kuh, Schuh, Whitt, & Associates, 1991; Pascarella & Terenzini, 1991) and institutional environments that clearly communicate high but reasonable expectations for performance and affirm and support students (Education Commission of the States, 1995; Kuh, 2001a; Kuh et al., 1991; Pascarella, 2001).

The clusters are (1) level of academic challenge, (2) active and collaborative learning, (3) student-faculty interaction, (4) supportive campus environment, and (5) enriching educational experiences.

The five clusters represent distinct educational concepts, but they are not mutually exclusive, nor do the institutional practices fit neatly into discrete clusters. In other words, although the student behaviors and institutional practices in each cluster can stand alone, they are complementary and interdependent in that student experiences in these areas interact to promote higher levels of engagement in other educationally purposeful activities, thereby fostering greater student learning. This symbiosis occurs in two ways.

First, student behaviors and institutional practices that constitute one of the clusters of effective educational practice overlap with and influence behaviors and practices described in other clusters. For example, when large numbers of students on a campus work with faculty members on research, student-faculty interaction is likely to increase. Student-faculty collaboration on research can also increase the level of academic challenge, especially if research activities are woven into other aspects of undergraduates' experiences, such as a senior capstone seminar or conference research presentations. Similarly, the activities that make active and collaborative learning a powerful pedagogy may be manifested in enriching educational experiences out of class. For example, serious conversations among students from different backgrounds, community service, and presentation of results of a senior capstone project all require that a student expend more effort in meaningful activities.

Second, learning and personal development are enriched and deepened when students actively participate in a variety of academic and social activities inside and outside the classroom, apply newly-acquired information and skills in new settings, and integrate these experiences (Chickering, 1974; Pike & Killian, 2001; Pike, Kuh, & Gonyea, 2003). Integration refers to students making connections between ideas from different courses and other learning activities such as diversity experiences, and using this information in their conversations with peers and others or applying knowledge to real-life problems and concerns. Moreover, different types of college experiences reinforce one another in facilitating learning and personal development (Davis & Murrell, 1993; Pike, 1995). For example, intellectual development is fostered in part by experiences with diversity and an environmental press that values academic achievement.

For these reasons, behaviors or activities that fall into one cluster of effective educational practice—while important in and of themselves—have even more influence on learning and student success when students experience a variety of effective practices. This principle of interdependence has implications for how different units work together on a campus.

CONSIDER THE POSSIBILITIES

We selected different types of high-performing colleges for the DEEP project, in part to recognize the fact that people tend to look to institutions similar to their own for examples of promising practices. But we also sought variety to encourage our readers to look beyond their own institutional type for ways to more productively engage students. We are confident that any institution can learn something about effective educational practice from every one of the 20 DEEP colleges and universities. The following pages demonstrate that large, public, research-intensive universities can implement initiatives that approximate the rich learning environments often associated with small, liberal arts colleges. At the same time, DEEP schools offer examples of liberal arts colleges that provide research and study-abroad opportunities as developmentally powerful as those experienced by students attending large institutions. Predominantly white institutions have enacted policies and programs that create supportive environments for students historically underserved by higher education. At the same time, many important lessons about preparing students to thrive in a diverse world can be learned from the several minority-serving DEEP institutions.

Before we illustrate a sampling of these policies and practices, we offer two caveats and a suggestion. First, do not lose sight of the fact that each of these practices is effective because it is tailored for its particular context. Including a promising program or policy in a cluster of effective educational practices and describing it out of its institutional context will invariably be somewhat misleading. We described some of the relevant contexts of each of the 20 DEEP institutions in previous chapters. To have the desired effect on student engagement and success on another campus, practices must be reinterpreted and adapted in appropriate ways to the new institutional setting and student characteristics. In other words, the history and the context of the institution matter a great deal.

Second, although many institutions have implemented initiatives that appear similar to those we describe later, do not assume that because the label is similar that the program is of the same quality or that it has the same positive effects on student success. First-year programs, learning communities, interdisciplinary seminars, and capstone experiences along with opportunities for community service, internships, and study abroad are nearly universal. As we said at the outset of this volume, what makes DEEP schools distinctive is that substantial numbers of students are involved in one or more of these effective educational activities. Equally important, the programs and practices are generally high quality, as evidenced by their positive impact on persistence and graduation rates and student-reported activities.

Finally, Chapters Eight through Twelve stand alone and each can be read independent of the others. But as with the six key properties of DEEP schools, the clusters of effective educational practice complement one another and, together, constitute an integrated approach to facilitating student learning and engagement. Therefore, we suggest that you read the chapters with a view to understanding and appreciating their complementarity and interdependence.

8

Academic Challenge

Challenging intellectual and creative work is central to student learning and collegiate quality. Colleges and universities promote high levels of student achievement by emphasizing the importance of academic effort and setting high expectations for student performance.

ACADEMIC CHALLENGE represents a range of activities from time spent studying to the nature of intellectual and academic tasks students are expected to perform at high levels of accomplishment. The activities and behaviors included on the NSSE survey are (1) the amount of time and effort students devote to preparing for class, (2) reading assigned and other books, (3) writing reports and papers, (4) the extent to which students engage in activities that require analyzing, synthesizing, applying theories, and making judgments, (5) performance standards that compel students to work harder than they thought possible, and (6) the degree to which the college environment emphasizes spending time on academic work.

Faculty members and administrators at many institutions equate academic challenge with rigor. Lack of rigor can be conceived as assigning relatively little reading or requiring few or no examinations, papers, or other evidence of student performance. Using this definition, the most rigorous or academically challenging undergraduate experience is one in which faculty members pile more and more work on students. Although the amount of reading and writing and other academic work certainly contributes to academic challenge, also important to a high-quality undergraduate experience is the nature of the work and whether the amount and nature of the work stretches students to previously unrealized levels of effort, understanding, and accomplishment. Equally important, faculty members at DEEP institutions carefully considered what constitutes academic challenge in their institutional context, given the backgrounds and aspirations of their students.

DEEP schools promote high levels of academic challenge by setting and holding students to high expectations and providing appropriate levels of support. Intentional efforts to socialize students to the values of the academy and to steer student energy toward educationally productive activities inside and outside the classroom sustain this ethos of challenge and support. For example, most DEEP institutions emphasize student writing and provide rigorous culminating experiences for seniors. In addition, NSSE data suggest that many of these colleges and universities require students to employ higher-order thinking skills to complete assignments and class projects. Finally, the 20 DEEP colleges and universities publicly celebrate student and faculty achievement.

HIGH EXPECTATIONS
FOR STUDENT PERFORMANCE

High expectations for academic excellence are the foundation for creating a campus environment that values and rewards academic achievement. When faculty members expect students to perform at high levels and support their efforts to meet their high standards, students generally strive to rise to the occasion. As mentioned in Chapter Five, DEEP schools establish standards for achievement consistent with their students' academic preparation, but at levels that impel students to stretch further than they think they can. One way they do this is by socializing students early on to high academic expectations and providing appropriate levels of support to assist students in meeting these standards.

Socialization to Academic Expectations

The vast majority of students applying for admission to the University of Michigan are well aware of the institution's reputation for academic excellence. New student orientation emphasizes that students should prepare themselves for an intense academic experience. An associate dean in the College of Engineering described the climate in the university as a "boot camp" atmosphere. As we noted earlier, Michigan students acknowledge that this high level of academic intensity continued throughout their undergraduate years, and is one of the attributes that make the Michigan experience distinctive.

At George Mason University's School of Information Technology and Engineering (IT&E), students and faculty described engineering classes as very difficult, and attrition of students from the courses tends to be high. Because retaining first-generation and transfer students in engineering is particularly challenging, the IT&E initiated a plan to help students make relatively smooth transitions between high school, through the first year of college, to graduation and beyond. The school sends letters to admitted students emphasizing the need to perform well in their classes throughout their senior year in high school and reminding them to take math placement tests and, in some cases, summer courses to be ready for college-level work. IT&E holds orientation sessions for their students and provides an array of support services (for example, peer counseling) to ensure that students get off to a strong start. IT&E reflects Mason's ethos—challenging learning environments bolstered by support to ensure that students can succeed.

Summer reading programs are another way to signal to newcomers that the campus is serious about academic achievement. For example, during its two-day summer orientation program, new students at Miami University register for classes and learn more about institutional resources while meeting other incoming students. The university also introduces students to its expectations through the summer reading program. Students receive a copy of a book selected as the common reading for the incoming class (for 2003, the book was *Nickel and Dimed* by Barbara Ehrenreich). Students are to read the book before the First Year Institute (FYI), which begins the weekend before classes start. Part of the FYI is a convocation, at which the author of the book usually speaks; afterwards, discussions based on the common reading are led by a Miami faculty or staff member and an upperclass student. The summer reading program reinforces the idea that the college experience will be much more academically challenging than high school.

For the first time in 2002, Wofford introduced "the Novel Experience," a common reading for all incoming first-year students. As described in Chapter Two, the eight best student essays about the novel are published and distributed to the new students. As one administrator explained, "How do you become a celebrity here? Academic excellence." In addition to reading a common book, incoming students at Wheaton College have access to a Web site that contains essays written by faculty in response to the assigned text and essays written by other scholars. The assigned readings and faculty responses combine to introduce new students to the ways the academic community at Wheaton examines an issue in depth. Wheaton students told us the summer reading prepared them for a high level of academic engagement and challenge once classes started. As one faculty member put it, "We want students to become young intellectuals." These reading programs provide students with interesting and important academic challenges even before they arrive on campus.

Most first-year experience programs aim to facilitate students' socialization to the academic expectations of undergraduate education. The University of Maine at Farmington offers a first-year course, LIA 101 "Explorations in Learning." The course is optional during the summer before school begins and required during the academic year. Approximately 20% of new students enroll in the intensive summer course, called the "Summer Experience," which has a common curriculum and readings from a number of disciplines and traditions. The course creates a learning community to introduce students to the liberal arts through active discussions of the readings. Students record their thoughts in journals and discuss the readings with peers both inside and outside the classroom. The Summer Experience emphasizes the importance of communicating thoughts clearly and effectively and reflecting on and integrating in-class learning with other college experiences.

Ursinus establishes academic expectations through the Common Intellectual Experience (CIE), which is required of all first-year students. According to the academic dean, a motivating factor in the development of the CIE was "to raise intellectual discourse on campus." Thus, its emphasis on writing and a wide range of challenging readings on complex philosophical topics sets appropriately high academic expectations. Although first-year students have mixed feelings about the course, several upper-division students described how CIE prepared them for the rest of their time at the college, especially through the development of writing skills. Indeed, as one junior told us, "The classes are pretty rigorous and the professors demanded a lot of us—a lot of time, a lot of work outside of class."

The first-year seminar courses at Michigan, Sewanee, UMF, UTEP, Wheaton, and Wabash all engage new students at high levels of intellectual discourse through a variety of provocative topical first-year seminars. Fall 2002 Freshman Tutorials at Wabash included "Representations of China on Film: A History of the Martial Arts Film Industry," "The Young Winston Churchill," and "Vietnam War Stories: Innocence Lost." Sewanee students had the option to enroll in "God, Death, and the Meaning of Life," "Sex and Gender Around the World: Common Issues and Diverse Perspectives," and "The Struggle Between Good and Evil: Fairy Tales in Literature and Music." UTEP offered "Fictional Women Detectives" and "Writers, Artists, and Places on the Rio Grande."

Support to Meet Academic Challenges

DEEP schools balance academic challenge with various types of support so that students are not left to fend on their own to figure out how to succeed.

Fayetteville State University's Early Alert System, described in Chapter Five, is one such supportive initiative. Another is FSU's Extension Grade policy which permits students in certain introductory courses to request a temporary "extension grade" in lieu of a D or F. To be eligible, students must have signed an Extension Grade Contract with the instructor no later than the end of the fifth week of the semester and re-enroll in the course the next semester. In addition, the student must have completed all requirements of the course and any others that may be a part of linked academic support services, such as supplemental instruction. This practice provides students "the support they need to measure up to the tough academic standards," as one staff member put it, and encourages them to take advantage of academic support services. An administrator in FSU's University College explained that it is important for "students to know from the onset that they have an 'extension grade' so that they have an incentive and a cushion . . . so they understand why they are required to participate in math tutoring each week." Another supportive practice is aimed at students who are suspended from the university. They can request a Contract for Educational Progress (CEP), which specifies strategies and requirements for the student to make educational progress, such as the number of credit hours a student must successfully complete to remain in good academic standing. In addition, students may also be required to participate in study skills workshops, meet with faculty or advisors regularly, or participate in study groups.

DEEP schools hold high expectations for students, while providing programs and support services to help students meet the institution's performance standards. Faculty and staff demonstrate their commitment to student success by holding students accountable while also offering encouragement and support.

EXTENSIVE WRITING, READING, AND CLASS PREPARATION

Research that compares and contrasts new students' expectations for college with their actual experiences during the first year of college suggests students are less engaged in most activities than they expected to be (Kuh, 2005; Kuh, Gonyea, & Williams, 2005). Students expect to read and write more, and take advantage of more learning opportunities outside the classroom than they actually do. Moreover, what students expect to do in college is comparable in many ways to what faculty members report as important, particularly regarding the amount of time students study. Yet many students appear to earn grades good enough to stay in school without spending even half the amount of time faculty members say is needed to do well in their courses (Kuh, 2003). This situation raises questions about the amount and nature of academic work assigned and the nature and range of intellectual skills required to produce the academic work at an acceptable level of quality.

At most DEEP institutions NSSE results indicate students read and write more than their peers at comparable institutions. A variety of programs and practices that reinforce the importance of spending time on academic work—particularly reading and writing—account for these differences. Descriptions of some of these programs and practices follow.

Emphasis on Writing

DEEP schools emphasize writing, though they use different approaches to this end. For example, Sewanee and Ursinus are "writing intensive" in that they emphasize writing across the curriculum. Others require a specified number of writing-intensive courses of students, such as Sweet Briar College, which requires three such courses, and Ursinus, which requires two. Another approach is to offer a distinctive writing experience, such as Wofford's "Modern Novel" course in which students write novels, one of which the college publishes.

Most DEEP schools emphasize writing by adopting some variant of a writing-across-the-curriculum approach, recognizing that a single English composition course in the first year is not sufficient to acquire and hone writing skills at the desired level. For example, until the 1980s writing was housed in the English department at Sewanee. When faculty wanted more in-depth attention on writing, they reduced the faculty load from four courses to three and instituted expectations for writing in all courses. This changed the burden on the English department while at the same time emphasizing that excellent writing should be an element of every discipline. It also opened up more time so that more faculty members could provide extensive feedback on student work. As a result, writing has become a cornerstone of the Sewanee experience, regardless of the major area of study. This is corroborated by 2002 NSSE data that put Sewanee in the 95th percentile in amount of writing required of students at comparable baccalaureate liberal arts colleges.

George Mason University implemented its Writing Across the Curriculum (WAC) program about 25 years ago. This effort is credited with creating and sustaining a focus on rigor and excellence across majors and courses. The writing-across-the-curriculum initiative began through the efforts of a faculty senate task force with funding from the Northern

Virginia Writing Project. Over the years, funds have come from grants from the Commonwealth and GMU. *US News and World Report* recently placed Mason fourth in the Writing in the Disciplines category, with Harvard, Cornell, Yale, and Princeton rounding out the top five positions. Since 1995, every GMU student has been required to take freshman composition, advanced composition, and at least one writing-intensive course in the major. Some writing-intensive courses require writing portfolios (for example, nursing) or design projects (for example, engineering). In some majors, such as Public and International Affairs, every course at the 300-level and above is a writing-intensive course. A faculty member involved in WAC commented that these requirements have "a big impact" on student learning: "They think more critically, they expect to work harder." In addition, WAC "creates a culture of writing in the disciplines; students just assume writing is part of any major or subject matter. They also learn that their ideas are taken seriously."

Communications is one of the eight abilities Alverno College students must master to graduate. Although the abilities are embedded in the disciplines, Alverno's sequence of Integrated Communication Seminars (CM 110, CM 112, and CM 212) provides students with opportunities to practice listening, reading, speaking, and writing, as well as hone skills in computer and media literacy—the full spectrum of communication abilities. Faculty organize seminars around the principle that all communication skills are related. For example, careful listening leads to meaningful speaking; clear, persuasive writing inspires a response from readers. Thus, Alverno believes it makes sense to teach and learn these abilities together.

Writing-intensive courses such as those at CSUMB, George Mason, Sweet Briar, and UMF ensure that students receive feedback and have adequate opportunities to rewrite their work based on that feedback. Students at UMF and CSUMB told of faculty members who allowed them to resubmit papers two or three times. CSUMB requires entering students to achieve a certain level of proficiency on a writing placement test; if they fall short, they must take a writing class to ensure their success in college. Even in the junior year, some CSUMB ProSeminar courses form writing tutorial groups that are linked to the course to help students develop the required level of writing proficiency. As a result, students continue to improve and gain confidence in their writing in the company of a supportive group of peers.

Writing across the curriculum encourages interdisciplinary efforts and challenges students to think critically and holistically about their assignments. Required coursework in writing ensures that everyone benefits from the extensive writing experience, and discipline-specific writing helps students realize the importance of writing well in their future professions.

Writing Centers

The importance that DEEP schools place on developing students' writing skills is illustrated by the fact that all but one has a writing center or organized writing support program. The presence of such centers and programs highlights the importance these colleges and universities place on developing and enhancing students' written communication skills.

The Writing Center at Evergreen provides programs, including day and evening tutors, vital to enhancing students' writing. A first-year student explained that a faculty member persuaded him to work with a writing tutor. "[This faculty member] challenges me to do my best work. . . . She gives me lots of feedback on my writing and won't let me turn in something that I have not worked on with the writing center tutors." Students taking a Core program are assigned Writing Center peer tutors who are familiar with the course texts and assist students as needed. Some students meet with their writing tutor on a weekly basis.

Depending on the time of year, the Writing Center at the University of Kansas has anywhere from three to five locations on campus. Tutors assist with a wide range of students and writing needs, ranging from "remedial" help for new students to providing feedback to talented undergraduates and graduate students. During the 2001–2002 academic year, more than 3,000 students took advantage of writing support services at the center, one of the highest repeat rates in the Big 12. Contributing to this level of use are convenient locations accessible to students and the welcome reception that students get when they visit a center. Two of the centers are located in high–student traffic areas near student living communities, a location that results in a lot of impulse or drop-in tutoring. According to students and tutors, the centers are "relaxed environments" where students can get both in-person assistance and online writing consultation. In addition, the director of the KU Writing Center sends an e-mail to faculty members with a standardized description of Writing Center services that they can easily insert in their syllabus.

The Gayle Morris Sweetland Center at the University of Michigan oversees writing in the disciplines from the first year of college through the dissertation, and brings together tenure-track faculty, lecturers, graduate students, and undergraduate peer counselors to discuss composition pedagogy, theory, and practice. By reaching out to individual departments, the center assists with the writing component in specific courses. The center also provides development on composition theory and writing pedagogy for both faculty and graduate student instructors through the Sweetland Writing Center Fellows Seminar, which meets weekly for one term each year. The goal of this seminar is to create a cohort of "writing leaders" across the disciplines who will spearhead writing efforts within their departments.

The Writing Lab at Wofford College is staffed by a faculty member and several student assistants. Open afternoons and some evenings, the lab offers help with study, reading, and research skills, but its primary focus is writing (for example, generating, developing, and supporting ideas; organization; grammar; punctuation; editing). By locating the lab on the second floor of the library, Wofford has provided students easy access to library resources as well as to computers for research and word processing. The director of the Writing Lab indicated that use of the center "jumped dramatically" with the move to the library and with the addition of evening hours. Student assistants help their peers improve writing through discussion and instruction; progress reports on the students with whom they meet are sent to faculty for additional follow-up. A student assistant in the Writing Lab explained that the progress reports "help students who might need more support from their professor on a paper get the attention they need." One senior writing assistant commented that his work in helping others has actually improved his own writing and described the experience as "very enjoyable." The director sees the lab as important in helping "first-year students feel there are people who care about them and that they get the sense of the 'Wofford community.'"

Tutors at the Wabash College Writing Center assist peers with all forms of writing assignments. Writing Center tutors receive training from academic support services staff in reviewing papers, ethics of tutoring, and "looking at themselves as writers first, teachers of writing second." Although their efforts tend to focus on freshman compositions and Cultures and Traditions assignments, the Writing Center is used by a wide variety of students. Open on weekdays, prior to finals the center is open for "Write All Night," from 10:00 P.M. until 2:00 A.M.

Intensive Reading

NSSE data indicate that students at most DEEP schools read more both for class and for pleasure than their peers at comparable institutions. Some DEEP schools, such as Miami, Wofford, and Wheaton, communicate expectations for high levels of reading through summer reading programs for incoming students. First-year students at Wabash and Ursinus read a book a week in Freshman Tutorials and Common Intellectual Experience courses, many of which are original sources.

Evergreen students also do a great deal of reading. A senior concentrating on environmental science explained that Evergreen's reading demands were necessary for students to develop an interdisciplinary understanding of their area of study. "I have to read a broad range of books in addition to the traditional science texts . . . in subjects like art, political science, and economics." A junior explained, "Doing the readings is vital to having a good seminar experience." A first-year student elaborated, "We had to read a book or two a week, plus a bunch of articles . . . and we were in class almost all day for four days a week." The richness and complexity of reading that Evergreen students do also is impressive. First-year students in the "So You Want to Be a Teacher?" seminar had read primary sources, including Plato and Dewey. A classroom observation of this seminar revealed that students had a command of the reading and were learning how to connect disparate ideas from different readings. Because many students take only one integrated program per quarter, faculty members are able to incorporate breadth and depth in reading assignments.

As with Evergreen, Macalester seminars require students to do extensive reading. Students average about eight to ten required books for each course. A typical example is a first-year seminar in which students read dense, heady primary sources such as Weber, Marx, and Saussure.

RIGOROUS CULMINATING EXPERIENCE FOR SENIORS

Nearly all DEEP schools require some form of culminating experience of their students. Some, such as Winston-Salem State, Alverno, and Miami, require senior capstone courses in the major. Others, such as Sewanee and Wabash, require senior comprehensive examinations. Seniors at a few DEEP schools, including Miami's School of Interdisciplinary Studies, CSUMB, and Evergreen, write senior theses. Despite the variation in form, all provide a rigorous culminating experience that contributes to high levels of academic challenge for all students, particularly seniors.

The senior capstone project at CSUMB required of all majors is designed so that students integrate and apply their learning in the major. This culminating experience enhances student learning in three ways. First, it provides students with a deep, engaging intellectual experience. Many seniors described the capstone as the highlight of their undergraduate education. One former student described her capstone as her "defining academic experience." The capstone has become almost ritualized. Juniors talked in animated ways about looking forward to beginning their projects. Even some first-year students had begun to think about their capstone project. Second, the capstone increases the amount of individual contact students have with faculty. For many students, the level of rigor expected in the final product is comparable, faculty members say, to a graduate-level thesis. Finally, the capstone project provides a personally meaningful experience that enriches the life of the larger community. That is, many students complete capstone projects that address community needs, such as "An Evaluation of the Salinas Community Food Security Collaborative Leadership Strategies." As a result, students come to better understand and appreciate their community and begin to see how their educational goals and interests can be applied in real-world settings.

Longwood also requires an integrative capstone course. Some capstones include a major research paper or portfolio in which students document their learning and which they can use when applying for graduate school or a job. One student, for example, described a senior capstone project that called for designing a questionnaire, analyzing the data, and presenting her results before a panel of several faculty members. Many capstone courses also include a review of major areas of thinking found in each discipline. Some students take the Major Field Achievement Test (MFAT) in their major as part of the capstone course. Departments whose students take the MFAT take pride in the generally high scores achieved on these standardized examinations.

Wabash students take comprehensive examinations in January of their senior year. A two-day written exam is followed by an hour-long oral exam given to a committee (faculty in the student's major and minor fields of study and an at-large representative). "Comps" require students to organize and synthesize information to address broad questions relevant to their discipline and to demonstrate competence in the major area of study. Another feature of the competitive Wabash student culture, comps push students to, as one faculty member observed, "strive to do better than just 'passing.' 'Passing' isn't good enough. Passing with Honors counts toward honors for graduation." In fact, for a period of time, "We abandoned the designation 'just passed,'" but "we found students trying to just get by, so we reinstated 'just passing.'"

Sewanee also requires comprehensive exams of all seniors. The exams are a part of the important senior "bookend" experience, described earlier, in which students apply and reflect upon their skills and knowledge, and they also serve a number of other important purposes. First, the exams help students integrate key concepts from courses in their major field of study. Second, they serve as a "culminating endeavor," a formal "rite of passage" symbolizing and signifying the mastery of knowledge associated with a Sewanee degree. A student in religion indicated that her comps were two full days: "I comped for 16 hours!" A student in geology reported that his department scheduled comps over an entire week.

At Sewanee and some other DEEP schools, the culminating experience is a source of motivation to persist, as well as a symbolic rite of closure, signaling completion of one stage and transition to the next.

CELEBRATIONS OF SCHOLARSHIP

Several DEEP schools provide a forum for celebrating excellence in student scholarship through opportunities for students to present their research or creative activities. These events reward outstanding academic performance and reinforce high expectations for all students.

Every fall, students in Miami's Summer Scholars Symposium present their summer projects to students and faculty. Michigan's Undergraduate Research Opportunity Program (UROP) conference is a popular campus event where students present research in poster sessions. The Wofford College Computational Science Department also hosts an annual conference on student research. A recent event featured the projects of several students who completed summer internships, including those at Lawrence Livermore Laboratory and Oak Ridge Labs. More than 30 students and a dozen members of the faculty and staff attended the session. Regardless of the scope of these community celebrations of scholarship, they communicate and reinforce high expectations for all students by publicly acknowledging students who have achieved excellence.

The University of Maine at Farmington cancels classes one day each spring so all students and faculty can attend "Symposium Day." The event recognizes students' intellectual and creative achievements in a context where they will be on the same stage as their faculty, and in which all are encouraged to listen, learn, and interact with the presenters. In addition, the celebration promotes additional contact among students, faculty, and staff focused on intellectual and artistic accomplishments. Students and faculty present research or artistic, intellectual, and other creative projects to members of the community in sessions scheduled throughout the day and across the campus. Symposium Day in April 2003 offered papers on scientific topics ranging from hydrogen fuel cells and global climate change to a screening of a locally produced movie to auditions for the senior commencement speaker. In addition, a panel of first-year students read their original compositions, students involved in service learning projects discussed the outcomes of their experiences, and education students described their involvement in promoting the use of computers in local school classrooms.

In January 2001, Wabash held its first "Celebration of Student Research, Scholarship, and Creative Work," which included research from student and faculty representatives from every academic department in the college. Students presented posters of scientific research, as well as poetry readings, dance, and music. This public display of student work "ratcheted up the quality when you make what goes on in a seminar public." Celebrations are scheduled at the same time that the board of trustees meets on the campus and all classes are canceled, which "validated the value of the Celebration to the community." The celebration is now a campus tradition, with approximately 80 students showcasing their research in 2003. As a result, more faculty members are encouraging students to do research, which opens up the possibility of graduate school for more students.

Each year, the Division of Instructional and Technology Support at George Mason offers "Innovations," a competitive showcase event similar to the EXCELebration at the University of Maine at Farmington (Chapter Three). At "Innovations," George Mason faculty and students describe initiatives that demonstrate unique and creative learning experiences, such as Best Use of Technology, Best Technology Learning Tool, or Best Research Project. As in similar events on other DEEP campuses, GMU students work on their projects for many hours over an extended time, thus generating considerable enthusiasm and excitement for the public presentation.

Presenting one's intellectual work or artistic creation in a public setting to peers and faculty experts is typically both challenging and immensely rewarding. Students gain self-confidence in creating and sharing their scholarly work. Equally important, such celebrations of excellence communicate the institution's high expectations for student achievement.

SUMMARY

DEEP schools provide ample opportunities for academic challenge buttressed by a good deal of intentional, organized institutional support. Whether selective or not in terms of admission policies, DEEP schools expect their students to perform at high levels. In addition, they hold students accountable for meeting established standards while providing the support structures many students require to successfully stretch to perform at these levels.

Among the practices DEEP colleges and universities employ in a coordinated manner are the following:

- Informing students of the institution's high expectations from the very beginning

- Expecting significant time-on-task for writing, reading, and class preparation

- Supporting students when they are in academic trouble or just wanting extra enhancement of their skills

- Providing a rigorous summative experience such as a senior capstone or a comprehensive examination

- Encouraging students to share the results of their work through various forms of scholarship celebration activities

9

Active and Collaborative Learning

Students learn more when they are intensely involved in their education and have opportunities to think about and apply what they are learning in different settings. Furthermore, when students collaborate with others in solving problems or mastering difficult material, they acquire valuable skills that prepare them to deal with the messy, unscripted problems they will encounter daily during and after college.

DEEP SCHOOLS employ a variety of active and collaborative learning strategies to accommodate diverse learning styles and engage students. As a result, students have opportunities to learn how to work effectively in groups and apply what they are learning to practical problems. Included among the effective active and collaborative learning practices used at DEEP institutions are those on the NSSE survey: (1) asking questions in class or contributing to class discussions or both, (2) making class presentations, (3) working with other students on class projects inside or outside of class, (4) tutoring other students, (5) participating in a community-based project as part of a course, and (6) discussing ideas from readings or classes with other students, family members, or others outside of class.

In this chapter, we illustrate how DEEP schools employ these and other active and collaborative learning vehicles, such as service learning and learning communities.

LEARNING TO LEARN ACTIVELY

Teaching students how to succeed is a hallmark of DEEP schools. A key step in this process is introducing students to active and collaborative learning as a preferred pedagogical approach. Some DEEP schools, including California State University at Monterey Bay (CSUMB), Macalester, Miami, Sewanee, Wheaton, and Wofford, do this through the pre-enrollment summer reading programs, described earlier. At Wheaton, Wofford, and Sewanee, the common reading is featured in orientation. Students discuss the readings with peers and faculty and are exposed early to academic expectations. Wofford students write a reflection paper on how the experiences of the main characters are similar to their own lives. On at least one occasion, the author of the text also visited Wofford's campus to discuss the reading with students. This provided yet another meaningful opportunity for students to delve into the text, hear others' perspectives, and begin to practice the level of intellectual discourse that Wofford expects.

New Macalester students talk about their summer reading in their first-semester classes. During class discussions, professors ask students to analyze the text in the company of their peers. Faculty members provide feedback to underscore the importance of critical thinking and model how to examine an argument from multiple perspectives. Such exercises help students refine and practice oral communication skills and raise their levels of confidence in public speaking. The common reading requirement also provides a shared experience in which all incoming students—sometimes for the first time in their academic careers—are expected to construct, not simply "receive," knowledge (Baxter Magolda, 1999).

Pre-enrollment summer readings establish a decidedly academic tone for the first days of college, something that most students expect. Moreover, new students at these schools begin to take responsibility for their own learning, a habit DEEP institutions expect—and expect to teach.

LEARNING FROM PEERS

As we discussed in Chapter Seven, the role of peers in creating vibrant learning environments cannot be overestimated. Teaching, assisting, and evaluating peers places students at the center of their learning experiences. They learn to work as colleagues with faculty mentors and realize they are able to help others learn. Instead of relying solely on faculty instruction and assessments, students critically analyze their own work and the work of their peers. Evidence from decades of research is clear: tutors typically benefit at least as much if not more from tutoring as those who are being tutored (Pace, 1979; Pascarella & Terenzini, 1991). DEEP colleges validate the power of peers in a variety of ways, including collaboration in and out of class, peer tutoring, and peer evaluation.

Learning in Groups

Alverno faculty facilitate peer teaching and learning by arranging classrooms for student interaction. Most classrooms are set up as collaborative work areas, with large tables and chairs clustered so students can work in groups of four. Most classes are small, which also helps students work intensely with peers and their instructors. But we observed similar practices at several of the larger DEEP institutions—GMU, Kansas, and Michigan—where faculty members created "human scale" environments to foster both group work and student learning. For example, GMU's New Century College (NCC) faculty are expected to use (and NCC students expect to encounter) collaborative learning techniques in all classes and for most assignments.

At a university the size of Michigan, one would expect students to have difficulty creating study groups on their own in large classes where they know few of their classmates. Therefore, many Michigan professors divide large lecture sections into small discussion groups; other faculty members promote active learning by requiring students to participate in study groups. Michigan's Science Learning Center was introduced in 1998 to address this and related challenges by incorporating collaborative learning activities in large, primarily lecture-based courses. An interdisciplinary resource center for the university's five natural science departments, the center provides computers, library resources, meeting spaces, and structured study time facilitated by trained peer leaders for introductory science courses. In a typical semester, more than 70 study groups of between 8 and 12 members meet weekly to engage in group problem solving, discussion, and other activities.

The North Carolina Louis Stokes Alliance for Minority Participation (NC-LSAMP) provides opportunities for Fayetteville students to explore content beyond their coursework by attending Saturday workshops, on topics related to science and math, off campus throughout the academic year. The program fosters active learning by supporting collaborative research efforts, trips to professional conferences, and tutoring assistance for math and science majors. NC-LSAMP concludes with a "student expo" where program participants present their final projects.

Peer Tutoring

Tutoring is taken seriously at DEEP schools. This means, for example, both a great deal of responsibility and a great deal of training for tutors. At UMF, student writing tutors must complete a three-credit class on how to tutor and an internship in a local school before tutoring their peers. Peer advisors in Evergreen's academic advising office are trained to diagnose students' needs and refer them to the appropriate persons or offices. Tutors at KU's Writing Center serve as paraprofessional peer educators, not just spell- and grammar-checkers, so they must complete a two-credit preparatory class, "Tutoring and Teaching Writing." Wabash's Quantitative Skills Center (QSC) tutors are selected by faculty after an application and interview process coordinated by Academic Support Services. QSC tutors receive training from Academic Support Services staff in principles and ethics of tutoring, as well as discipline-specific training from faculty.

At UTEP, Tutoring Learning Center (TLC) tutors must obtain certification from the College Reading and Learning Association. To be considered for a TLC tutoring position, a student must (among other requirements) have a cumulative and major grade point average (GPA) of 3.0 and strong recommendation letters from two faculty members. Students also must complete formal training (the cost of which is borne by the university), maintain the GPA in both areas, and work a certain number of hours. Because these students must be able to communicate expertise in their area(s), they have an opportunity to "practice" what they learn in class and become even more proficient in those areas.

CSUMB, Evergreen, Longwood, UMF, Wheaton, and Wofford employ the junior professor or "preceptor" model of peer teaching. A preceptor is an academically accomplished upper-class student who collaborates with faculty to design and teach courses. Wofford preceptors help develop learning experiences and teach in the freshman humanities-science learning communities, and receive academic credit and a modest stipend for their efforts. Students work with their professors before tutoring peers. Acknowledging the educational value of the preceptor experience, Wofford offers a three-credit "Independent Study in Teaching Learning Communities" course. To earn this credit, preceptors attend and facilitate the class and complete an end-of-the-semester project on their experience.

Faculty identify peer mentors for Longwood's first-year seminar from among the students who complete the seminar successfully. The peer mentors serve with the faculty and staff in each of the seminar sections and receive a stipend for their work. They are trained to tutor students in relevant academic subjects and serve as advisors and role models. Some also co-teach the seminar class with faculty and student affairs staff.

At Sweet Briar, two natural science departments use student mentors to assist students to conduct research. A mentee, usually a first-year student, spends the first semester working with a junior or senior who is the primary investigator for the research project. The advanced student mentors the first-year student, and the faculty member overseeing the research project mentors the advanced student. First-year students become acclimated to the laboratory environment, learn laboratory research techniques, and gain experience using instrumentation. Both students are involved in drafting a publishable article, which is especially valuable preparation for graduate school. Using students as mentors also increases the number of students who can participate in a meaningful way in research and connects faculty with both advanced and beginning students.

Peer Evaluation

Peer evaluation adds another dimension to student learning. Assessing and being assessed by peers enhances students' sense of responsibility to their study or work group and encourages students to reflect continually on the quality of their own effort and outcomes. Peer evaluation is a key component of Alverno's assessment model. One student explained, "You're evaluated by the instructor and your peers as a team and as an individual. . . . Sometimes it's formal; sometimes it's informal." Through self assessments, students evaluate their own performance on class assignments. Peer evaluations offer opportunities to review others' contributions to the group's performance. After receiving feedback from the instructor, students have yet another opportunity to reconcile any differences among the three assessments.

At Fayetteville State, the freshman seminar requires students to give constructive feedback to peers after class presentations. Education majors work together in pairs on lesson plans and critique one another's work.

LEARNING IN COMMUNITIES

Learning communities on college campuses take many forms (Cross, 1998; Gabelnick, MacGregor, Matthews, & Smith, 1990; Shapiro & Levine, 1999; Smith, MacGregor, Matthews, & Gabelnick, 2004). Most consist of groups of students taking two or more courses together. Some have a residential component in that students enrolled in the same classes live together. Living and learning with other students and faculty creates a community based on shared intellectual experiences and leavened by social interactions outside of class. As a result, students often are more actively involved with the course material than if they simply attended classes.

George Mason's New Century College (NCC) aims to be a place of constant learning among students and between students and faculty. To achieve this goal, NCC fosters frequent and meaningful interaction between students and faculty, team teaching within interdisciplinary learning communities, and experiential learning requirements, including writing-intensive projects. NCC faculty describe their experiences as "transforming": "Learning from other disciplines, reflecting, modeling, and debriefing—it transforms your teaching." Faculty members teaching in Wofford's Integrated Learning program (described more fully in Chapter Six) report similar experiences.

Among Michigan's 11 living learning centers is Couzens Residence Hall, home to the Michigan Community Scholars Program (MCSP).

Residents come together because of their common interest in civic engagement. Relationships form early, as the students live together and take at least one MCSP course together each semester; these are typically small classes focused on the theme of civic engagement. Students have free access to academic tutors hired specifically to support them, along with a resident advisor, peer mentor, or peer advisor.

Gonzaga University designated two new residence halls, Dillon and Goller Halls, housing approximately 180 students, for Positive Choice living, where residents commit to a life free from alcohol, tobacco, or illegal drugs. In addition, a coeducation floor in Dillon Hall is dedicated for engineering students, who share many personality characteristics and study habits. In addition, each year Gonzaga designates a couple of academic living communities, such as the Community Service Learning Experience, in partnership with the Center for Community Action and Service Learning, instituted in 2003–2004. Together, these communities add a dimension of academic vibrancy to student life outside the classroom and foster collaborative learning by integrating academic requirements and living situations.

At UTEP, course clustering—students enrolled in two or more of the same courses—is the lever for creating learning communities. Clustering insures that students will see some of their peers regularly, which also makes it easier for them to determine times they can study together. UTEP first employed course clustering in Circles of Learning for Entering Students (CircLES) to ease the transition to college for science, engineering, and math (SEM) students. Institutional research shows that the program encourages students to study more and helps them make friends more easily, form study groups, work closely with faculty, and connect ideas across courses. The success of this initiative led to course clustering (that is, learning communities) in other academic disciplines and programs. As a result, other forms of learning communities at UTEP include first-year seminars linked with English or math and interest-specific clusters in law and education. In fall 2003, more than 70 learning communities were offered in science, engineering, anthropology, art, English, history, pre-law, English as a second or other language (ESOL), sociology, psychology, and math. Almost all entering students at UTEP now participate in a learning community.

SERVING AND LEARNING
IN THE LOCAL COMMUNITY

Active and collaborative learning take on additional meaning when students—as part of their academic requirements—apply what they are learning to the community and in some cases improve the quality of life of residents in nearby communities. In general, DEEP institutions link students to their communities through programs ranging from enrichment for elementary school students to enhanced awareness of environmental issues. In addition, the colleges use connections with local employers and graduates to structure opportunities for students to interact with professionals in their field and apply principles learned in class to the world of work.

At Longwood, a faculty member and a local stockbroker (who is also an adjunct faculty member) work with College of Business and Economics students to manage $250,000 in institutional funds. Students use knowledge gained from their accounting and business courses and practice their oral presentation skills in meetings with the Longwood University Board and Longwood Foundation. Longwood's Executive-in-Residence lecture series brings distinguished business leaders from across the nation to the campus for events attended by local executives. Faculty prepare students to interact with these professionals on topics covered in class, as well as career-oriented issues. The discussions provide students with insights into the norms and expectations of the "real world" and validate the utility of their program of study.

The goals of Sewanee's Lilly Summer Discernment Institute are to raise students' social consciousness about ethical values and encourage them to explore careers in service-oriented fields, including the ministry. Students complete a week of reflection before and after a service assignment, which range from placements in a domestic abuse shelter, an AIDS hospice, the Make-A-Wish Foundation, an orphanage in Russia, and a medical research laboratory. Because cohorts are relatively small—about 30—students can easily interact with guest speakers. Sewanee also uses its "Domain" as a learning laboratory for its environmental studies program (Chapter Four). Forestry and geology majors present the results of their collaborative capstone research projects to the faculty as though they were potential clients. The findings from a recent project examining the effects of land development on water quality are being used by administrators and the Domain manager in developing new housing options for faculty and staff.

Miami's "Over-the-Rhine Design/Build Studio," a collaboration between Miami's Department of Architecture and Interior Design and community organizations, is set in a low-income Cincinnati neighborhood that is racially more diverse than Oxford, Ohio. The program allows faculty and students from different disciplines to work with neighborhood residents on projects for the cultural and economic enhancement of the community. The experience also exposes students to the architectural challenges of inner cities and provides them an opportunity to apply theoretical concepts to these challenges.

Applying principles learned in class to problems in the community also is the focus of a wide array of experiences for Fayetteville State students. For example the "professional development school model" of FSU's College of Education requires upper-division students enrolled in methods courses to spend one day a week in the public schools. Students work with a university faculty member, public school teacher, and principal and learn how to function as members of professional teams. Students are involved in developing approaches to addressing challenges associated with K–12 student learning needs. Members of FSU's Elementary Education Club tutor children in the Fayetteville public schools, and health and physical education students in Majors in Motion volunteer in prisons and assist prisoners through exercise and fitness activities. Art faculty at FSU work with their majors to produce artwork for the Fayetteville Museum and Rosenthal Gallery, and students assist gallery staff on various projects. Chancellor's Scholars at FSU must provide six to eight hours of service in an approved and supervised activity on or off campus each week. Some students meet the requirement by tutoring peers in the Student Support Services program; others work as tutors and mentors in Fayetteville's public schools. Such cocurricular experiences help students connect knowing with doing, theory with practice, and problems with solutions. In its accreditation report of FSU, the Southern Association of Colleges and Schools (SACS) noted students' involvement in these community-focused learning activities as an institutional strength.

Through a variety of initiatives, UTEP reaches out to El Paso groups as varied as elementary school students and corporate executives. The engineering department, for example, offers "Discover Science and Engineering Day," which features monthly presentations by UTEP science and engineering students at area high schools. For part of the day, the program is something of a science fair. High school students observe interactive experiments developed by UTEP student organizations and learn about studying science and engineering at UTEP.

Three faculty members collaborate on KU's School of Journalism "campaigns course." They secure a client, such as Coca-Cola, Hallmark, or Russell Stover Candies, for whom students develop a campaign to address an issue the company faces. Students work in six- or seven-person teams; each team assumes responsibility for one aspect of the campaign, such as background research, creative initiative, and media relations. During the last week of the semester, student teams present their portfolio to the client and receive extensive feedback about the strengths and weaknesses of their campaign strategy.

Research on the college experience shows that service learning—integrating work in the community into course assignments and other requirements combined with reflection—has numerous positive benefits (Astin & Sax, 1998; Eyler & Giles, 1999). Longwood, Ursinus, Kansas, CSUMB, and George Mason require students to complete a certain number of experiential learning opportunities, one of which may be service learning. Other schools include a service component in academic programs, such as CSUMB, George Mason's New Century College Integrative Studies program, and Gonzaga's College of Arts and Science. Although several of the examples in the previous paragraphs on using the community as classroom reflect a commitment to serving the community, the illustrations in this section are more explicit service learning experiences.

Service learning at CSUMB is tied directly to the curriculum through a general education or lower division requirement and a major-based requirement. One major-based program links faculty and students of the university's Watershed Institute with students and teachers in K–12 schools to create greenhouses and grow native plants for area restoration. Time during class is devoted to discussing and reflecting on issues of social justice.

Challenged by the Jesuit education community to promote justice in curricular and cocurricular programs, Gonzaga implemented a "social justice" (SJ) core requirement. Students in the College of Arts and Science must complete one or more "SJ courses," which include a service learning component. Faculty developed and revised courses to address Gonzaga's mission to develop students' "thirst for justice."

The University of Michigan's Project Community, begun in 1961, is linked to Sociology 389 and Education 317. The courses foster students' social and civic responsibility through service in local and urban schools, correctional facilities, health care facilities, and women's agencies.

Sewanee has expanded the number of service learning courses. Its Center for Teaching helps faculty develop courses to engage students through community service and a reflective component and to challenge students to apply ethical and moral concerns to real life. The goal of these courses is to highlight ethical issues and concerns in multiple areas of the curriculum and in their related professions. For example, students may be asked to discuss the moral consequences of research and development of biological weapons, or how environmental concerns interplay with the dispensation of public utilities. New courses with service learning and reflective components include "Buddhism and the Environment" (religion), "Ecology: An Integration of Service and Ethics" (biology), and "Microfinance Institutions in South Asia" (economics). In a summer course called "Food for Thought," students study ecology and sustainable agriculture in depth. At the same time, they live together in an on-campus house and produce their own food in their organic garden. Another summer course engaged students in service to the Grameen Bank in Bangladesh. Other courses involved students in a conservational study of the Ocoee River area, east of the university Domain, and in ecological projects with the South Cumberland Regional Land Trust.

Ursinus and Macalester are two of 10 pilot colleges in Project Pericles®. Project Pericles is based on a conviction that democratic institutions and processes offer the best opportunity to improve the condition of society. The project seeks to renew campuswide engagement in the community, promote public scholarship in coursework, and identify and strengthen the civic engagement of academic departments. Project Pericles colleges will modify their curricula to address the project's goals of educating students for social responsibility and participatory citizenship.

At all these institutions, students complete service learning projects with a deeper sense of meaning about what they are learning. They also see more clearly and appreciate the connections between the university and the community while coming to know their faculty members and peers in more authentic ways by working closely with them over an extended period. As a result, everyone benefits.

RESPONDING TO DIVERSE LEARNING STYLES

Active and collaborative pedagogical approaches and alternative evaluation techniques—such as project- and portfolio-based assessments instead of test-based—permit many students who have been frustrated in traditional educational environments to demonstrate what they know and can do. Moreover, these approaches foster their learning. A CSUMB student expressed sentiments similar to those of many students at DEEP institutions:

My family was just amazed. I had never received good grades. I always struggled with tests. People thought I was not smart. No one expected me to go to college. But I got in here. The environment here allowed me to demonstrate the knowledge I was acquiring, which had never happened before. I always thought I was not smart, but I soon realized that I just didn't perform well on standardized tests. I brought my report card home and my parents could not believe it was mine. I have been very successful here and I appreciate that this environment allowed me to realize I was smart and could learn after all.

According to a CSUMB faculty member in the sciences, CSUMB's outcomes-based curricular approach reflects an institutional commitment to design learning environments and activities responsive to individual student needs and skills: "Because you have explicit objectives you're trying to hit, you devise a course approach and pedagogy that speaks to these. This forces you to devise a pedagogy where students learn, and demonstrate what they learn. . . . It is not just you lecturing and them memorizing, it is much more hands-on. It has profoundly affected teaching, as it forces you to constantly review what you're doing and ask 'are students hitting these outcomes?'"

This approach demonstrates how designing and assessing student learning outcomes can lead to more responsive pedagogy. In addition, when faculty honor and celebrate students' backgrounds and encourage students to make use of their prior knowledge, they empower students as learners. Valuing students' prior knowledge is a bridge to connecting students to the curriculum and to helping them make meaning of their educational experience.

Recognizing students' talents and preferred learning styles empowers them and also makes it possible to raise standards for academic challenge. A CSUMB faculty member noted that he had to be much more thoughtful in his teaching because students were not just passive learners, rather they would push him to explain and justify his approach. Because students were empowered as knowers, they felt free to challenge faculty and their classmates. More important, this exchange of views created a dynamic and engaging classroom.

Faculty members at George Mason assess students' skills and needs and revise their use of class time and assignments according to the assessment results. One faculty member said, "I used to make assumptions about what will work within my teaching. Now I cannot go in and assume students will get the material dished out from the textbook. I am challenged to be a better teacher and to present material in multiple ways." Another GMU faculty member devised a contract system to recognize students' different learning styles. The syllabus set forth competencies and technical skills (for example, research, critical analysis, retention of course material) and students were asked to determine how they would demonstrate these skills and competencies, as well as the weight each assignment would contribute to the course grade. In effect, the students designed their own learning experiences. The instructor asserted this "co-creation of the learning experience" empowers students because they must think about what they want to learn and exert some influence over how—and how well—they learn it.

SUMMARY

DEEP colleges and universities use active and collaborative learning pedagogies in a variety of educationally effective ways. They recognize that, when used appropriately, such approaches are very powerful aids to student learning. Furthermore, these schools do not presume that students can figure out on their own how to productively engage in active and collaborative learning activities. Rather, they teach students how to "learn actively" and collaborate effectively with others on complicated problems. In addition, DEEP schools create physical and programmatic structures that induce interactions with peers. They employ undergraduate "preceptors," mentors, and tutors, and build in ways (sometimes optional, sometimes required) for students to provide constructive feedback to their peers. Service learning and volunteer activities create purposeful, mutually beneficial links between students, the campus, and the surrounding community.

Taken together, these activities encourage students to work together to facilitate learning, improve their problem-solving skills, and help them apply knowledge gained in class in a variety of settings. Moreover, practices such as those listed below increase students' engagement in their own learning, thereby enhancing desired educational outcomes:

- Teaching new students the value, and skills, of active and collaborative learning

- Designing physical and programmatic structures that encourage group study and other forms of student interaction

- Using undergraduates as "junior professors" to teach, mentor, and provide guidance for their peers

- Using credit-bearing courses that prepare and provide incentives for undergraduate tutors and mentors

- Requiring students to provide feedback to their peers through structured course assignments

- Offering academic credit for service learning opportunities

- Cultivating ties with the community to create learning opportunities for students

10

Student-Faculty Interaction

Students learn firsthand how to think about and solve practical problems by interacting with faculty inside and outside of classrooms. As a result, teachers become role models, mentors, and guides for lifelong learning.

MEANINGFUL INTERACTIONS between students and their teachers are essential to high-quality learning experiences. Toward this end, DEEP schools fashion policies and programs to encourage such interactions. The types of contacts students have with faculty include the handful of behaviors measured by the NSSE survey: (1) talking about career plans with a faculty member or advisor, (2) discussing ideas from readings or classes with faculty members outside of class, (3) receiving prompt feedback from faculty on academic performance, (4) working with a faculty member on a research project, (5) working with faculty members on activities other than coursework (for example, committees, orientation, student-life activities), and (6) discussing grades or assignments with an instructor.

Faculty and staff members at DEEP colleges and universities are generally accessible and responsive to students' needs, both in and out of classrooms. Academic advising is framed by a holistic philosophy of student development. That is, advising is about being available to students, being responsive to their educational needs and career interests, and helping them develop as independent thinkers and problem solvers. In addition, faculty members at DEEP schools provide timely and extensive feedback on student work, and work closely with students on research and scholarly projects. DEEP schools also use electronic technologies to facilitate and enrich interactions between and among students, faculty, and staff.

ACCESSIBLE AND RESPONSIVE FACULTY

Students at most DEEP schools perceive their faculty to be available when needed. At some schools, students are expected to take initiative to obtain assistance from faculty. At others, faculty go out of their way to help students.

From their first day on campus, new students at the University of Michigan are told by orientation leaders, faculty, and peers to take advantage of faculty office hours. As a student tour guide told us, "Anyone who teaches has to hold office hours." The expectation that students seek out their teachers creates a culture in which both faculty and students expect to see students during office hours. It also sets the expectation that student e-mails to faculty members will be answered, neither of which is necessarily the case at other large universities. Academic departments at Michigan increase contact with students by sending electronic reminders to students about academic functions. Many students told us that they rely on their major departments' listservs as sources of information about such events. One senior noted, "There's a lot going on all the time on campus. Tonight, Madeleine Albright is speaking and there is another lecture in the B-school I want to go to. . . . Both were listed on the [departmental] e-mail." Moreover, encouraging student participation in department-sponsored events increases opportunities for interaction with faculty outside the classroom.

Evergreen also acculturates new students to the importance of getting to know faculty and being known by faculty. Its view book declares: "Social life . . . begins in the academic community." In this case, "the academic community" refers to the Program, which connects a small group of students with a team of two to five faculty members, often for an entire academic year. As a result, virtually every student at Evergreen is known—and known well—by at least a few faculty members.

At Longwood University, Gonzaga, and UMF, almost every student we spoke with mentioned the ready availability of faculty members outside of class. Faculty members signal their accessibility by listing their home phone numbers on the course syllabus, asking students to baby-sit their children, and inviting students to meet during office hours for informal chats that often evolve into advising sessions. When one student was asked what she would *never* change about Longwood, she replied, "The way that faculty are willing to help students and how they recognize students for trying to make positive change. They inspire it in people." It is no wonder that Longwood students report that they could acquire letters of reference from 10 to 15 faculty members if they asked. A KU faculty member confirmed what we observed firsthand: "We leave our doors open [in my unit]," a clear signal to students that they are there for them.

Faculty members at most DEEP schools are perceived as accessible and responsive to students. At FSU and WSSU, for example, many students praised faculty members for caring about students. In turn, students pushed themselves toward academic success because they really felt that faculty cared about them. One stated simply and eloquently: "We don't want to fail our faculty."

Socially Catalytic Spaces

Many of the DEEP institutions arrange physical space to increase accessibility to faculty and promote student-faculty interaction. For example, Macalester designed work space in its new science building with faculty offices opening out into an atrium filled with tables and chairs for group study. Faculty offices seem to spill out into hallways, making it easy to engage in impromptu discussions with students and other faculty members.

By situating space used by students near faculty and department offices, interaction between students and faculty is naturally occurring. For example, Ursinus placed well-appointed group study carrels near science and math faculty offices. Wofford College surrounded the language lab with faculty offices and also placed comfortable couches and chairs near faculty offices in the new science building to increase the time students spend close to faculty. By locating student space in greater proximity to faculty offices, students are more likely to naturally bump into faculty. This regular contact can reduce the psychological distance between faculty and students and increase perceptions of accessibility.

Faculty members at some DEEP institutions are highly visible beyond the classroom. For example, Alverno's emphasis on assessment creates an "intense working relationship between students and faculty." As a result, students and faculty get to know one another more personally and have frequent occasions to come into contact out of class. The college also provides venues, such as the Common Lunch Hour, Thursday student-faculty "Roundtables," and the Mug, a relatively new student-run coffeehouse, where students and faculty can spend time together. Many students—including commuters as well as on-campus residents—routinely eat alongside faculty and administrators in the Commons, the central dining hall.

The Campus Center at Macalester also facilitates student-faculty interaction. Faculty, staff, and students eat together in the café, although a faculty dining room is available. Students also occasionally dine at faculty members' homes. The college encourages this hospitality by providing funds (a "virtually inexhaustible" supply) to reimburse faculty for food costs. Thanks to a student affairs–led-effort at Michigan to help make food preparations easy (entrées are prepared by the campus food service), students eat meals in faculty members' homes, or faculty may partake of a free meal on campus if accompanied by a student resident.

On Wednesdays and Thursdays at the University of Maine at Farmington, faculty members can eat lunch free at the dining hall when escorted by a student. Two things are important about this arrangement. First, the dining hall food at UMF is quite good, so eating there is an attractive option for faculty. Second, that a faculty member must be escorted by a student inverts the typical power relationship between students and faculty, a role reversal that encourages students to initiate interactions with their professors and faculty to welcome that initiative! These examples illustrate some ways that space can be designed and programmed to increase student-faculty interaction.

Campus Governance

Student participation in policymaking and decision making facilitates student-faculty interaction, as well as student learning and satisfaction (see Chapter Seven). Student-faculty engagement in campus committees has several educational benefits, including increasing students' understanding about how the institution works and learning about governance.

At George Mason, many colleges and departments have student advisory committees to provide feedback about students' experiences, communicate with the student body, and brainstorm ideas for campus improvement. An advisory committee of 25 students performs the same functions for the entire university. Students also serve on campuswide committees and participate in various aspects of campus decision making. Furthermore, students oversee, or are central to, several processes, such as the campus judiciary. All these experiences bring students in contact with faculty while providing meaningful opportunities for interaction outside the classroom.

The president of UMF is committed to increasing the role of students in making changes in the campus community, such as antismoking and antisweatshop policies. One student leader commented, "They know this is our school and they want to know how we want the university to be run." Understanding the process of policy development and the implications of policy decisions for the campus and community members is vital. "Students have a different mindset and they know it's important to tap into that." And opportunities for responsible positions are plentiful: "It's not just the same people doing everything. They want new perspectives and are looking for different feedback."

As we reported earlier, all decision-making committees at KU, including search and screen committees, have 20% student representation. Therefore, new faculty recruits have contact with students from the start. Student involvement in campus committees not only builds trust between students and the institution and incorporates students' voice, but it has the additional benefit of providing a meaningful context outside of the classroom in which students and faculty can interact.

Faculty Mentors

Several DEEP schools foster meaningful student-faculty interaction through mentor programs. Some of these programs are formal; others are less so in that mentoring relationships evolve out of advising, first-year seminars, and other routine contacts. Several programs focus specifically on first-generation college students or students from groups historically underserved by higher education.

Michigan's University Mentorship Program matches up groups of four first-year students with an advanced student and a faculty or staff member who share similar academic interests. The goal is to provide students with networking opportunities, yearlong guidance and support, and help with the transition to college (http://www.onsp.umich.edu/mentorship). One faculty mentor told us that attending plays, taking trips to a Detroit ballet, or just meeting for coffee helps connect her with "what's going on with students." Such relationships also make students feel as if they are part of a smaller community within the large university, and they learn firsthand about faculty and their academic interests. We were told that "Everyone who wants [a faculty mentor] gets one," implying that students are aware of the program and participate if they desire to do so.

As a Hispanic-serving institution, CSUMB enrolls a significant number of migrant students and students from other special populations. CSUMB's Faculty Peer Mentor Program is designed to foster interaction between professors and first-generation students. First-year students, particularly those who are the first in their families to attend college, tend to be intimidated by faculty. Developing relationships with faculty is, however, essential for many students to feel comfortable seeking necessary information about class work and other aspects of college. The mentor program ensures that students view faculty as accessible and supportive, and faculty help students receive timely assistance.

Sewanee's Faculty Minority Mentor Program served approximately 70 students in 2003. Founded in 1989 to augment the existing advising system, the program is administered by the offices of the Dean of Students and Minority Affairs. The 60 faculty mentors meet with students throughout the school year, attending concerts in a nearby city or dining together. Most important, perhaps, the faculty mentors are available to "provide guidance about life" and assist with the various trials and tribulations associated with adjusting to college life.

In 2003, 30 departmental clubs and organizations at Fayetteville State, including the Accounting Society, Political Science Club, Bio Phi Chem Science Club, and the Society for the Advancement of Management, had a faculty advisor. Because many of the students involved in these organizations were majoring in the respective area, faculty members and students had numerous serendipitous opportunities to interact with one another. As a result, the science club advisor explained, faculty members develop a "personal relationship with all the students in the club." Some of these contacts blossom into research activities with faculty. Students at FSU are quick to credit major field clubs for their involvement in experiential learning related to their major, and report having better relationships with FSU faculty members.

ACADEMIC ADVISING

Many academic advising models exist. Some DEEP institutions, such as the University of Kansas and Miami University, have well-established first-year student advising programs staffed by professionals; faculty serve as academic advisors once students are accepted into a major. At other DEEP schools, faculty members advise new and undecided students as well as majors. To the extent possible, most DEEP institutions attempt to connect students with faculty members in their major department early in their college career and create innovative advising structures for student-faculty interaction.

At Longwood, a faculty member may well serve as a student's advisor from the first year through graduation, with students and advisors meeting on a regular basis. Several faculty told us that they chose to work and stay at Longwood because advising is valued, rewarded, and supported.

Almost all first-year students at Fayetteville State University enroll in the University College, an administrative unit that coordinates programs designed to facilitate transition to college. Because every student is assigned a faculty advisor who also teaches the freshman seminar course, students are in contact with their advisors several times a week. This regular contact opens up frequent opportunities to talk about academic, career, and personal matters that might affect the student's academic performance. Also, because advisors are seminar instructors, they have first-hand knowledge of what students are learning in class. Macalester, Sewanee, and Wheaton have similar advising models, in which faculty teaching a first-year seminar course serve as new students' advisors. Wheaton faculty receive special training to deal with the needs of first-year students, including a series of workshops that take place throughout the academic year.

Some DEEP schools use more traditional advising models. For example, Gonzaga assigns each new student a faculty advisor who typically is from the student's intended field of study. In addition to providing advice about academic and course registration matters, the advisor also orients students to the norms of the major.

At FSU, UTEP, and WSSU, faculty members told us that advising students is intrinsically rewarding. At these institutions, advising is viewed as a way to connect students to the campus and help them feel that someone is looking out for them. As with other forms of student-faculty interaction, academic advising is encouraged, supported, and rewarded at DEEP colleges and universities.

UNDERGRADUATE RESEARCH

It is hard to imagine a richer educational setting for student-faculty interaction than working side by side with a faculty member on a research project. Students not only observe an expert at work, but they also contribute to that work by applying in-class learning to the research project. And because many such projects extend beyond a single academic term, they provide students and faculty with many opportunities to discuss topics related and unrelated to the research. According to NSSE national norms, about 25% of all undergraduates participate in research projects with a faculty member. At most of the DEEP schools, the percentage is higher. In fact, some DEEP schools require an undergraduate research experience.

Ursinus College requires all students to complete an Independent Learning Experience (ILE), which may be a research project. The ILE resulted from discussions among students, faculty, and administrators about what students considered their most meaningful learning experiences. Beginning with the Class of 2003, 76% of Ursinus students have participated in at least one of these learning opportunities. The ILE requirement acknowledges the educational relevance of experiential learning. Each academic unit determines what type of experience is most appropriate for its majors. The range of options includes an independent research or creative project, an internship, study abroad, student teaching, summer fellow program, or a summer research program. As one psychology major told us, "research enriches everything I do. It's great to work with a professor and see what you can do when challenged."

At Miami, the University Summer Scholars program enables students to work with faculty on proposals for research or creative activities and implement the projects under faculty guidance. About 100 students, distributed among the sciences, the arts and humanities, and the social sciences, are selected as Summer Scholars each year. Students use other opportunities, such as Miami's undergraduate research program, to work closely with faculty on research projects, about three-quarters of which are in the sciences. Another 70 students each year serve as "undergraduate associates," assisting faculty members with courses, including reading papers and helping develop syllabi.

The University of Kansas has used institutional funds to support undergraduate research since 1957. It also was a pioneer in obtaining National Science Foundation (NSF) funding for undergraduate research. Today University Undergraduate Research Awards support more than 60 students each year. Faculty and students come together each spring at the "Undergraduate Research Symposium," a full Saturday devoted to student presentations of original research and other creative activities. The event is similar to UMF's Spring Symposium, at which students, faculty, staff, and administrators share their research, creative projects, and other talents with the community in a day-long celebration.

Across all the DEEP schools, students who worked alongside a faculty member on a research project considered the experience a highlight of their undergraduate career. Collaborating with faculty on such investigations gave students a better understanding of their teachers, deepened their learning, and in more than a few instances opened new opportunities beyond college, such as graduate school.

ELECTRONIC TECHNOLOGIES

Electronic technologies and instructional technologies can be effective vehicles for promoting student-faculty interaction, as well as important means to enrich learning. As one Alverno professor observed, "E-mail has changed the nature of [student-faculty interaction]." Furthermore, e-mail is not just exchanges between individual students and their instructors. Electronic group discussions and Blackboard (a Web-based learning tool) activities bring students and faculty members in frequent contact on academic matters and provide additional opportunities to spend more time on task, thus enhancing the learning process.

The Laptop Initiative at Ursinus provides a computer to all new students and promotes interactions between students and faculty. According to one faculty member, the laptop program increased students' e-mailing faculty; more students also use electronic technology to submit drafts of papers for feedback. As one student told us, "E-mailing a professor is a much more efficient way to interact. . . . It reduces the wait between when I have a question and when I can get a response from my professor." The increased frequency of student-faculty interaction via e-mail has, in turn, increased the amount and timeliness of feedback from faculty to students.

At Fayetteville State University, more than a quarter of the students regularly use Blackboard to communicate with faculty, submit assignments, complete assignments online as a group, take quizzes, and get immediate feedback on their academic performance. Blackboard also supports faculty efforts to provide regular feedback to students, particularly in the process of writing papers. For example, the English and history departments require that students upload rough drafts of papers onto the institution's course management software prior to the submission of the final paper.

CSUMB also uses course management software to promote regular interaction between students and faculty. As at other schools, students at CSUMB rely on e-mail to communicate with their faculty, especially when they need feedback on their projects and assignments. Faculty members frequently return the favor, e-mailing students with feedback about class participation and reminders about assignments. A student leader indicated that many "profs will e-mail or call if you are not in class." Student activities staff estimated that students receive three e-mails a week from their professors. A professor told us that she makes efforts to respond to student e-mails within 24 hours. More important, she explained that e-mail provided her more opportunities to interact with students who were quiet in class. One academic administrator explained how this approach springs from CSUMB's mission: "Some students are too timid to come to office hours. Vision students might pour their heart out over e-mail, and sit silent in class. As a learning community we can acknowledge different styles of participating in community. Once you are on record as advocating active and collaborative learning, you have to acknowledge different forms of participation. . . . E-mail can honor our different communication styles and allows more student-faculty interaction."

The CSUMB example demonstrates how instructional technology used appropriately can facilitate student-faculty interaction for students who might not otherwise interact with faculty. It can be especially useful with students who are intimidated by the idea of speaking up in class, those who cannot spend much time on campus, or those who for whatever reason may not feel comfortable meeting face-to-face with a faculty member.

Technology can be a conduit for increasing student-faculty interaction. Moreover, electronic technology, particularly e-mail and other interactive features of course management software, invites students who might be less inclined to meet with faculty members face-to-face to communicate online. In Chapter Eleven we describe additional ways that technology is used to enrich student learning.

SUMMARY

Students at DEEP schools interacted with their faculty at levels higher than predicted. However, probably more important than the frequency of contact is the quality of the interactions. Students at DEEP schools praised the accessibility and responsiveness of faculty, especially those who were available beyond formally posted hours. Timely e-mail exchanges and inquiries about students' social and academic well-being personalize the learning environment. Many students told of faculty members who treated meetings with students as moments for individual consultation, as opposed to inconveniences. Others easily named one or more professors and administrators whose genuine interest encouraged their academic progress. Academic advising frequently evolves into mentoring and, occasionally, friendship.

Among the policies and practices that encourage student-faculty interaction are the following:

- Structuring opportunities for undergraduate research

- Designing first-year seminars and capstone experiences to put students in regular contact with faculty members

- Encouraging students to use electronic technology to communicate easily and frequently with peers and faculty and staff members

- Recruiting and rewarding faculty members who are willing to spend time with students outside the classroom

- Using mentoring and other programs to link students directly with a faculty member with similar interests

- Arranging physical facilities to encourage informal interaction, such as setting chairs at the ends of hallways or in other places to permit students and faculty members to continue conversations started in class

11

Enriching Educational Experiences

Complementary learning opportunities inside and outside class-rooms augment academic programs. Experiencing diversity teaches students valuable things about themselves and other cultures. Used appropriately, electronic technologies facilitate learning and promote collaboration between students and instructors. Internships, community service, and senior capstone courses provide opportunities for students to synthesize, integrate, and apply knowledge.

DEEP SCHOOLS present students with an array of learning opportunities that complement their academic programs. Activities in the cluster of enriching educational experiences represented on the NSSE survey are (1) having serious conversations with students of a different race or ethnicity than one's own, (2) having serious conversations with students with different religious beliefs, political opinions, and values, (3) using electronic technology to discuss or complete assignments, (4) participating in internships or field experiences, foreign language study, study abroad, community service, independent study, or a culminating senior experience, (5) participating in cocurricular activities, and (6) having an institutional climate that encourages contact among students from different economic, social, and racial or ethnic backgrounds.

Most DEEP institutions weave diverse perspectives throughout the curriculum and cocurriculum. In addition, many students participate in cross-cultural learning experiences, use electronic technologies in productive ways, and take part in programs that connect them with communities near and far in meaningful ways. Two of the most distinctive characteristics of this set of colleges and universities are the number of students who take advantage of the opportunities available and the quality of the experiences students report.

INFUSION OF DIVERSITY EXPERIENCES

DEEP schools demonstrate their commitment to diversity by socializing newcomers to this value, encouraging students to experience diversity by featuring diverse perspectives in the curriculum and cocurriculum, and recruiting and supporting students, faculty, and staff from backgrounds historically underserved by higher education.

Signaling the Educational Value of Diversity

Some DEEP schools have been particularly effective in communicating the value of diversity before, and immediately after, new students arrive on campus. Their reason for doing so is because students are more likely to recognize the importance of experiencing diversity if they hear about the value of such activities prior to and early in their college career.

Fayetteville State, for example, features the importance of diversity in its Freshman Seminar by requiring students to attend four cultural events every semester. Assigned weekly readings describe real-life situations relevant to students' lives. One such scenario involves two roommates of different races who are having problems getting along; the students are asked to consider what they would do in a similar situation. To foster self-reflection, students write and get feedback on papers integrating what they learn from the readings and cultural events.

UTEP socializes newcomers to the value of diversity through its University 1301: "Seminar in Critical Inquiry" (Chapter Two). Students can choose from an array of options that present different perspectives on topics, which often involve race and gender issues. The titles of University 1301 sections offered recently illustrate the array of offerings: "Chicano Literature," "Entrepreneurship and Opportunity Evaluation," "Fictional Women Detectives," "Writers, Artists, and Places on the Rio Grande," and "Government Information: What's in It for You?" In addition, some University 1301 courses are taught primarily in Spanish, allowing certain students to build on their strengths by using their native language to establish themselves academically in this important foundational course.

Physical properties on DEEP campuses also reinforce institutional commitments to diversity and communicate this commitment to newcomers. For example, as we mentioned in Chapter Four, George Mason's high traffic, multipurpose Johnson Center (Chickering & O'Connor, 1996) is decorated with international flags to honor and recognize Mason's diverse student body. Similarly, Wabash hangs flags representing the country of origin of its international students in International Hall, the large foyer of its administration building. Macalester does something similar, displaying the United Nations flag in the middle of campus to publicly declare its commitment to human rights and multiculturalism, as well as to acknowledge the international stewardship of Kofi Annan, the UN Secretary, who is a Macalester alumnus.

Classroom Infusion

DEEP schools ensure that students' experiences with diversity do not wane after the first year of college, as is the case on many campuses. For example, NSSE data indicate that seniors are less likely to report experiences with diversity than first-year students (Umbach & Kuh, in press). These institutions are serious about promoting diversity throughout the curriculum and other aspects of campus.

At Alverno, students encounter diversity in many forms and forums. First, more than a third of the student body is of a racial or ethnic minority group (28% are African American, 7% are Latina, 2% are Asian American, and 1% are Native American). Students of color with whom we spoke described the college as "embracing women of color" by offering courses that explicitly address their experiences. In addition, many Alverno courses have a cultural or global focus and include opportunities to study abroad, either for a semester or more, or for three weeks; the latter short cross-cultural experience was designed for students who cannot go abroad for a semester or year. We say more about such opportunities later.

To deepen its commitment to diversity, George Mason created a campuswide committee to generate synergy among the diversity efforts under way. The committee's efforts were intended to better integrate diverse perspectives in the curriculum and encourage the use of innovative pedagogical approaches. Since about 1990, between 1,200 and 1,500 Mason students annually have participated in the dialogue series sponsored by its chapter of the National Coalition Building Institute (NCBI). All students new to New Century College and first-year students in University 100 courses participate in NCBI events. Students, faculty, and staff are trained by the NCBI and are instrumental for making diversity work in the classrooms as they help lead and facilitate difficult discussions related to diversity and social justice issues.

CSUMB not only espouses multiculturalism and globalism as academic values, but students must also demonstrate competency in these areas to graduate. Consistent with the institution's mission, CSUMB expects faculty members to infuse diverse perspectives in their courses. Toward this end, the Teaching, Learning, and Assessment Center initiated a series of brown bag discussions for faculty about race in the classroom. The conversations were so popular and productive that what was intended to be a one-semester program was extended. This was, perhaps, predictable, given that, as one administrator put it, the campus is "passionate" about stamping out racism. Many faculty told us that multiculturalism is nearly always on their minds, so they feel compelled to weave related topics into class discussions. As one first-year student noted, "We talk about social justice and multiculturalism in a lot of classes." Other students told us diversity topics are "in your face every day," beginning with the First Year Seminar course and continuing in the rest of their CSUMB experiences. As a result, according to one science professor, "CSUMB students are more tolerant of one another, accepting diversity in all shapes and sizes." By specifying multiculturalism as an academic value and requiring students to demonstrate competency in this area, CSUMB places diversity squarely in the center of the undergraduate experience.

The University of Michigan's Center for Research on Learning and Teaching (CRLT) helps faculty develop engaging approaches to teaching a student body of increasing racial and ethnic diversity. CRLT staff members consult with instructors on such topics as facilitating controversial discussions in class, managing group dynamics, and assessing the effectiveness of multicultural classroom initiatives. One of its more innovative efforts to stimulate discussion is the "CRLT Players," a theatre troupe that performs interactive skits on diversity topics, including race relations and cultural identity. The players perform at faculty development workshops to demonstrate the effectiveness of role playing and skits and can be booked for presentations in courses. The CRLT's Multicultural Teaching and Learning Services Program also conducts workshops on learning styles and other topics for faculty and graduate student instructors to help them serve the needs of the university's diverse student body.

Because some DEEP schools, such as Michigan, George Mason, UTEP, and Macalester, have relatively diverse student bodies, students at those institutions can become involved with many forms of diversity with relative ease. But even the more homogeneous institutions within this set of schools have found ways to present students with diverse perspectives and expose students to many forms of cultural diversity. Wheaton is a case in point, given its origins as a women's college. When the College decided to enroll men, it declared its commitment to gender-balanced education: the academic and intellectual accomplishments of both sexes would be addressed explicitly in classrooms. Today the learning styles, aspirations, and expectations of men and women are explored equally to examine similarities and differences. Wheaton's commitment to gender-balanced education has evolved to include issues of class, race, and ethnicity. Principles of "connection" and "infusion" were adopted by the faculty to more effectively integrate the curriculum. "Connections" are courses linked across any two of six academic areas: creative arts, humanities, history, math and computer science, natural sciences, and social sciences. All students must take either two sets of two-course "connections" (a total of four courses), or one set of three connected courses. For example, one connection comprises a basic anatomy and physiology course and an art course in which students are expected to draw the human form. The "infusion" principle encourages faculty to feature topics such as race, ethnicity, gender, and sexuality in their courses.

Kansas also is committed to infusing diversity issues throughout the curriculum. Goal Four of its general education program asks that students "understand and appreciate the development, culture, and the diversity of the United States and of other Societies and Nations." All majors in the College of Liberal Arts and Sciences must take a course in a non-Western culture, such as those from Africa, the Pacific Islands, or the Middle East. Multicultural Resource Center staff members consult with faculty in designing academic programs and help ensure that the learning environment emphasizes inclusion of cultural, racial, ethnic, religious, and other differences.

At the University of Maine at Farmington, students in sophomore-level education methods course correspond as "pen pals" with a first-grade class in a Chicago public school. Every few weeks, UMF students read aloud a few of the letters they received to the class to discuss the development of the children's writing skills and consider the role and impact of equity, racial prejudice, and socioeconomic status on K–12 education. This illustrates one way that a relatively homogeneous campus can introduce issues of diversity in the context of course objectives.

Out-of-Class Diversity Experiences

In addition to sowing diverse perspectives into the curriculum, DEEP schools create opportunities outside classrooms for students to experience diversity.

Alverno developed two approaches to cocurricular diversity programming. Once a week over the noon hour, when no classes are scheduled, students, faculty, and staff at Alverno come together for "Roundtable" to talk about local, national, and international current events. Frequently, issues related to multiculturalism and internationalism are discussed. Attendance varies depending on the time of year and topic, with a typical Roundtable drawing two dozen or so Alverno people. Students select the topics and facilitate the discussion with the help of a faculty advisor. In addition, one of the more popular and active student groups is Programming Activities and Great Events (PAGE), which is responsible for bringing a mix of multicultural entertainment options to campus. For example, during the academic year we visited Alverno, PAGE sponsored performances by several world music artists.

Many DEEP schools have institutionalized their commitment to diversity by sponsoring activities, events, and organizations that help underrepresented students, such as adult students and those with special needs, help each other and discover and celebrate their unique histories. They also went to great lengths to affirm underrepresented students.

Michigan offers a variety of initiatives, programs, and services that feature diversity. Some efforts appeal especially to students of color, such as the Office of Academic Multicultural Initiatives (OAMI); King, Chavez, and Parks College Clubs; Multi-Ethnic Student Affairs (MESA); Leaders and Best (LAB); Black Celebratory; and the Dr. Martin Luther King Jr. Symposium. Recent Michigan keynote speakers include such prominent people as Cesar Chavez, Nikki Giovanni, Edward James Olmos, and Benjamin Carson, whose presence and messages enriched the dialogue on diversity, social justice, and pluralism. Alpha Phi Alpha fraternity sponsored a tribute to Dr. Martin Luther King Jr. to affirm the organization's support of students of color. Finally, the Talk to Us Theatre Troupe performs during orientation and other events to stimulate thinking and discussions on such topics as sexual orientation, living with students who have disabilities, and the learning climate for women in ways that challenge unexamined ways of thinking about these issues.

The Bi-National Leadership Development Program at UTEP, funded in part by the Ford Foundation, creates occasions for students to interact with their counterparts at The Autonomous University of Juarez (UACJ), just across the border from El Paso in Mexico. One goal is to engage in conversations about key ethnic and racial issues in both locales. One of the initial experiences brought students to a retreat site in northern Mexico to examine differences in culture, language, and ethnicity. A faculty member involved in the program told us he has seen some progress in "erasing barriers" that are perceived to exist between both locales, though much more remains to be done to address this gap in understanding. Toward this end, efforts are under way to develop a formal partnership between the UTEP and Juarez student bodies called "encuentro" or meeting. The idea is that students from both schools participate in social, academic, and community service initiatives "on both sides" of the border, such as cleaning up one of the many bridges that connect El Paso and Juarez. Students meet at the mid point of the bridge to symbolize the two cultures coming together in pursuit of a common goal.

George Mason University sponsors more than 200 student clubs and organizations and goes to considerable lengths to involve students of different ages, ethnicities, and socioeconomic backgrounds in these and other out-of-class activities. The university attracts nontraditional-aged students to such activities by offering academic credit for certain bona fide learning experiences. A peer advisor who is a traditional-aged sophomore described working with another peer advisor who was over 60 years old. An older married senior said that his involvement with student government was one of the highlights of his college career; "it was," he said, "as if they invited me into 'the family.'" Dozens of students of color hold leadership positions on campus, which put them in visible positions as role models and give them a platform from which to encourage others to get involved. The Vice President of University Life at George Mason serves as the institution's conscience with regard to diversity issues, regularly challenging her staff with such questions as, "What would this situation be like for a gay, lesbian, bisexual or transgender (GLBT) student or one with a disability?"

INTERNATIONAL AND STUDY ABROAD

DEEP colleges and universities value international and study abroad experiences and infuse them throughout the curricula and the cocurriculum. Miami, Wofford, Gonzaga, and George Mason are among the ten universities with the highest proportions of students who study abroad. But all have semester- or year-long study abroad experiences, as well as shorter cross-cultural immersion options. Miami and George Mason even have campuses abroad, in Luxembourg and Italy, respectively. Across the DEEP institutions, students who studied abroad described the experiences uniformly as "transforming," "life-changing," and "the best experience of my life." A Wofford administrator observed wryly, "It's interesting that what takes students away from campus makes the Wofford experience what it is." A Wheaton junior mentioned that students who study abroad bring a lot back to campus: "Every student who goes abroad has a story about a different culture—and that story resonates." Thus, at many DEEP institutions, students who study abroad bring their experiences and learning back to campus, thereby enriching the learning environment for their peers.

International Experiences Linked to the Curriculum

Many DEEP schools have integrated international experiences into the curriculum, either through academic programs or foreign language study. For example, one way Ursinus students can meet the Independent Learning Experience (ILE) requirement is through study abroad. Kansas lists study abroad as one of several enriching experiences (for example, service learning, doing research with a faculty member) students should do during their undergraduate studies, a point that is emphasized in their PRE 101 orientation seminar. Study abroad is one way to meet the experiential learning requirements of Mason's New Century College Integrative Studies program. With support from a Freeman grant, Alverno's Center for International and Intercultural Programs sponsors faculty and staff to travel for three weeks in Japan and China over several years to expand Asian studies at Alverno, infuse Asian culture into courses, and expose Alverno students to Asian culture.

Sewanee maintains rigorous language study requirements and has expanded its foreign study opportunities. Most language majors study abroad; German majors are required to do so. Four campus Language Houses (French, German, Spanish, Russian) are sought-after residences. Each has a native-speaking resident director. In 2002, for example, the director of the Spanish House had been a matador in Spain. Students who desire to live in the Language Houses commit to speaking the new language while in the house. Language faculty assist students to organize events in the houses to promote social interaction in which students can use their newly acquired language skills.

DEEP schools seek to make these "life-changing" experiences available to as many students as possible through structures to facilitate the entire process—from applying for the programs to arranging financing and transferring credits to debriefing and assisting reentry for students upon their return. Ursinus, Wheaton, and Wabash allow institutional aid to travel with the student, regardless of whether or not they attend a program affiliated with the home institution. This increases the number of students who can afford to study abroad. At Wheaton, for example, in addition to a student's regular financial aid, the college has a fund of $350,000, half of which is available to students for international study or other types of internships. In addition, peer advisors who have studied abroad are available to work with students planning for, and returning from, an international experience. Wheaton also offers two credit-bearing courses, one to prepare students for international experiences and the other to welcome and prepare students for their return to the college community.

At both Wofford and Sewanee, students pay only the cost of tuition at the host institution, even if it is lower than at the home campus. Furthermore, at Sewanee, where according to an administrator the prevailing attitude is, "We'll get them abroad no matter what," the university has a number of grants available to students to supplement the cost of a trip. At Alverno, the Travelship Program, administered by the Department of Student Life, provides modest funding to assist students in their travel experiences, and awarded about $3,700 in spring 2002 to seven applicants.

Short-Term Cross-Cultural Experiences

Many DEEP institutions, especially those with large numbers of older or part-time students, have created cross-cultural opportunities for their students who cannot be away from work or family for extended periods. DEEP schools with large numbers of first-generation college students—who might be less familiar with the advantages of cross-cultural study or for whom long-term foreign study may be too expensive—also provide abbreviated international experiences. George Mason, Alverno, Kansas, Wabash, Fayetteville, UMF, and Sewanee offer short-term immersion programs (for example, three weeks or less), both within and outside the United States. Such experiences are particularly valuable at institutions such as UMF and FSU, where many students have never left their home state, let alone the country.

Many of these short-term trips occur during spring break and might include service learning opportunities. Kansas offers "the London Review," a two-week trip planned and coordinated by students. UMF sponsors a two-week Spanish immersion program in Mexico, replete with a home-stay program, daily language instruction, and visits to cultural sites. Upon their return, some students share their experiences with the community during UMF's Symposium Day. An Alverno faculty member spoke of the value of these trips for their regional student population: "We're a work in progress and it excites me that Midwestern women will take the risk associated with foreign travel and learning."

Cross-Cultural Experiences at Home

Certainly international travel can be a powerful educational experience. At the same time, there are other ways to learn about cultural differences. As one Sewanee faculty member noted: "You don't have to go to Ecuador to learn about diversity." Discussions at Sewanee often focus on issues related to poverty and racism in the proximal Appalachian region. Sewanee students can also choose from spring break trip options to experience life in the inner cities of Chattanooga, Atlanta, Miami, and New York. Recent examples of cross-cultural experiences include a student who worked with the Hmong community in Milwaukee and a nursing student who spent time on a Navajo reservation. The Wofford president along with his counterparts at other colleges in the Spartanburg area are developing ways to promote diversity within the city limits. They meet regularly to devise strategies for building in more experiences with diversity for their students and faculty. Because few UMF students have traveled outside of Maine, the university uses a small fund to offset travel costs of students who attend regional conferences with faculty members. One faculty member arranged for 25 students to travel to New York City for such a meeting so they could see professional conference behavior firsthand as well as experience "the city that never sleeps."

ELECTRONIC TECHNOLOGIES

At most DEEP schools, electronic technologies play a large role in enhancing educational environments. In Chapter Three we described some of the specific ways such technologies facilitate engaging pedagogies. In Chapter Ten we highlighted how technology can facilitate student-faculty interaction. DEEP institutions also use computing and information technology to help students improve their communication skills and connect students with one another, with faculty, and with the campus community.

Widespread Access to Technology

George Mason offers Internet access in all dorm rooms, staffed computer labs, and state-of-the-art electronic classrooms. The library offers more than 400 databases, many of them full-text; an e-mail reference service; the Ask-a-librarian virtual reference; and the MasonLink+ software linking searchers of bibliographic databases with full-text articles, authors' biographical details, and book reviews.

Ursinus's Laptop Initiative provides first-year students with a computer, which is replaced after the sophomore year. As one student explained, "If I didn't receive the laptop I would have purchased a desktop computer. The laptop allows me to get out of my room to study. I can take my laptop to the library and it allows me to avoid the distractions in my room." Another student observed that the Laptop Initiative "put everyone on an equal basis" in access to and assistance with computer technologies.

The "equal access to technology" principle also fueled CSUMB's Presidential Access Loan (PAL), a need-based financial aid program that provides computers to up to 200 students each year. Each semester that a student is in school, the university writes off one-eighth of the amount of the computer loan.

In 2001, UMF expanded its network access from "one port per pillow" to a wireless network covering 70% of the campus. EXCEL (Excellence through Connected and Engaged Learning), a dual platform wireless computing and computer lab project that supports technology to improve instruction, is another major institutional commitment (Chapter Three). A faculty member noted that EXCEL "creates deeper and more meaningful connections between courses and technology and between students and faculty." Another commented, "EXCEL is an opportunity for intellectual play." Another observed, "Technology can be an instructional scaffold . . . it helps us implement good teaching for more students because it can address different learning styles."

George Mason offers online mentoring and advising, "virtually" pairing first-year students considering psychology as a major with a current psychology major. Undeclared students can learn about departmental expectations and requirements, workload, and potential career choices in the field by e-mailing their mentor. As an incentive for their time and support, mentors are offered one credit. In addition, the Academic Support and Advising Center provides an "Ask an Advisor" Web site for students who are undeclared, pre-med, or changing their major.

Electronically Enhanced Learning Opportunities

Especially noteworthy are the ways that faculty and staff at DEEP schools use computers to enrich learning opportunities for students. Alverno's Diagnostic Digital Portfolio program, an Internet-based system, allows students to document and monitor their academic progress online. UMF's "PT3: Preparing Tomorrow's Teachers to Use Technology" electronic student portfolio initiative is supported in part by a U.S. Department of Education grant. Ursinus students also use electronic portfolios to archive their work in a variety of multimedia formats. Used in this way, computers can be an assessment tool and vehicle for student self-reflection.

Fayetteville State's School of Business and Economics uses computers to introduce students to how the stock market works. Three-quarters of the courses in the College of Arts and Sciences are Web-enhanced. Music classes are also technology-enriched. Two students composed a classical work on the computer, and the piece was performed by the Richmond and Fayetteville Symphony Orchestras.

User Support

DEEP schools do not simply put computer technologies in place and assume that people have the skills to use them. Rather, these institutions create support structures for both students and faculty to use computer technologies for teaching and learning. For example, to support its students and help level the playing field in technological knowledge, all first-year students at CSUMB must take a TechTools course. The course is projects-based and emphasizes using computers to engage in research. The Academic Skills Achievement Program at CSUMB offers a one-credit tutorial workshop as supplemental support for the TechTools course.

Ursinus provides similar computer support, sponsoring training sessions to expand students' skills and confidence in using computers.

Several faculty development centers, such as Fayetteville's Center for Teaching and Learning, help faculty to experiment with technological applications to enhance teaching and learning and to learn how to use course management software. UMF's EXCEL program (Chapter Three) provides resources for faculty and course development, funding for students who serve as tutors and troubleshooters for both students and faculty, and minigrants for developing course-based technology and student assistants. More than 30 mini-grants had been awarded to faculty by 2003. One faculty recipient of a minigrant noted, "You can try one thing, rather than adapt your entire course." Another explained, "You can address something that's not going well."

The STAR (Student Technology Assistance and Resource) Center at George Mason serves students, faculty, and staff, working with more than 15,000 walk-ins each year. This conveniently located "one-stop shop" offers assistance with multimedia production, graphic imaging, video editing, desk-top publishing, presentations, and Web development. It also provides equipment, studio space, and free workshops. In addition, STAR staff offer technology sessions in classes, using a "hands off" approach in assisting students, meaning they provide support in terms of how to use learning technology but do not perform or produce any work for the student clients.

Tap Student Expertise

In many cases students know more about information and instructional technologies than faculty. UMF students involved in implementing EXCEL programs and projects told us about the "powerful learning" from teaching their peers and faculty members about how to use instructional technologies effectively. One student described her growth in the role: "I feel like the technological guru—teachers are asking for my help. People are looking at me as this technological person, and a semester ago I had no idea about any of this." They also recognized the "enormous responsibility" they had for helping faculty develop course activities and materials. A full-time EXCEL staff member told us: "A lot of faculty don't call me anymore. They call the student assistants." At the UMF EXCELebration, students and faculty demonstrate how they incorporate computer technology into teaching and learning, such as an electronic environmental audit of the campus, "discussion boards" to address common class questions, photo essays on international travel, and course-related Web pages.

Mason's Technology Assistants Program (TAP) trains undergraduates to assist faculty, departments, and instructional units with computer technologies. TAP participants receive academic credit and obtain hands-on work experience. TAP students might begin as a front desk worker, a role in which they serve as the first line of contact for clients of the center. Depending on their goals and interests, they might move into a student mentor position in which they work one-on-one with students on projects, teach workshops, and help design instructional materials for training and mentoring.

At Longwood, student technology assistants coach faculty on using computer technologies, which can lead to informal interaction and opportunities for students to improve their speaking and teaching skills. Resident technology associates and assistants (RTAs) who live in the halls provide one-on-one support for their peers and also teach computer classes. Sewanee also employs student "residential computer assistants" to manage technology integration and perform technology troubleshooting and support in the residence halls.

CIVIC ENGAGEMENT

DEEP schools enrich student learning and prepare students for success after college by involving them in community service, service learning, and related leadership activities. Most of these institutions promote service systematically through campus centers and organized programs that connect students with the community and offer opportunities to apply what they are learning, programs that we described in Chapters Three and Eight. What is equally important at a handful of the schools is that service is well integrated in the campus culture. At others, the value of service is expressed in curricular requirements.

Service as a Cultural Value

Some DEEP schools articulate their service commitments in succinct values statements that guide service-related initiatives. For example, Longwood University has created and maintained strong institutional and student identities via a powerful, yet simple, concept of student development: "Preparing citizen leaders for the common good" (Chapter Two). Faculty and staff incorporate themes related to character and citizenship in their classes and cocurricular programs. The "citizen leaders" concept also resonates with students. According to one, "A citizen leader is someone who strives to do their best, sets an example, and encourages others." "Longwood wants to produce leaders, not followers," said another. Still another student stated "citizen leadership" is "whatever I make of my involvement and how I apply the concept in my own life." In other words, there is no standard definition of this Longwood tradition.

Longwood's Student Government Association (SGA) promotes this spirit by tying funding allocations to community service. For each $1,000 an organization receives from the SGA, the organization's members must perform at least 10 hours of service. The prestigious "Chi" and "Princeps" service organizations also raise the visibility of service and volunteerism within the student body. Campuswide service events include "Saturday Citizen Leader Day," a morning of volunteerism followed by time for reflection about the meaning of leadership, a spring banquet to celebrate and recognize leadership, and a service banquet that draws as many as 300 faculty members and students.

Winston-Salem State's motto, "Enter to learn, depart to serve," introduced in Chapter Two, plainly declares the institution's commitment to service. Community service sites include on- and off-campus agencies, offices, and programs such as Big Brothers/Big Sisters and a nearby church, where students tutor local youth. Although some WSSU students told us they were initially uncomfortable with the community service requirement, they admitted the experience was "life changing."

Support for Service and Civic Engagement

DEEP schools create structures to promote and support service and civic engagement. Often, these structures are campus centers with staff who are brokers for various service activities. In addition, these institutions intentionally create mutually beneficial ties with the local community.

In 1995, Gonzaga established a full-time community service director and service learning office, the Center for Community Action and Service Learning (CCASL). The epicenter of Gonzaga's service learning initiatives, CCASL coordinates both community service and academic service learning and reports to the president and the vice president of Student Life. Collaboration between academic and student affairs has helped foster curricular and cocurricular service and has proved to be most helpful in terms of resources, as both areas share responsibilities for funding. CCASL staff promote and coordinate campus, local, state, and national service projects, connecting students with agencies and raising funds for worthy causes. CCASL has garnered more than $250,000 in grants each year and relies on students to perform every aspect of the multitude of service learning programs, such as an Alternative Spring Break and after-school tutoring programs. In addition, most academic departments and the law school offer service learning courses.

The University of Michigan's Ginsberg Center for Community Service and Learning both symbolizes the university's commitment to service and is a vehicle for enacting this commitment. The center's curricular and cocurricular programs engage students, faculty members, university staff, and community partners in activities that promote civic participation and build community capacity by linking service with academic learning experiences. Consistent with the university's smorgasbord of cocurricular experiences, the Ginsberg Center offers powerful curricular and cocurricular programs, such as Advocacy Day, Alternative Spring Breaks, the Detroit Initiative, Volunteers Involved Every Week (VIEW), and Lives of Urban Children and Youth (LUCY). Many of these programs are facilitated by students, thus creating opportunities for students to develop important leadership skills.

More than 800 Macalester students get involved in some form of community service each year. Its Community Service Office promotes service activities as a "tool kit" for social change, a concept that appeals to the predilections of students who choose Macalester.

Wheaton's Filene Center, which one person affectionately called a "career center on steroids," helps students explore the connections among a liberal arts education, internships, jobs, and volunteer or service learning experiences. A clearinghouse for volunteer experiences, the center's mission is to help students acquire "insight into the lives of others, into complex social issues and into their own talents and aspirations."

INTERNSHIPS AND EXPERIENTIAL LEARNING

Internships and other experiential learning activities are plentiful at DEEP schools. These experiences are venues for applying knowledge and gaining real-world experience. In addition, they enrich campus learning environments when students reflect on and share what they've learned from class presentations and informal conversations beyond class. Some DEEP schools built internships and experiential learning into their academic programs.

Evergreen, George Mason, UMF, Ursinus, and Wofford require experiential learning, one form of which may be an internship. Integrating liberal arts with professional preparation is an ongoing challenge at UMF, as it is at many other institutions. One approach to integration is to induce students to grapple with the challenges and problems they encounter outside the classroom. Most major fields at UMF encourage or require internships and practica. Several programs at UMF place students in practicum experiences early in their studies to help them identify career interests and potential. A faculty member described the situation this way: "We try to reach out to students to help them either stay in their major or help steer them into another area of study. Regardless, we want them to be successful."

Aiming to prepare women for successful careers, Alverno provides its students with "practical tools vital for success" and "the abilities needed to put knowledge to use." According to one faculty member, "Students come to Alverno expecting to go to work." Alverno's curriculum focuses on developing skills employers find attractive and useful, such as written and oral communication, self assessment, good citizenship, and problem solving. Because these skills require practice, Alverno requires all weekday students, regardless of major, to participate in at least one off-campus internship. Some majors require students to participate in two internships;

some require more. For example, education requires four field placements before student teaching, and environmental science requires three internships. Recent Alverno interns served Wisconsin College Democrats and in the national office of Amnesty International.

As at many other colleges and universities, career services offices at DEEP schools connect students with internship opportunities. Wheaton's Filene Center for Work and Learning, mentioned earlier, was founded to "put careers in the minds of liberal arts students." A "reflective component" is built into all of the center's programs so students "can make clear connections to their experiences in class." When asked why she decided to attend Wheaton and why she stayed, a senior stated, "The Filene Center really sold me." She attributed her interest in a career in environmental sciences to her internships: "No one ever encouraged me in the sciences before." This student had internships every semester, spring break, and summer of her Wheaton career; the lone exception was the semester she studied abroad. And although she said she is "extremely unique" in the extent of her internship participation, she noted that any Wheaton student could do the same thing.

As noted in Chapter Four, George Mason's location provides innumerable opportunities for applied learning through internships, and its Career Services Office is organized to leverage this advantage. Staff do not wait for students to come to the office; they conduct extensive outreach through the University 100 college transition courses and orientation programs. Career services staff also visit classes to advertise their services and describe the possibilities for cooperative learning, community service learning, and internships.

Career services staff at Sewanee, FSU, and UMF make sure students know about their services by reaching out to students where they live, work, and play. As one Sewanee staff member commented, "We take our show on the road to the dorms, the dining hall, orientation, and any place they want us." FSU's "Careers on the Move" initiative puts staff in touch with students by making suite-by-suite visits in designated residential facilities.

Sweet Briar taps into its "old girl network," as one student put it, to develop internship and career opportunities for students. Stipends are available from the college to make the typically no- or low-paying internships financially viable. Students seek their own internships and, based on the quality of the proposed experience, career services provides stipends, some as high as $3,000, to cover students' expenses. Students must submit a reflective project paper at the conclusion of the internship. Sewanee has a similar program developed under the auspices of the Lilly Summer Discernment Institute. The program now is supported by endowment funds that provide stipends for up to 10% of the student body to engage in summer internships.

Experiential learning is a distinctive feature of students' experiences at Evergreen. In 2001–2002, more than 1,900 independent learning and internship contracts were sponsored, accounting for about 25% of all seniors' credits.

At the University of Kansas most schools and colleges offer a variety of field experiences. A journalism student described the "invaluable experience" she gained working on the *Daily Kansan,* the University student newspaper, where she managed a budget of over $1 million. School of Architecture and Design students constructed a plan and vision for the urban area in the core of Kansas City, conducting a detailed economic and demographic analysis of the urban core and preparing conceptual design proposals for an array of possible developments that fit the site.

COCURRICULAR LEADERSHIP

DEEP schools provide a wellspring of other cocurricular offerings that involve students in campus life, connect them to the institution, and provide leadership opportunities. As we mentioned in Chapter Seven, from the beginning these colleges and universities encourage their students to "get involved." Some students do this on their own. Others are "pushed" gently by a staff or faculty member to take on a role or responsibility. Students also often convince other students to get involved.

The Leadership Scholars Program at Ursinus, a program spanning academic and student affairs, includes a course in leadership theory as well as funding for student projects. Each year, 20 to 25 students are Leadership Scholars. One scholar humorously noted that "It's really annoying how all those leadership theories stick in your head. It really has developed me as a person and a leader."

A Student Life–communication studies department partnership makes it possible for Kansas to offer a 19–credit hour leadership minor designed to help students explore and enhance their knowledge of leadership trends, theories, and best practices. In addition to formal coursework in ethics, community development, leadership, diversity, and culture, students completing the minor participate in supervised community service, as well as practicum or field experiences.

At Longwood, where cocurricular involvement is a lifestyle, the "New Student Leadership Program" brings 80 first-year students to campus prior to the beginning of the fall semester to explore leadership skills, build support networks for leadership development, and provide opportunities for faculty and staff to identify potential student leaders. Longwood students, faculty, and staff consider extensive cocurricular involvement part and parcel of the undergraduate experience. One student restated this philosophy in his own terms: "No one looks at you in the future and says you earned a 3.3 GPA. It's the nature of who you are that defines what you've learned."

SUMMARY

DEEP institutions provide students a broad sampling of enriching educational experiences from which to choose, including diversity experiences, community service, internship, and study abroad and enrichment options. Thus, students have an abundance of opportunities to apply their knowledge, serve their communities, gain hands-on experience in real-world settings, and enhance their leadership and career development. Whether it is doing an internship, studying abroad, or using technology, most DEEP schools have made it a priority to encourage widespread participation. In addition, they are particularly effective at communicating the value of diversity to new students, and they address multiculturalism and social justice issues through the curriculum and out-of-class experiences. Important to the success of these initiatives is the strong sense of administrative support found across the 20 schools. Some schools believe so strongly in the value of enriching experiences that they expect students to participate in at least one before they graduate. Why? As a Macalester student explained, "Ruminating too much separates you from the topic. You have to go and touch it."

Among the policies and practices that merit consideration are

- Communicating the value of diversity, not only to newcomers, but throughout students' college experiences

- Requiring students to participate in courses or activities that promote cross-cultural understanding, civic engagement, and self-reflection

- Providing short-term study abroad opportunities to increase the numbers of students who benefit from such cross-cultural experiences

- Using electronic technologies to increase communication among students and between students and faculty, improve instruction, and enhance learning

- Providing ample administrative support and resources to implement and use new technologies

- Encouraging and even requiring students to participate in experiential activities such as internships, practica, and field placements so that students gain experience in applying what they are learning to real-life situations

12

Supportive Campus Environment

Students perform better and are more satisfied at colleges that are committed to their success and cultivate positive working and social relations among different groups on campus.

D EEP INSTITUTIONS employ a variety of approaches to support their students, academically and socially. They provide resources to those who need them *when* they need them and create the conditions that encourage students to take advantage of these resources. In addition, relations among students, faculty, and administrators are cordial and helpful. The conditions characterizing a supportive campus environment represented on the NSSE survey include (1) an institutional emphasis on providing students the support they need for academic and social success, (2) positive working and social relationships among different groups, (3) help for students in coping with their nonacademic responsibilities, and (4) high-quality student relationships with other students, faculty, and the institution's administrative personnel.

In this chapter we illustrate a sampling of the many supportive programs, services, and practices DEEP schools make available to their students. These include affirming transition programs, advising networks, peer support, multiple safety nets, special student support initiatives, and educationally purposeful living environments. Once again, as with programs and practices associated with the other clusters of effective educational practices, a supportive campus environment does not exist in a vacuum or independent of other policies and practices. Rather, the properties of a supportive campus environment are situated in a complex network of cultural assumptions, beliefs, values, norms, and perceptions. For example, the operating philosophies of DEEP institutions value and embrace all students, whether adequately prepared for college or not. Services tailored for students with specific needs are many and varied. At the same time, academic performance standards are set at reasonably high levels and not compromised. Although this is a component of academic challenge, the message that because "you are a student here, you are capable of learning anything" affirms one's potential as a learner and signifies full membership in the academic community. This ethic of care and belonging stitched into the institutional fabric is the glue that holds together the many different supportive mechanisms these institutions have developed.

TRANSITION PROGRAMS

As discussed in Chapter Five, DEEP institutions provide guideposts to show students how to succeed in college. One of the key mechanisms for doing this is a set of transition experiences that intentionally acculturate first-year and transfer students to institutional values and academic expectations and introduces them to campus resources and opportunities. The University of Maine at Farmington gives its students a head start by offering admission to them late in their junior year of high school. This allows ample time for them to learn about the UMF culture before making a final decision to attend. By November of the senior year in high school, most members of the matriculating class are familiar with the campus. Prospective students are then encouraged to participate in one of two summer orientation programs (the orientation and advising program or the Summer Experience course) to get even better acquainted with the undergraduate program. As a result of these early socialization experiences, UMF students (the majority of whom are the first in their families to go to college) told us they were well prepared for what they encountered when they started college. Among those welcoming newcomers is the UMF president—often in her jogging suit—who assists families moving their first-year student into the residence halls.

First-Year Experience Seminars

Many institutions across the country offer seminars and other programming that attempt to demonstrate to new students how to "do" college. Many of the DEEP institutions either require these courses or provide additional programs and activities that serve this function. Moreover, these high-quality efforts are well conceived and delivered.

At Kansas, the objective of the two–credit hour, semester-long course for first-year students, PRE 101: Orientation Seminar, is to ensure that every student understands what is required to succeed academically and becomes connected to a club, organization, or other group during the first semester. Students keep an experiential journal organized by weekly topics. One of the topics, "KU organizations," requires students to collect information handouts from three separate organizations in which they are interested and how they intend to become involved on campus. PRE also presents a variety of student success topics, including financial management, goal setting, and time management. One African American undergraduate told us, "PRE 101 was really instrumental in my success. Once I became involved in various clubs and organizations, the campus became much smaller and, as a result, I felt much more comfortable and confident that I could succeed at KU."

George Mason sponsors a series of credit-bearing courses that teach students how to make the most of their collegiate experience. For example, 33% of first-year students enroll in University 100, a course that focuses on academic success skills. Classes are kept small and address a wide variety of topics relevant to student success, including the traditional adjustment to college issues. According to students, University 100 was instrumental in making them aware of the amount of effort they need to put into their studies and introduced them to campus resources they could use.

Wheaton students extolled the virtues of their First Year Seminar (FYS), indicating it was helpful both for preparing them to do college-level work and for fostering meaningful relationships with peers. A sophomore explained that the FYS is "definitely a challenging course because you have to think and write and rewrite. It was a great introduction to the college." Others commented that the course helped them "develop a sense of unity with students and faculty" and instilled in them a "sense of confidence that you can discuss things." Overall, the first-year students identified the seminar as one of the things they "would not change about the college."

At Gonzaga, upper-class students are an integral component of its supportive campus climate. For example, more than 250 upper-class students return to campus early in the fall to welcome new students to campus. They help newcomers move in and perpetuate endearing Gonzaga traditions. One such event is the "serpentine," where upper-class students, resident assistants, student government, and other student organization leaders line up in a serpentine in the field house and cheer and applaud as the new students walk through the middle of the lines. This student-initiated display of goodwill and support by upper-class role models is a powerful way to welcome newcomers and affirm that they are now members of the Gonzaga community.

Comprehensive Programs

DEEP institutions such as Longwood, University of Maine at Farmington, Wheaton, Winston-Salem, UTEP, and Fayetteville align and integrate their first-year programs with advising, the residence halls, faculty, and other campus resources.

Fayetteville State's University College is an administrative unit organized to help students with varied academic preparation learn to do what is necessary to perform at acceptable levels, inside and outside the classroom. To this end, University College provides mentoring and advising for all first- and second-year students. It also coordinates reading, writing, mathematics, science, and critical-thinking tutoring and support programs. In addition, FSU requires that new students take a two-semester freshman seminar course that teaches them about the university's academic expectations, emphasizing the skills needed to do well during and after college. A sophomore communication major described how his freshman seminar instructor helped him become a "serious student" through participation in "Professional Image Day." "PID" (as it is called) emphasizes how doing well in college is related to success afterwards. The instructor "related everything to school and our lives." A junior said her seminar instructor "saved my life" by helping her work through some personal issues that were affecting her academic performance.

The Entering Student Program (ESP) at UTEP, established in 1999, is one of the main components of the University College that assists students with their academic and social transition to university life. The program brings together in one place all the services that an entering student may need to learn how to succeed in college: enrollment services, undergraduate recruitment, new student orientation, Academic Advising Center, university seminar and academic programs, and Tutoring and Learning Center.

As Chapter Two indicated, the Common Intellectual Experience (CIE) at Ursinus brings together multiple effective practices to fashion a challenging, yet supportive academic experience. As one CIE instructor explained, "What's so neat about this—my class is a family. There's a sensitivity as we talk about topics. There's a level of trust that develops over time. My students feel comfortable enough to challenge me—but they'll also go look things up and bring it in." One upper division student said, "You have to do reading you probably wouldn't, but you really talk about it." In addition to establishing a decidedly academic tone to campus life for first-year students, CIE also facilitates the formation of affinity groups among students. A first-year student told us, "It unites the freshman, because it throws you into college reading with a bunch of other freshmen. It's a common bond right away, more than just being in class together." As first-year students tackle the same dense readings, friendships form that help students cope with these and the other challenges that college presents, inside and outside the classroom.

Teaching students how to use their institution's resources for learning is common to all DEEP institutions, though the methods they use differ markedly. More often than not, their policies and practices have the desired effect, as students cultivate a sense of ownership and figure out together how to take advantage of educational and social opportunities to navigate their way through college.

ADVISING NETWORKS

Many DEEP schools tie advising to first-year experience initiatives to provide students early on with the information and tools they need to make good decisions about course sequencing. At Kansas, the Freshman-Sophomore Advising Center (FSAC), described in Chapter Five, is one part of a large-scale comprehensive academic program, an intentional effort to encourage students to use FSAC resources throughout their entire educational career. Other DEEP schools have created advising networks, drawing on the combined resources of professional advisors, faculty members, peers, and others.

All new Macalester first-year students take a discipline-based First Year Seminar (FYS) in their first semester. Sections are limited to only 16 students, and the seminar instructor serves as the advisor to FYS students for the first two years or until the student declares a major. A peer "writing preceptor" works with students on their written work. A series of workshops through the academic year prepare faculty to deal with the needs of the current first-year student cohort. Because of the FYS instructor's dual role—seminar leader and advisor—faculty learn firsthand a good deal about their advisees' intellectual interests and relative strengths and weaknesses. Moreover, they see their advisees several times a week, which provides frequent opportunities for informal conversation about various matters as well as to monitor students' academic and social adjustment. As a result, Macalester students have at least one faculty member who knows them very well by the end of the first term and is in a position to know whether students seem to be struggling and, if so, to make appropriate referrals.

Staffing the First Year Seminars (FYS) at Wheaton are a faculty member, administrative mentor, librarian, and two preceptors who are junior- or senior-level students. All serve as advisors to FYS students. The faculty member is the student's academic advisor throughout her or his first year, or until the student selects an academic major. Preceptors serve a similar role by assisting the faculty in a peer mentoring role. Throughout orientation, new students meet daily with their preceptors either individually or in their advising teams. After orientation and throughout the student's first year, the preceptors work with the faculty advisor and administrative mentor to help students obtain the academic and life skills they need. In addition, one of the two preceptors lives in the residence hall with the students to maintain frequent contact. Preceptors are trained to serve as study skills tutors and offer workshops focusing on test taking, study strategies, time management, and note taking. Faculty members regularly meet with the rest of the team to discuss the progress of the class and individual students. Some students call this carefully designed support network the "freshman family."

Administrative mentors work with first-year students, a practice that began at the urging of the president. Mentors meet with new students in their advising team meetings during orientation, attend or host social gatherings throughout the first year, and connect with new students individually and in small groups to help students "work through the system." For example, how do you deal with a financial aid problem, a roommate dilemma, or a need to go home early? Mentors have a thick training manual to rely on and meet monthly to discuss issues related to helping the new students with their transition. Some assist with the First Year Seminar by reading student papers and helping with library training. First-year students really appreciate the different perspective on college life and coursework the mentors provide. One student told us that his mentor sent handwritten cards to all her FYS students before Halloween and again at winter break. Others send postcards from different locations while traveling during breaks. These small gestures go a long way to welcoming newcomers into the Wheaton freshman family.

At Sewanee, the faculty member teaching a student's First Year Program course also is the student's primary advisor. As with similar models elsewhere, faculty members get to know their advisees academically and personally. Some FYP instructors send letters to their students "before they hit the Mountain," which helps connect new students to Sewanee. As one first-year student put it, "I get to know my advisor much better because I see him in class."

At Alverno, professional support staff members advise many students aided by peer advisors who work with new students during orientation. The adviser typically works with advisees for the first two years, a period during which the curriculum is fairly well prescribed. Once the student selects her major, a faculty advisor from that area takes over. Throughout the student's time at Alverno, the professional advising staff work closely with the faculty to support an ethic of collaborative learning, which is key to succeeding at the college.

At George Mason, academic advising center staff members work closely with department faculty, the career center, orientation, and other offices to make sure students get the information they need to make good decisions. At Ursinus and Miami, representatives from student and academic affairs work collaboratively to provide academic advising. Miami follows a well-established model that has a full-time, live-in professional who serves as both the resident director and the academic advisor to all first-year students living in that residence hall. First-year advisors counsel students on personal, judicial, academic, and career concerns and shape the environment and experiences of first-year students by providing services and programs that foster academic success, promote the multifaceted development of first-year students, and encourage responsible involvement in campus and community life.

DEEP institutions employ a variety of models for academic advising. The common thread is that a network of competent, skilled people provide good, timely information buttressed by an ethic of support. In addition, advisors generally enjoy good working relations with one another and with their advisees.

PEER SUPPORT

Many DEEP colleges are almost intrusive in the degree to which they encourage peers to interact in educationally purposeful ways (see Chapter Nine for more examples of peer support). As with many other effective educational practices, such efforts require contributions from faculty, staff, and upper-division students, who lead both by example and exhortation.

Academic Support

Though the content and structure of orientation and first-year seminars differ, they all emphasize the importance of students connecting in meaningful ways to their peers. For example, as mentioned earlier, one of the sessions in KU's PRE 101: Orientation Seminar introduces students to the benefits of joining a club, organization, or other group during the first semester. There is ample empirical support that associating with peers with similar interests is linked with persistence and other positive outcomes (Pascarella & Terenzini, 1991; Tinto, 1993). As with most other DEEP schools, KU does not leave such matters to chance but intentionally stitches such opportunities into the PRE curriculum.

GMU peer advisors assist in University 100 courses by facilitating discussions, occasionally lecturing, and helping evaluate student performance. They also meet with new students informally outside of class, which provides opportunities to point out ways to get involved on campus and to refer students to resources when appropriate. In many instances, they stay in contact with one another after the course ends.

At Wofford, peer tutoring involves students teaching other students in a given subject area. Tutoring takes a variety of forms, from one-to-one tutoring by more experienced students (for example, in the writing lab), formal student presentations in seminars and community events, to students actively assisting other students informally outside of class contact hours.

Wheaton College employs peer mentors extensively in First Year Seminars, study abroad advising, in the Filene Center for internships, and as writing tutors, just to name a few. First Year Seminar preceptors help facilitate the discussion sections of large introductory courses and serve as teaching assistants in laboratories. Peer writing tutors are also trained via a half-credit course to assist first-year students, especially those who are struggling and may be embarrassed or intimidated to seek help from a faculty member at this early point in their college experience.

Faculty members at DEEP schools also recognize the value of peer interaction and facilitate such contacts by designing group projects that bring students together to work on intellectual tasks, both in and out of class. We highlighted many of these collaborative activities in Chapter Nine, but it's worth reiterating their value in helping students develop supportive peer networks. For example, a Kansas faculty member uses group quizzes in his large, primarily lecture-oriented course that require students to work together to answer the questions. By talking with different classmates over the course of the semester, they eventually come to know one another. As a result, he found that students in this class were more likely to study with peers and were more willing to pose questions to their peers when they were unclear about class material.

Peers also play a central role in the delivery of advising and tutoring at CSUMB's Academic Skill Achievement Program (ASAP), which offers tutoring and supplemental instruction in computer technology, math, science, writing, languages, and study strategies for students at all ability levels. ASAP offers a comfortable environment for students to meet with tutors one on one and in study groups. Although small, the space has a relaxed feel, with soft chairs, numerous round tables and computers, and bulletin boards with helpful suggestions and photos of the friendly tutors and staff. Since many students with limited English skills may feel ill at ease in the classroom, ASAP tutors work hard to reframe students' ability to speak Spanish as a talent and not a deficit, as we said in Chapter Eleven.

Michigan's psychology department uses trained upper-division peer advisors to help students assess their progress in meeting course requirements. They also aid students with planning class schedules, considering graduate school and career options, and reviewing research opportunities and departmental independent study options.

UTEP's Student Leadership Institute (SLI) annually trains a cadre of peer educators to assist students in the Entering Student Program. Student leaders participate in two 12-week, intensive training sessions, as well as an additional three hours of classroom instruction and weekly two-hour field placement either in a department on campus or community service organization. They also work in an administrative office and are expected to model "good student behavior" and maintain a minimum 3.0 cumulative grade point average. In addition to performing an invaluable university service, SLI participants also benefit personally, in that they develop leadership abilities, polish communication skills, and learn firsthand about group dynamics as they collaborate with other student leaders and faculty.

Through its student organizations, such as Student Educators for Active Leadership (SEAL), Longwood students actively recruit newcomers to join and become involved in one or more organizations. SEAL is especially adept at getting students to deal with personal issues as part of their leadership development strategy. The organization emphasizes the importance of reflection and attention to process as a leader, and cosponsors leadership programs that provide experiential activities and retreats.

The effectiveness of these peer academic support programs depends on proper selection and training of student peers and preceptors, collaboration between faculty and the student preceptors or tutors, and public recognition of their contributions to student success and institutional effectiveness.

MULTIPLE SAFETY NETS

Unlike many colleges and universities, student success trumps territoriality at DEEP schools. As we emphasized in Chapter Seven, faculty and administrators at these institutions realize that educating students is everyone's business. Student affairs staff, campus librarians, support staff, and faculty work together to make sure no student falls through the cracks. Although each of these schools loses some students they believe could and should have stayed, in relative terms there is much to admire and emulate from their work.

All DEEP institutions have variants of an early warning system, such as FSU's Early Alert System, described in Chapter Five. Another key partner in this vein at FSU is the Student Government Association (SGA), whose members are on hand as soon as new students arrive, helping them move into residence halls. SGA's "Four Years or Less" initiative sponsors programs and events to increase retention and graduation rates. Perhaps most powerful are the SGA officers themselves, who model how to succeed in college and exhort their peers to do the same.

To make sure students know the college is committed to helping them succeed, Ursinus "tag teams" students. That is, two or more staff or faculty members will contact a student individually if they sense that the student is struggling academically or socially, and make others who have routine contact with the student aware of the situation. Faculty, selected student affairs staff, and the director of the Bridge program receive academic warning slips from faculty members for students who are not performing up to expectations. It is not unusual for a faculty member to call a staff member or the first-year coordinator to talk about issues that might be affecting student performance.

Similarly, Wheaton's Student Life department holds weekly meetings that include residence life staff, athletics staff, and a representative from the academic advising office. The objective is to identify students who may be in need of academic or social support and to identify the most appropriate staff member who might successfully intervene, given the circumstances. A hall director told us that she often sits in these meetings to provide another view of how students are doing. Because she lives in the residence halls, she brings to the discussion a different, but helpful and informed perspective on the issues students are dealing with. Occasionally others are consulted to determine what the best approach might be to help a student, such as the dean of students, academic advisor, and the student's parent.

Winston-Salem creates redundant safety nets through its First Year College (FYC) and Academic Support Services division, which is home to all new first-year students, second-year and readmitted students, undecided students, and transfer students with fewer than 12 credit hours. The FYC aims to enhance academic performance and adjustment of students by providing specialized advising and support services, including counseling, monitoring, tutoring, developmental advising, computer-assisted instruction, and other learning assistance programs. Most of the offices and programs associated with the FYC are conveniently housed in one building near the center of campus. In addition to the required freshman seminars (see Chapter Two), students in need of additional academic monitoring and counseling are referred to the Center for Student Success (CSS); those in need of learning assistance can take advantage of computer-assisted instruction available in the Academic Resource Center (ARC). Staff in the CSS work closely with faculty to monitor students' academic performance. In addition, by employing tutors and peer leaders such as Campus PALs (peer advisor leaders) to help mentor students and keep faculty informed of services available in the center, the FYC maximizes the impact of support provided to students.

SPECIAL SUPPORT PROGRAMS

Some students come to college inadequately prepared to perform academically at acceptable levels. DEEP schools recognize that if they admit these students, they have a moral and educational obligation to provide the academic and social support they need to acquire the skills needed to succeed. As we've said before, this is not about lowering academic standards but about making available to students what they need to improve their performance to meet their school's achievement standards. Different groups of students need different types of academic or social support. Given the heterogeneity that characterizes students today, it is not possible in one chapter to describe the large variety of programs and services DEEP colleges provide to meet students' needs. In this section we focus on programs with properties that appear to be important to large numbers of students, including historically underserved students, commuter and adult students, transfer students, international students, and students of color. Because of their pervasive talent development philosophy, DEEP schools also reach out to students with other defining characteristics, such as those with disabilities and students of different sexual orientations, though we do not discuss such efforts here.

Historically Underserved Students

High-quality programs for underserved students were numerous at DEEP institutions. For example, Ursinus's Bridge Program, described in Chapter Five, introduces students to the college's academic standards and connects them with a faculty advisor and other students from underrepresented groups.

A goal of Sewanee's Summer Bridge program is to substantially increase the size of the applicant pool for talented minority high school students. It now focuses primarily on high-ability Hispanic, Asian, and African American students interested in science and math. Prior to their senior year of high school, these students attend, at no cost, a three-week summer program where they take calculus and physics courses.

The Office of Multicultural Affairs (OMA) at Kansas aims to enrich the educational experience of all students, with a special emphasis on meeting the needs of African American, Asian American, Hispanic American, and Native American students. OMA sponsors HAWK Link, a program that reaches out to students of color as soon as they are admitted to the university. Fundamentally a retention initiative, HAWK Link coordinates the work of several different offices to form an early-alert system, provide faculty mentoring and free tutoring, and connect students to existing services and programs. The program is demonstrably effective, as the persistence rate for students involved in HAWK Link is 89% from the first to second year of college compared with 78% for students who do not participate in the program. Noel-Levitz (2003) recognized HAWK Link as one of the three most effective retention programs in the nation.

Evergreen's First Peoples' Advising program provides services for "minorities" or "people of color." The term First Peoples was adopted in the mid-1980s to recognize the heritages of indigenous students from varied racial and ethnic backgrounds. The First Peoples' Scholars Program, a fall pre-orientation activity, helps new students with their transition into the Evergreen community. The First Peoples' program also provides a variety of other services and informal contacts that make up a network of support resources for First Peoples students.

Complementing Michigan's national leadership in the area of affirmative action is a series of programs and events that provide meaningful experiences for underrepresented students. The Comprehensive Studies Program (CSP) is an academic support program. Of its 2,000 annual participants, about 90% are students of color representing every college or school. Centrally located, CSP offers academic advising, personal counseling, and supplemental academic instruction. Several students described CSP as their "home away from home" because CSP staff members make their overall experience at the university more enjoyable while also holding them to high expectations. Another student offered an alternative interpretation of the value of CSP: "You can't make a small university large, but you can make a large university small."

Commuter and Adult Students

At Fayetteville State University, commuter students formed the Achieving Understanding Towards Off-Campus Students (AUTOS) group to meet the needs and advocate on behalf of the commuter student population. The group keeps commuter students informed about campus events, sponsors workshops, and other activities designed to promote academic achievement, and promotes commuter student involvement in campus organizations.

In an effort to address the needs of its commuter students, who are in fact the majority, UTEP's University 1301 instructs them about institutional policies, procedures, and resources. Because commuters are often still more closely tied to their friends from the neighborhood and high school, the class—organized as a learning community—connects commuters to others with similar goals and interests, thus helping create a support network they can rely on as they move through their program of studies.

Evergreen's Campus Children's Center provides affordable child care. In addition to regular daytime hours throughout the week, it is open late into the night as well as on Saturdays to accommodate students enrolled in the Evening and Weekend Studies courses, a large number of whom are older and have dependents.

Transfer Students

Most institutions pay far more attention to new first-time first-year students than they do to transfer students. As a result, transfers often do not know enough about the resources available to them. Equally problematic, they have little by way of common academic and social experiences with their peers who started at the institution and cannot easily connect with other transfer students. Thus, they often feel disconnected from the institution. Some DEEP colleges and universities have addressed this unfortunate circumstance with events that welcome and introduce transfer students to their new school.

Almost two-thirds of the incoming class at Evergreen annually are transfer students. To address their transition needs, the college adopted a number of transfer-friendly policies, including automatic acceptance of all credits for students who have completed an associate degree at a Washington community college. Moreover, Evergreen's Upside Down Degree program enables students with specified technical degrees to complete a bachelor's degree, thus inverting the traditional model, which begins with general coursework followed by specialized training.

About half of the incoming class each year at George Mason is transfer students. Unlike many campuses, transfer students are not invisible at GMU. A separate orientation program and support services are tailored to their needs and specially designated sections of the semester-long University 300 course reviews university policies, requirements, and procedures and covers available campus resources. University 200 appeals to students currently enrolled at a community college and helps them learn more about various majors before they have arrived on campus. Once on campus, career services reaches out to transfers to inform them about internship opportunities and, if they are still undeclared, provides more information about majors. The retention committee examines transfer student data to ensure that adequate services are provided for this population.

International Students

Thirteen percent of UTEP students are international; most cross the border from Juarez to attend classes. Given UTEP's student-centered ethos, it is not surprising that several support organizations exist to work with international students, including Programa Interamericano Estudiantil, the Mexican American Student Association, and the Center for Inter-American Border Studies. The present situation is a far cry from 30 years ago, when Mexican students created Mu Epsilon Chi (cleverly abbreviated MEX) as a vehicle for Hispanic students to connect and support one another because the institution generally ignored them.

The Center for Global Education (CGE) at Wheaton College is home away from home for 45 international students. In addition to providing ongoing support on an individual basis, the center orients new students, including an overview of immigration regulations, a visit to the local Social Security Office, and a tour of the city. An international sophomore student told us when she had visa trouble upon trying to reenter the United States, she called her international advisor at home, who quickly negotiated a happy resolution to the problem.

Michigan provides an extensive orientation program for international students to teach them about relevant cultural issues in the United States, including how people interact socially, where to live, and how to find transportation, as well as helping create a sense of community among international students. Students also visit the International Center in the Michigan Union, a kind of "buffer zone" for international students, providing them with a nurturing environment to help ease their transitions to American life and life at the university.

Women and Men

As we mentioned earlier, the female-dominated environments of Alverno and Sweet Briar are powerful and affirming, surrounding their students with intelligent women in positions of authority. The effect on intellectual self-esteem is palpable. As one Alverno senior said, "It's given a huge boost to my confidence, my belief in myself and what I can do."

Wabash College empowers its students by the college's Gentleman's Rule, which places both trust and responsibility on the student, essentially impelling them to become "a Wabash man." According to one junior, "The ideal Wabash man is an excellent student, very involved, and the consummate gentleman." Another said, "From the moment you're 'rung in,' you begin to understand what it means to be a Wabash man. But it's an intuitive process. You observe others and compare yourself to them." Faculty and staff along with strong peer and alumni networks are centrally involved. As one student told us, "They very self-consciously try to turn all of us into Renaissance men." For example, "They make us more than bookworms by getting [us] involved in concerts and plays."

Consistent with its position on affirmative action, Michigan worked hard to create a campus climate that values, recognizes, and appreciates the achievements and contributions of women. As mentioned earlier, its WISE research and residential program supports women majoring in science, mathematics, and engineering and maintains a list of women faculty members who are available as resources. They make up a key thread in the institution's safety net.

RESIDENTIAL ENVIRONMENTS

Students living in campus residences now constitute only about 15% of all undergraduates. Nonetheless, for this group of students and for their commuting counterparts attending residential campuses, the residence halls can be an important locus of support and intellectual vitality, which can have a significant influence—for better or worse—on the quality of campus life for everyone. DEEP institutions offer a variety of effective models.

FSU, Longwood, Miami, Sweet Briar, Ursinus, and Wheaton require that all first-year students live in the residence halls. With adequate, competent staff and programming, this encourages newcomers to bond in desirable ways, to study together, and discuss topics covered in class. As one FSU student affairs staff member told us, "We reserve space in the halls for our freshman class because we want to nurture them and keep them in an environment that will provide for their needs." FSU's Center for Personal Development sponsors a variety of outreach programs in the halls including "Suite Talk," a program that engages students in their residence hall suites in candid conversations about relationships, roommate problems, personality differences, health concerns, and other personal issues.

Longwood assigns students to residence halls based on intended major field (including undecided majors) with hall programming developed to match student interests. Sewanee also requires all first-year students to live on campus, but it intentionally mixes first-year students with upper-class students because staff members believe that the presence of responsible upper-division role models helps curb some typical first-year student antics related to psycho-social development that detracts from the nature of the living-learning environment it wishes to foster in campus residences.

To harness the educational advantages of the residential campus, many DEEP institutions intentionally connect residence life programs with first-year experience courses and related activities. For example, Ursinus recently moved all first-year students into common campus housing to strengthen the sense of community and belonging among first-year students and to enhance the impact of the Common Intellectual Experience (CIE). Clustering first-year students together in Freshman Centers capitalizes on the propinquity principle; because they live next to one another, they have frequent opportunities to informally discuss ideas presented in class. Some CIE sections are held in the halls where students in those sections live. One hall recently initiated a lecture series to further promote a sense of intellectual vitality while providing an opportunity for new students to interact with the faculty and administrators who give the lectures.

Sewanee uses a similar approach with its First Year Program, housing new students in small groups of six to eight, which also serve as their advising group. These students take the same FYP class and work with a faculty advisor and an assistant proctor, who is typically a sophomore. A junior or senior student manages each hall. Along with the proctor and assistant proctors, the halls also appoint "environmental residents" who volunteer their time to raise awareness about environmental concerns, and also "residential computer assistants" to manage technology integration and troubleshooting in the halls. It's worth noting that cable TV is not available in students' rooms, a situation that students seem to take some pride in. They told us, "We don't need cable because we all go to the lounge areas if there is something good to watch." Taken together, this integrated approach is well conceived and helps promote friendships as well as inculcate Sewanee's academic values.

The Michigan residence halls help shrink the physical and psychological size of the campus, which can be overwhelming for some students. Michigan has made extensive efforts to connect life in campus residences to academics and the intellectual life of the campus. As with some other DEEP schools, some sections of the faculty-led First-Year Seminars meet in the residence halls. Also, Michigan offers a variety of small, theme-oriented classes in the halls as part of one of the many formally designated learning communities. Many faculty members have offices in the Residential College, which provides opportunities for informal student-faculty contact in the hallways as well as at meals or in evening discussion groups. In addition, Michigan relies on a network of people to enhance the intellectual vitality of student residences. Along with a library in every hall, students also have access to an academic advisor, minority peer advisors, and technology assistance dedicated to their residence.

Similarly, first-year students at Sweet Briar have an impressive amount of support available to them in campus residences, including 12 peer communicators (PCs) (who are returning students), 24 resident assistants, resident coordinators (who are professional staff), and the director of first-year programs, in addition to their faculty advisor.

It's worth noting that not all DEEP schools do extensive programming in campus residences. At several of the smaller schools, notably Sewanee and Macalester, the focus is on campuswide events.

SUMMARY

Colleges and universities with supportive campus environments are characterized by high-quality student relationships with other students, faculty, and the institution's administrative personnel. These institutions not only make available resources that students can use to enhance academic skills or to enrich the quality of their social life, but they also find ways to induce students to actually use these resources. In some instances, a DEEP school intrusively makes it plain to students what they need to do to succeed. But at the same time, these efforts are motivated by a deep, abiding concern for students and their success, and students know and appreciate it. Supportive, knowledgeable, and helpful peers are also important to creating the conditions that make students feel welcome and affirmed as full members of the academic community.

Peers are very important in helping students understand faculty performance expectations and standards, managing time commitments for academic work and other activities, and connecting students to the institution and to other students in meaningful ways. By becoming involved with people with similar interests inside and outside the classroom, students develop support networks that are instrumental to helping them deal effectively with academic and social challenges. Though every DEEP college or university agrees that some of their students fall through the cracks, it is not for lack of trying.

Among the policies, practices, and conditions that are worth emulating are

- Transition programs that welcome and affirm newcomers

- Redundant early-warning systems that identify and respond to students whose academic performance or other behaviors put them at risk of failure or dropping out

- Advising networks that respond effectively to the academic and related needs of students

- Mentoring and other initiatives that help students understand and successfully navigate institutional policies and comply with procedures

- Learning support resources that are available and used by students when they need them

- Peers who provide academic and social support in formal and informal ways

- Residential living environments that provide academic and social support

- Faculty and staff members who are perceived by students as accessible and helpful

- Campus administrators who are responsive and supportive

PART IV

Summary and Recommendations

It's difficult to do justice, even in a book-length presentation, to the variety of complementary policies and practices that the 20 DEEP colleges have in place, especially to the intricate way these features are woven together to create and sustain a campus culture that fosters student success. Equally important, these institutions are works in progress. What we learned during our 18 months of data collection and reported here is a snapshot in time. All DEEP colleges and universities are almost certainly different in some ways from how they were in 2002 when we started this project. But given their collective penchant for improvement, we expect they will do even better by their students, though many variables come into play that make such a prediction risky, some over which a school has little to no control.

As we said at the outset of the book, many of the policies, programs, and practices we found at DEEP colleges and universities may—at first blush—appear familiar. Indeed, hundreds of institutions have in place many initiatives that are similar to those we found at DEEP schools, such as orientation programs, first-year seminars, learning communities, peer tutoring, student-faculty research, student support services, senior capstone projects, and the like. We mention this again now for two reasons. First, simply *offering* various programs and services does not foster student success. Programs and practices must be tailored to and resonate with the students they are intended to reach, be of reasonably high quality, and actually touch large numbers of students *in a meaningful way.* Second, we strongly discourage using a checklist approach to determine whether your school is doing what it can to promote student success. That is, there is more—much more—to creating a culture that promotes student achievement and success than having many different programs in place. We'll say more about this in the final chapter.

With this mind, Chapter Thirteen discusses the major principles that four-year colleges and universities can use to organize their human, fiscal, and physical resources to focus on student success. These build on the six major properties and conditions described in Chapters Two through Seven, as well as the numerous examples of effective educational practices presented in Chapters Eight through Twelve. We also call attention to perennial challenges facing these strong-performing institutions. In the final chapter, we offer recommendations for colleges and universities that are ready to make success a reality for more of their students.

13

Principles for Promoting Student Success

IN THIS CHAPTER we distill guiding principles for promoting student success based on what we learned from DEEP colleges and universities. We've organized the principles into three categories:

1. *Tried and true.* These are well-known policies, practices, and institutional conditions that have been empirically confirmed across multiple studies. Many of them are frequently mentioned as "best," "good," or "promising" practices in national reports. Thus, they are thought to be worthy of emulation by large numbers of colleges and universities.

2. *Sleepers.* These are policies or practices that have been mentioned in the literature, have a compelling conceptual or theoretical foundation, but have little in the way of empirical validation to support their use broadly. One example is the notion of developing a "culture of evidence" that accreditation agencies are emphasizing, which is an aspect of the "positive restlessness" feature we found at DEEP schools.

3. *Fresh ideas.* These are innovative initiatives and approaches about which to date little to nothing has been written or said. These efforts appear to us to be generally ahead of the curve, in that schools have developed responses to contemporary challenges

presented by changing student characteristics and expectations of institutions of higher education.

Reasonable people differ in terms of which category to assign a given principle. One or more of what we've called a "tried and true," well-documented institutional condition or promising practice may be a revelation to some. Even within the research team, consensus was sometimes elusive as to where a given principle should be placed. We raise this point to discourage quibbling over the assignment of an idea. A far more productive exercise is to consider each in terms of its utility and applicability within the context of a specific institution. Indeed, we view all of these ideas as DEEP nuggets worth emulating, provided they can be appropriately adapted to complement the institutional mission and educational purposes.

TRIED AND TRUE

Some of the ideas in this category have been around so long and are so widely accepted that they are articles of faith. The power of a clear, coherent mission is one example (Keeton, 1971; Chickering, 1969; Kuh, Schuh, Whitt, & Associates, 1991). Another is that students are more likely to benefit from college in desired ways if they are actively engaged in educationally purposeful activities both inside and outside the classroom (Astin, 1993; Chickering & Gamson, 1987; Pascarella & Terenzini, 1991, 2005).

Please resist the urge to skip over the tried-and-true principles because they've been discussed before or sound familiar. The fact of the matter is that many colleges do not consistently use these principles or enact their policies and practices as effectively as they could. It's worth pondering both what the principle represents and the various approaches DEEP schools used to weave them into the fabric of their campus cultures.

STUDENT SUCCESS STARTS WITH AN INSTITUTIONAL MISSION THAT ESPOUSES THE IMPORTANCE OF TALENT DEVELOPMENT AND THEN ENACTS THIS VISION.

Occasionally, trite, well-worn phrases capture truisms. Such is the case for cultivating a *shared vision* of what is desirable and possible in terms of student development, persistence, and satisfaction. As we said in Chapter Two, all schools have a mission—whether it is clearly and widely understood or not. A "living mission," however, may or may not be what the institution writes or says about itself. It is what happens when a college delivers the curriculum, organizes human talent, and allocates resources in a manner that enables it to realize its aspirations. In addition, various groups on a campus use similar language to describe what the institution stands for and is trying to accomplish with its undergraduate programs. Moreover, living missions are not mandated or legislated. They represent what people do on a daily basis.

Clear, focused, and compelling, a living mission is eminently practical. Contemporary life is increasingly hectic and complex. People at DEEP colleges are stretched thin with responsibilities and work just as hard (some maybe more so) as their colleagues at other schools. In a noisy, cluttered world, the living missions of DEEP colleges make it relatively easy for people to decide what they should be busy doing. More so than at many other colleges and universities, faculty, staff, and students "stick to the knitting," as Peters and Waterman (1982) put it, focusing on student learning and success as a priority.

Equally important is that DEEP schools express their missions in language that animates institutional will to encourage and support students to develop their talents. Among the best examples of this are CSUMB, FSU, UTEP, Wabash, and WSSU. In addition, people at these colleges and universities *believe* in their school's mission. In fact, DEEP colleges select faculty and staff in part because of their predisposition to understand the mission and socialize them to appreciate its value. Thus, for these 20 institutions, their living mission is much more than florid and often tendentious prose. It is a pragmatic lever, mobilizing and channeling effort, the yardstick by which proposed new initiatives are measured and preferences become priorities.

Remember, too, as we discussed in Chapter Two, living missions are not set in stone. They are continually being revised, in large part because DEEP schools are constantly striving to deliver what they say by minimizing the gap between their espoused and enacted mission. And as we underscored in Chapter Six, DEEP colleges have not settled once and for all the "Why are we here?" and "Where are we going?" questions. These and other fundamental aspects of campus life are frequently revisited and occasionally contested, a predictable outgrowth of the positive restlessness that characterizes these institutions.

STUDENT SUCCESS IS ENHANCED WHEN AN INSTITUTION PROVIDES MANY COMPLEMENTARY POLICIES AND PRACTICES TO SUPPORT STUDENTS ACADEMICALLY AND SOCIALLY.

DEEP colleges stand out from the pack because of the variety of high-quality programs and practices they make available. They also are especially good at effectively front-loading multiple resources to help students learn what it takes to succeed and to establish themselves as independent and then interdependent learners. As discussed in Chapter Five, these socialization efforts are tailored to students' needs and begin long before and continue well after students arrive on campus.

Indeed, DEEP schools provide guideposts to clearly mark key transition points during the college years that help channel student effort toward the right activities at the right time. Occasionally this takes the form of intrusive advising—telling students directly what they need to do when, sometimes *requiring* them to do it—to attain their educational objectives. Early warning systems and not-so-invisible safety nets are in place to "catch" students who are teetering on the edge. Competent, caring faculty and staff are seemingly everywhere, especially when students need them. DEEP schools exemplify what Pascarella and Terenzini (1991) meant when they wrote, "rather than seeking single large levers to pull in order to promote change on a large scale, it may well be more effective to pull more small levers more often" (p. 655).

MAKING PROGRAMS AND RESOURCES AVAILABLE IS NECESSARY BUT NOT SUFFICIENT TO PROMOTE STUDENT SUCCESS. SCHOOLS MUST INDUCE LARGE NUMBERS OF STUDENTS TO USE THEM.

Student success is not a function of osmosis, just as joining a gym does not automatically make someone physically fit. One has to *use* the resources of the setting to realize such benefits. Most colleges assign students to an advisor, offer some form of first-year seminar, and provide opportunities to work with faculty members on research or do an internship or community service. But these cannot have the desired effects if few students take full advantage of one or more of them. Institutions contribute to student success by making certain these programs and experiences are of uniformly high quality and large numbers of students participate in one or more of them. A complementary set of offerings that touches large segments of the student body is essential, with a special emphasis on reaching those students who are least well prepared to succeed in college—especially when they need it. For this reason, we cannot overemphasize the importance of a dense web of student success-oriented initiatives held together by redundant early warning systems and safety nets, such as FSU's early-alert system and Ursinus's academic warning slips described in Chapters Five and Twelve. The content and structure of these interventions may vary, depending on student characteristics and institutional factors. What does not vary much is their quality.

Many students, of course, can find their own way. Some are fortunate to become involved early with an activity that morphs into a lifeline to persistence, graduation, and a rich harvest of learning. We heard countless stories of students whose entire outlook on their institution and their potential as a learner changed once they became connected with the student newspaper, or found a job on campus, or began to work with a faculty member on a research project, or helped teach a course. Journalists, teachers, medical doctors, lawyers, librarians, and other professionals tell similar stories when talking about highlights of their college experience.

Good things go together. Once students engage in a meaningful way with something that excites them, doors to other educationally purposeful activities often open up, and students discover that being in college is the single best place for them to be. We'll return to this important point in Chapter Fourteen when describing the "sticky" features of effective educational practices at DEEP schools.

STUDENT SUCCESS IS PROMOTED BY SETTING AND HOLDING STUDENTS TO STANDARDS THAT STRETCH THEM TO PERFORM AT HIGH LEVELS, INSIDE AND OUTSIDE THE CLASSROOM.

Setting high expectations and then supporting and holding people accountable for reaching them is *modus operandi* at DEEP schools. Students, faculty, and staff all take student achievement seriously, recognizing there are no shortcuts. Faculty establish high but appropriate performance standards and provide frequent feedback to nudge students toward improvement. Similarly, administrators provide feedback to faculty and staff for the same purposes. And it's not uncommon for students to reciprocate, freely offering suggestions to their teachers and coaches about what could and should be improved. This interactive network of high expectations, student work, and feedback loops ensures that students perform at high levels and that faculty and staff members deliver what they promise.

Performance matters to students as well. Most we spoke with were willing to trade a modicum of social pleasure for academic substance and meaningful learning experiences. The most compelling stories in this regard were from partly marginalized students—those who did not feel as integrated or mainstream as others on campus. And yet they persisted because they recognized they were getting something valuable from their experience.

STUDENT SUCCESS BECOMES AN INSTITUTIONAL PRIORITY WHEN LEADERS MAKE IT SO.

DEEP schools chose their leaders wisely. They were right for the times and the challenges facing their institution. Paradoxically, perhaps, while presidents, provosts, and other senior administrators were "good fits" for their institutions, they also were focused on tweaking elements of their school's culture to further the student success agenda. Their approaches to leadership varied. Some presidents were very involved in campus policy and decision making that directly affected undergraduate curriculum and support programs; others were less involved. But almost to a person they persuasively championed efforts to enhance student learning and effectively balanced multiple priorities. Worthy of note is that all 20 DEEP presidents had academic appointments prior to assuming their current role. We'll return to the relevance of this observation in the final chapter.

In addition, DEEP institutional leaders were often imaginative, sometimes inspirational, and occasionally visionary. Equally important, most personified institutional values and commitments. Academic leaders with this combination of qualities are not nearly as numerous as one would think or hope. On too many campuses, executive leadership falls far short of persuasively expressing and modeling the talent development philosophy in ways that inspire others to do the same. There are many reasons for this, not the least of which is a lack of understanding about what an institution needs from its cabinet leadership and senior faculty to promote student success and the competing and sometimes conflicting priorities of the governing board that chooses the president.

As important as senior administrators are, effective leadership for student success is not concentrated exclusively in the executive ranks. DEEP schools are blessed with senior and junior faculty and staff members who find ways to creatively weave their shared talent development philosophy into policies and everyday practices. Typically, they learned what works and what doesn't through reflecting on their experiences and by swiping good ideas from their colleagues elsewhere. Indeed, at many DEEP schools some of the more powerful innovations described in this book were introduced by faculty members. Thus, DEEP colleges and universities had lots of people pulling in the same direction at the time we conducted this study.

FINANCIAL AND MORAL SUPPORT FOR PROGRAMS ARE BOTH
NECESSARY AND IMPORTANT FOR SUSTAINING EFFECTIVE
EDUCATIONAL PRACTICE.

As much as we would like to say money doesn't matter, it does. But not in the way most people think. In *Moneyball,* Michael Lewis (2003) sought to answer the question, "What was it about baseball success that resisted so many rich men's attempt to buy it?" (pp. xii–xiii). As with over-achieving in professional baseball, what seems to be important to promoting student success in college is not necessarily the *amount* of money an institution has, but that it spends it wisely. That is, on average, DEEP schools do not seem to spend more money than other institutions with similar structural or student characteristics nor do their resource allocation patterns differ (Gansemer–Topf, Saunders, Schuh, & Shelley, 2004; National Center for Higher Education Management Systems, 2004). This is not surprising, given that high-performing institutions seem to find ways to accommodate their resource needs (Fullan, 2001). Indeed, DEEP schools span a substantial range in terms of slack resources that can be used for discretionary purposes. Even those that in relative terms are advantaged in this regard—Miami, Michigan, Wabash, and Sewanee, for example—cannot fund all the attractive programs and initiatives they would like. But DEEP colleges with fewer resources still found a way to support worthwhile efforts that promise to add value to the student experience. For example, Wofford made developing learning communities a priority, supporting participating faculty members with course load reductions and opportunities to acquire pedagogical skills to effectively implement the innovation. UMF earmarked $86,000 from the president's discretionary fund to jump-start its campus work program. Because the program has been so successful, the fund has now doubled, allowing more students to work on campus and increasing the odds that they, too, will persist and succeed in college.

So, why and where an institution invests in student success can make a big difference, both in terms of what gets funded and the messages sent about institutional priorities and values. Resource decisions are mission driven and informed by data, with the salient question being: What will this investment produce in terms of student learning and success?

STAYING THE COURSE

DEEP schools did not become high-performing institutions overnight. In one form or another, DEEP schools were advantaged by having people at the institution who worked on one or more initiatives for an extended period of time in order to establish them and demonstrate their efficacy. Some of the key people who championed improvements had been at the institution a long time, such as the provost at KU and the vice president for student affairs at Miami. The academic dean at Evergreen was a graduate of the college, and a key actor who helped to maintain fidelity between the college's mission, educational philosophy, policies, and practices.

ULTIMATELY, IT'S ABOUT THE CULTURE . . .

A focused mission, institutional will, money, talent, and more are necessary but yet insufficient to foster student success. Sooner or later studies of high-performing entities conclude that distinctive features of the organization's culture are key to its effectiveness. Indeed, as Ewell (1997) observed, change initiatives in a college or university typically are "trains on their own track," running parallel rather than being meaningfully connected to other interventions in a way that stitches them into the campus culture.

Culture represents in part tacit assumptions and beliefs that influence the substance, policies, programs, and practices as well as how they are implemented. Culture gives people a common language with which to communicate. At the same time, a campus culture is not monolithic. In addition, cultures have their "shadow sides"—aspects of institutional life that are problematic. Moreover, the meaning of cultural properties and interpretations of events and actions are sometimes ambiguous. Who and what are privileged and valued are often contested, especially as students, faculty, and staff members become more diverse in every way. This is true for our 20 DEEP colleges as for any college or university.

At the same time, a strong institutional culture can bring a measure of coherence to campus life that helps people make meaning of events. Moreover, student success is advanced when the culture values talent development, academic achievement, and respect for human differences. Another book can be written focused squarely on the cultural properties of DEEP colleges and universities. We have alluded to many such elements in piecemeal fashion throughout this book—the drive to excel in everything at Michigan, the multiple affinity groups Sweet Briar women join to express different dimensions of their personalities, the pull of the Populist legacy of Kansas even today that impels people to work together for the good of the university, the invitation to a Sewanee angel to ride along for good luck by touching the roof of the car when leaving the campus, the call to service symbolized by the arches at Winston-Salem State University, and the list goes on and on. These visible manifestations of norms and values give clues about what's important and what isn't. They shape how people behave. And they are a window into the values at the core of the institution's operating philosophy, which we discussed in Chapter Two.

As with their missions, the operating philosophies of DEEP schools differ one from another. Their philosophies—the principles they use to make decisions and conduct other business on and off the campus—complement their missions, students' characteristics, and institutional aspirations, all of which combine to influence policy and decision making. Yet there are commonalities as well. For example, each DEEP college has its own variant of talent development and related beliefs about teaching and learning. For example, though they express the talent development philosophy differently, FSU, Michigan, Evergreen, CSUMB, Wheaton, Miami, WSSU, and the other DEEP institutions all communicate a similar message—"any student we admit can learn what there is to learn here."

At the same time, students at these 20 institutions of higher education believe their school is a very unusual, "special" place, that there is no other college or university like it—very distinctive if not unique. Almost every student we talked with said something akin to this, that "this is really a wonderful, special place. I can't imagine any place that could be better for me than this. It's such a great fit for me!" How can this be?

One explanation is the Hawthorne effect—that students think they are expected to say things like this when talking with outsiders, especially those who are visiting because the institution has been singled out as "special" for some reason. This very real possibility aside, many students didn't fully understand why we selected their school for the DEEP study; some were added to focus groups at the very last minute as institutional contacts scrambled to fill out our schedule, though all willingly agreed to participate in the study. Such is the real world of site visits.

A more likely explanation is that the cultures of these institutions *are* special, though they are not unique, at least in the ways students believed. The uniqueness paradox from organizational theory partially explains how this is so. People think aspects of their school (or office or synagogue) are unusual or distinctive, even though other organizations have similar features. Joanne Martin and her colleagues (1983) described organizational stories that have variants in other settings, such as how people are treated, or how "the boss" reacts when getting good or bad news. This is true of DEEP schools as well. Although each differs from the others in certain ways, some share certain cultural nuances. For example, Evergreen and CSUMB favor egalitarianism, whereas Wofford, Sewanee, and Miami tend to be more meritocratic in terms of how they operate. At UTEP, CSUMB, UMF, FSU, and WSSU, support mechanisms are very visible; at Michigan and Wabash less so though they are in ample supply.

This does not diminish the fact that students at every DEEP school believed that their campus was "special." And this is the point: if every institution in this diverse set of colleges and universities has been able to create a palpable sense of specialness about itself, so can many others. And this is the reason we embarked on this project, to find out what they do that makes students feel this way. So we move on to discuss some "sleepers": less-well-known aspects of what makes DEEP schools "special" in terms of fostering student success.

SLEEPERS

The literature describes many institutional policies, practices, and conditions that promise to promote student success. Too few examples exist of where and how some of these key conditions have been successfully implemented. DEEP schools are exceptions.

PROBLEMS AND CHALLENGES ARE CONVERTED INTO OPPORTUNITIES.

Owing in part to their improvement-oriented ethos and overall sense of institutional confidence, DEEP schools typically found ways to convert challenges into initiatives that would leverage the institution's current or potential strengths into advantages for students. Chaffee's (1989) interpretive strategy comes to mind to explain how leaders and key staff viewed the circumstances they were facing and how to make sense of them in ways that would move the institution forward.

For example, UTEP changed its mission to take advantage of the inexorable shift in the demographics of its region. Wofford's failure to obtain an NSF curricular reform grant it was confident of getting prompted it to revisit what it was doing and why, resulting in a renewed commitment to an interdisciplinary approach to general education with learning communities as the featured delivery vehicle. In some instances, events triggered concern about the state of affairs and turned the institution in a different direction. Longwood used its state's assessment mandate to design a student assessment system to guide decision making and resource allocation with a focus on student learning and success. Wheaton responded to enrollment shortfalls by changing its mission and reinvigorating its curriculum with a gender-neutral educational philosophy.

Conversely, enrollment challenges pressed Wabash and Sweet Briar to review the efficacy of their single-sex missions. After difficult and sometimes contentious debates, both affirmed their commitment to single-sex collegiate education while at the same time prompting them to consider ways to improve the quality of the undergraduate experience.

Gonzaga faced a different type of challenge to its mission and philosophy. Its successful men's basketball program stimulated an increase in applications for admission and matriculating students. The campus was embroiled in discussions in 2002–2003 about how to respond. One administrator told us, "Despite the tensions and rifts, all the parties care about GU and our students, which is the glue that keeps us together." As a result of grappling with these issues, the University discerned a clearer sense of its mission and purposes.

Although DEEP schools are predisposed to improve, as we discussed in Chapter Six, not every improvement effort was born of a constructive impulse. In some instances, the triggering event was a negative reaction to current circumstances. As Kezar (2002) emphasized, organizational change requires openness to surprises, a focus on creativity, and an appreciation for chance occurrences. What turned these problems into opportunities was when someone—usually administrators, but often faculty members and occasionally students—identified and successfully lobbied to have the issue addressed in an open forum. A faculty member at Evergreen State University called this "sensing negative restlessness." He elaborated: "Working out problems is vital. . . . We have to learn to collaborate and help faculty, staff, and students to have faith in the process." Skills like "taking the temperature of the group" and "building group consciousness" are part of Evergreen's ethos and take different forms at other DEEP schools.

ENGAGING PEDAGOGIES ARE MAINSTREAMED, RATHER THAN MARGINALIZED.

One of the surprises from the first few years of national NSSE results was the substantial number of students who engaged in various forms of active and collaborative learning activities (Kuh, 2001b, 2003). Group and collaborative learning activities inside and outside the classroom were common at DEEP schools. Indeed, several were early adopters of engaging pedagogies, such as Alverno, Evergreen, and CSUMB. The other DEEP institutions are not far behind. Moreover, this shift from passive, instructor-dominated pedagogy to active, learner-centered activities is not limited to handfuls of faculty and departments. Indeed, we were struck by the widespread use of pedagogical approaches at DEEP colleges and universities that emphasized practical application and situated learning. Such approaches have desirable effects on learning because they take students to deeper levels of understanding and meaning, encouraging them to apply what they are learning to real-life examples in the company of others (Lave & Wenger, 1990; Tagg, 2003).

Adaptations of engaging pedagogy were also evident in campus programming at DEEP colleges and universities. Urban and other institutions with substantial numbers of commuter and older students with families face challenges in involving these students in meaningful out-of-class experiences held on campus. GMU and UTEP warrant attention in this regard because of their innovative, successful approaches for involving commuter students in campus programming. Their pervasive talent development orientation is one key factor. Faculty and staff readily acknowledge the assets that nontraditional students bring to the classroom and campus in terms of their prior and current work experience, and they design class assignments and institutional events to build on and promote the application of their knowledge and experiences.

ORGANIZATIONAL STRUCTURE DOESN'T MATTER (MUCH) TO STUDENT SUCCESS.

This principle is a "sleeper" because of the tendency of newly appointed administrators to look for a quick fix to organizational performance challenges through reorganizing the administrative structure. We are not against reorganizations or other efforts to energize and improve institutional effectiveness. But in the absence of compelling evidence to the contrary, reorganizations by themselves are not likely to enhance student success.

There was no common or dominant organizational structure across the DEEP schools. Academic departments were clustered variously. Faculty members at some of the schools did the academic advising; at other institutions, advising was done by professional staff. At some institutions, student affairs reported directly to the president or chancellor; at other schools to a provost or executive vice president. And so it goes. Thus, tweaking bureaucratic reporting lines isn't likely to have much effect on student performance. Ultimately, program effectiveness and the quality of working relations are a function of competent personnel mediated by a host of intertwined cultural properties, not an organizational model.

DATA WERE USED TO GUIDE INSTITUTIONAL REFLECTION AND ACTION.

Collecting evidence for accountability and improvement is important to effective educational practice, and DEEP schools used data extensively to inform decision making. Faculty and staff frequently combined anecdotes and personal experience with systematically collected information about student and institutional performance to draw data-based conclusions about the efficacy of their initiatives. Moreover, they publicly reported on their performance. Examples include UTEP's comprehensive review of its first-year seminars, CSUMB's assessment culture, and the feedback loops systematically built into the Evergreen and Alverno curriculums.

At many DEEP schools, institutional research identified areas of institution and student performance that were worrisome. FSU and UTEP were not satisfied with their poor graduation rates and went to work to do something about them. Sewanee was disappointed in its NSSE active and collaborative learning scores and decided to revise the first-year program to encourage more such activities. In the early 1990s, Macalester commissioned a retention task force to examine first-year student retention, which was about 80%, well below the 90% level to which campus leaders aspired. The task force determined that part of the persistence problem was due to some problems with academic advising and a less-than-desired amount of student-faculty interaction. Macalester decided to require its successful, but optional first-year seminar course for all students and to formalize the academic advising responsibilities of the faculty member teaching the course. To increase early contact between students and faculty, the college encouraged faculty members teaching the first-year seminar to correspond with their students in the summer prior to enrolling; students were similarly encouraged to respond with information about their personal interests, goals, and other relevant information that would help their teachers better understand them.

Equally important, to varying degrees DEEP schools were, as Collins (2001, p. 70) put it, willing to confront "the brutal facts of reality." For example, feedback from external agencies became levers for action at some DEEP schools. Wofford's application for an Olin building grant in the late 1980s was turned back, in part because the College's espoused mission was viewed as provincial and its aspirations limited. This caused the institution to rethink its philosophy and goals. UTEP is now confident enough to productively use the feedback it receives on its unsuccessful grant proposals in revising and resubmitting them.

ASSESSMENT SERVES MANY IMPORTANT INSTITUTIONAL PURPOSES, ONLY ONE OF WHICH IS MEASURING STUDENT PERFORMANCE.

Alverno's Eight Abilities and CSUMB's outcomes-based education (OBE) model are vehicles for coordinating and revising curricular offerings and improving instructional practices as well as an academic accountability template. CSUMB's Center for Teaching, Learning, and Assessment (CTLA) incorporates the institution's assessment mandate into its faculty development initiatives. Through workshops and other events, faculty members gain expertise in developing common achievement criteria, become more consistent in judging the quality of student work, and learn to more clearly communicate performance expectations to students. Thus, faculty are able to create better conditions for learning and to assess student learning in different ways. A positive byproduct of engaging in these discussions about curricular goals is an increased appreciation for the scholarship of teaching and learning.

Equally important, doing assessment right also contributes to a supportive campus climate. By making students aware of their strengths and weaknesses and giving them frequent, specific feedback about how to improve their performance, students get a sense of what they need to do to succeed, *provided* the institution also sends unequivocal talent development messages—"You can do it!" and "We are here to help you."

WIDESPREAD USE OF STUDENT PARAPROFESSIONALS ENHANCES THE CLIMATE FOR LEARNING.

Using talented students in paraprofessional roles has been encouraged for decades but we have not seen such widespread *effective* use of them as we did at DEEP institutions. Not only do paraprofessionals stretch precious institutional resources further to reach more students, but paraprofessionals themselves typically benefit in numerous ways from the experience. For example, tutors usually learn as much or more about the respective subject than those they tutor (Pascarella & Terenzini, 1991). Especially noteworthy at DEEP schools is the sophisticated training required to serve in such roles. Tutors at UTEP, for example, are required to complete formal training, maintain a high GPA, and work a certain number of hours to remain eligible to tutor. Wofford preceptors work alongside faculty for eight weeks in the summer and help design a learning community, and then earn academic credit for attending and facilitating the learning community courses.

Faculty members and administrators also benefit from working with paraprofessionals. They learn from student preceptors how undergraduates today respond to class assignments and activities and how to modify policies in ways that are likely to have the desired effects on student behavior. Most important, perhaps, paraprofessionals provide new ideas about how to improve their course and teaching. Indeed, faculty at many DEEP schools told us working with a preceptor or peer tutor helped renew and deepen their enthusiasm for teaching.

SUBSTANTIVE, EDUCATIONALLY MEANINGFUL STUDENT-FACULTY INTERACTION JUST DOESN'T HAPPEN; IT IS EXPECTED, NURTURED, AND SUPPORTED.

Student Success in College

Simply put, DEEP colleges seek out, select, and socialize new faculty members who are interested in teaching and working with undergraduates. From initial contacts and telephone interviews, search committee members, deans, and others make it clear to prospective faculty members that student learning is a high priority. New faculty workshops, tours of the region from which students come, and ongoing socialization activities involving senior faculty colleagues reinforce this message, as does the institutional reward system. Some institutions subsidize housing and offer meal discounts to bring students and faculty together informally. Other institutions make funds available for students to do research opportunities with faculty members, and invest and train faculty and staff to use technology to augment communication with students. A key step is identifying faculty and staff who are psychologically accessible to students. That is, although faculty members hold office hours or communicate with students via e-mail, many do not reveal their inner selves in an authentic way, which is the foundation for a meaningful human connection. Faculty members who forge authentic relationships with students often are able to connect with students at deeper levels and challenge them to previously unrealized levels of achievement and personal performance.

STUDENT SUCCESS IS ENHANCED WHEN THE STUDENT AFFAIRS' OPERATING PHILOSOPHY IS CONGRUENT WITH THE INSTITUTION'S ACADEMIC MISSION.

The range of student affairs programs at DEEP institutions is similar to what can be found at many other colleges and universities. And, as with other elements of effective educational practice, student affairs at DEEP schools were organized in different ways and their contributions took different forms. What distinguishes student affairs policies and practices at DEEP colleges and universities is the degree to which they were aligned with and complemented the institution's educational purposes and objectives. This desirable state of affairs has been continually emphasized in such foundational documents as the American Council of Education's 1949 *Student Personnel Point of View,* NASPA's 1987 *Perspective on Student Affairs,* ACPA's 1994 *Student Learning Imperative,* and the 1998 ACPA, AAHE, and NASPA *Powerful Partnerships* joint statement. For example, student affairs plays a central role in developing citizen leaders at Longwood University by providing cocurricular programs emphasizing applied learning and leadership opportunities, venues for practicing the skills and competencies citizen leaders need to help enrich the civic life of their communities. The collaborative academic and student affairs model at Miami University is responsible in large part for the diversity of rich out-of-class learning opportunities available to students. Similarly, at Michigan, the collaborative efforts of student and academic affairs are especially evident in various living-learning programs described in earlier chapters, such as Residential College, Michigan Community Scholars Program, and the Women in Science and Engineering residential program (WISE).

ELECTRONIC TECHNOLOGY COMPLEMENTS INTENTIONAL
FACE-TO-FACE STUDENT-FACULTY CONTACT.

Technology is altering virtually every aspect of campus life. For this generation of students, e-mail and instant messaging are essential communication modes. DEEP schools recognize this and are seeking innovative, educationally purposeful ways of using technology. At Winston-Salem, the savvy use of e-mail and listservs keeps people informed and reduces the amount of junk paper pasted on bulletin boards and other places. CSUMB hosts an all-campus listserv as a campuswide forum. Various forms of information technology enliven peer interactions as students more frequently communicate and share diverse perspectives beyond the classroom. Equally important, virtual and synchronous contacts do not appear to substitute for face-to-face contacts between faculty and students or between students at DEEP schools, but are additional avenues students use to communicate with one another and with their teachers (Nelson Laird & Kuh, in press). Quieter students are often encouraged to come out of their shells, and more extraverted students learn how to "listen," because commentary unfolds asynchronously and they do not dominate the discussion.

One persuasive source of evidence in this regard is from the Pew-funded Course Redesign Program directed by Carol Twigg at the Center for Academic Transformation. Twigg concluded that by using technology effectively, "student success can be achieved in class without increased student-faculty contact." One key, as mentioned above, is being more intentional about the nature of the contact, such as being available on an as-needed, "when students get stuck" basis, which was the approach used to redesign mathematics courses at Virginia Tech, the University of Alabama, and the University of Idaho. However, the jury is still out as to the relative benefits of face-to-face interactions compared with virtual contacts between students and between students and their teachers.

A POWERFUL SENSE OF PLACE CONNECTS STUDENTS TO THE INSTITUTION AND TO ONE ANOTHER.

As Wendell Berry put it, if you don't know where you are, you don't know *who* you are. DEEP schools have found ways to develop in students a strong attachment to the campus as a physical place so that the campus becomes a part of their identity. Some students told us they "felt it"—this meaningful connection with the physical setting—as soon as they stepped foot onto campus for their campus tour.

As we described in Chapter Four, DEEP institutions created attractive, human scale campus environments in the context of their natural surroundings. For example, Sewanee students repeatedly mentioned the physical majesty of the "Domain." Renovations and new buildings such as Wofford's Milliken science building, Macalester's student center, and George Mason's Johnson Center include socially catalytic spaces to encourage spontaneous and informal educationally purposeful interactions among students and among students, faculty, and staff. Physical spaces can even inspire student achievement. One such example is Marvin Hall at the University of Kansas, known by students as "the KU lighthouse" because the lights in the architecture studio space are always on, indicating that architecture majors are working round-the-clock to complete their design projects.

FRESH IDEAS

Most of the principles we have discussed so far have been described to varying degrees of specificity in the literature. The kinds of policies and practices that logically flow from them can be found on many campuses across the country. DEEP schools are atypical, however, in that they touch in meaningful ways large numbers of students with high-quality programs and practices. At the same time, we also found some practices and conditions at DEEP colleges and universities that have not received very much attention.

NSSE studies and research done by many other scholars show that student engagement in effective educational practices is related to many desirable outcomes. Moreover, students who are exposed to one form of effective educational practice, such as active and collaborative learning, are also more likely to report higher levels of participating in other desirable activities, such as challenging academic work, diversity experiences, contact with faculty, and so forth. Equally important, they are more likely to get higher grades, report being more satisfied, and are more likely to persist and graduate. As we said earlier, good things go together. At DEEP schools, students tended to engage in such practices in bunches, because instructors in several classes used active and collaborative pedagogies and set high standards for their performance. These practices in turn led to more frequent feedback and typically more meaningful contact between students and their teachers, coaches, advisors, and so forth.

A similar pattern can be seen in the results from the Faculty Survey of Student Engagement (Kuh, Nelson Laird, & Umbach, 2004). Faculty members who report setting high standards and using active and collaborative learning techniques are also more likely to present diverse perspectives in class, give prompt feedback, and so forth. As a consequence, students attending these institutions report engaging more frequently in these practices.

Though DEEP schools use different combinations of policies, programs, and practices, there was considerable synergy across these activities. Thus, the sum of their collective impact on student performance was greater than the influence of any single practice. In this sense, effective educational practices seem to be "sticky," borrowing Gladwell's (2000) phrase from the *Tipping Point*. That is, they clump together. Thus, it stands to reason that the more a school exposes students to effective educational practices, the more likely it is that any given student will be positively affected.

STUDENTS FLOURISH WHEN THEIR PRIOR LEARNING IS VALUED AND THEIR PREFERRED LEARNING STYLES ARE RECOGNIZED.

Accommodating diverse learning styles has long been espoused as a principle of good practice in undergraduate education (Chickering & Gamson, 1987). Many faculty and staff members at DEEP colleges have taken this several steps further to systematically assess what students know and then design learning activities that build on their knowledge and skills. Such an approach flows from the talent development philosophy as extended by Dweck's (2000) work on self-theories about intelligence. Dweck found students tend to hold either an entity view or an incremental view of their ability. In the former, intelligence is essentially fixed; in the latter, intelligence is something that can be enhanced through continued learning and experience. Dweck further discovered that it's possible to influence how students view their abilities by structuring early learning experiences in a new subject by starting with what students are good at. This has powerful implications for many historically underserved students who have doubts about their abilities to do college-level work and who, like UCLA Professor Mike Rose (1989) when he started college, think that their fate was determined at birth. We now know, as Dweck (2000) says, that "those who are led to believe their intelligence is a malleable quality begin to take on challenging learning tasks and begin to take advantage of the skill-improvement opportunities that come their way" (p. 26). The challenge for institutions that wish to enhance student success is to figure out how to introduce this thinking to faculty members in ways that will persuade them to use it in course design and instruction.

STUDENTS ARE MORE LIKELY TO THRIVE WHEN SUPPORT COMES FROM MULTIPLE SOURCES.

One reason DEEP colleges seem to work so well is that they have done what some observers have been recommending for several decades: concentrating institutional resources on first-year students to increase the chances that they will get off to a good start in college, academically and socially. As with many other institutions, DEEP schools offer summer bridge programs, summer orientation and registration, first-year programs, student support services, and other efforts. Such efforts, when well conceived and implemented effectively, seem to have salutary effects, though the empirical evidence is not nearly as plentiful as we might like (Patton, Morelon, Whitehead, & Hossler, 2004; Upcraft, Gardner, & Barefoot, 2005).

In addition to precollege initiatives that serve fairly small numbers of students, DEEP schools mount a full-court press with a variety of coordinated, complementary programs for new students that start with precollege socialization activities and continue through much or all of the first college year. We described many of these earlier, such as the summer common reading experience at Wofford; the summer orientation program at KU; the pronounced emphasis on student learning as part of the residence hall living experience at Miami, Ursinus, and Longwood; the compact disks made available to students at Michigan that describe how students can get involved with faculty; and the numerous extended orientation experiences and courses at many of the DEEP schools.

As we said earlier, DEEP institutions take a somewhat different approach from many of their counterpart schools that have pretty much delegated the responsibility and authority for new student transition and first-year programs to the student affairs division. As with other aspects of the undergraduate program, DEEP colleges and universities have successfully blended the contributions and talents of academic and student affairs to form powerful partnerships that result in high-quality transition experiences for new, first-time students and transfers alike.

CURRICULAR IMPROVEMENTS THAT ENHANCE STUDENT LEARNING ARE TYPICALLY GROUNDED IN A CONTEMPORARY FUSION OF THE LIBERAL AND PRACTICAL ARTS.

At most DEEP schools, what has been traditionally called the liberal arts or liberal arts education is anything but static. In the 19th century, the liberal arts emphasized living the examined life via a circumscribed body of knowledge accessible only to the privileged class. By the mid-20th century, the focus shifted to critical thinking as defined by rational Western thought. Today, the contemporary conception of liberal arts education values different life experiences and perspectives and privileges the skills, competencies, and sensibilities needed to understand, navigate, and participate in meaningful, responsible ways in a diverse, increasingly complex postmodern world (Kimball, 1986; Orrill, 1997).

As with many of the institutions mentioned in the Association of American Colleges and Universities' (2002) *Greater Expectations* report, DEEP colleges seem to be on the leading edge of this transition, in that their successful curricular revisions mitigated contentious debates about the relative value of exposing students to the "pure" liberal arts traditions or preparing students for life after college. They developed their own fusions of liberal arts discipline-based offerings leavened with healthy doses of personal reflection and practical application, both through class-based active and collaborative learning activities and capstone projects and through learning experiences beyond the classroom, including internships, service learning, study abroad, and related opportunities. The learning communities at Wofford, UTEP, and CSUMB are excellent examples, as is CIE at Ursinus, Wheaton's gender-balanced curriculum, Alverno's Eight Abilities Curriculum, the Miami Plan Core Curriculum, Evergreen's "Program" curriculum model, Gonzaga's Core Curriculum, and Longwood's institutionwide "Citizen Leader" emphasis.

PERENNIAL CHALLENGES

As we've said before, as good as these 20 institutions are, they are by no means perfect. But there are lessons to be learned from imperfections as well as strong performance. In this section, we discuss several nettlesome issues that DEEP schools were dealing with when we visited. Most other schools are facing these challenges as well.

How Big Is Too Big?

Thirty-five years ago, Astin (1977) concluded that allowing undergraduate enrollments to swell to more than 15,000 was a regrettable mistake in terms of creating the conditions that optimally foster student development. Chickering and Reisser (1993) explain why as colleges and universities get large, it becomes more difficult to create among their members a sense of collective purpose and individual self-efficacy. For students, as institutions increase in size, it becomes easy to be anonymous and more difficult to get involved in meaningful ways in campus governance and other activities. Although DEEP institutions have more or less successfully struggled with ameliorating the disadvantages of large size, several institutions are being asked by their states to increase enrollments without commensurate increases in resources, such as UTEP, CSUMB, FSU, WSSU, and Evergreen. Others, such as Michigan, Kansas, and George Mason, already enroll more students than some believe can sustain a high-quality undergraduate experience. Although human scale facilities and initiatives such as learning communities can help shrink the psychological size of a university, at some point systems such as safety nets, early warning systems, and special support programs may not be able to ameliorate the deleterious effects of large size without taking a significant toll on faculty and staff.

Balancing Teaching and Research

A perennial challenge faced by most colleges and universities—even those focused on undergraduate education—is balancing the desire to provide high-quality learning experiences in classrooms, laboratories, and studios as well as in various out-of-class venues with faculty scholarly inquiry. The University of Kansas and the University of Michigan are, by definition, research-intensive institutions, which makes it especially difficult for them to maintain an institutional commitment to high-quality undergraduate education, given the multiple claims on faculty time and energy. At the same time, most of the other DEEP schools also wrestle with this issue. Indeed, at most of the 20 institutions, faculty reported that the expectations for scholarship were as high as they've ever been, even increasing.

For example, at Miami University, where teaching has long been the espoused priority, academic administrators are emphasizing scholarship more. In his 2003 State of the University address, Miami President James

Garland observed: "Despite our growing commitment to research, it is clear we still have very far to go before our scholarship is as highly ranked as our teaching. . . . I want to emphasize that a commitment to research excellence does not detract from a commitment to instructional excellence. On the contrary, at the best universities research and teaching inevitably go hand in hand."

In an article in the campus newspaper, a Miami University faculty member described this shift as "an assault on Miami's core values and commitment to the liberal arts." Others are concerned about juggling the expectations to produce more scholarship while continuing to spend as much time with students as in the past. Another worried aloud, "We're pretty good at what we do right now and I'd hate to see us become a second-rate Big 10 university."

Similarly, even small liberal arts colleges, including Macalester and Ursinus, struggle with maintaining high expectations for teaching and research. Ursinus strives to balance its commitment to liberal arts education with high expectations for faculty scholarship. In 1991, the faculty voted to increase the role of scholarship in faculty work, a decision that resulted in national searches for faculty members (previously regional searches were the norm) and modifying the promotion and tenure criteria to emphasize scholarship as well as high-quality instruction. Now the college uses external reviewers much as larger research-intensive universities do to evaluate the faculty productivity as part of the promotion and tenure review process. To support scholarly work, the college now makes pretenure leaves available on a competitive basis. Bringing in faculty who are active scholars helped to increase expectations for student performance as well.

Although all these schools were sympathetic to expanding constructions of scholarship consistent with Boyer's (1990) framework and The Carnegie Foundation for the Advancement of Teaching scholarship of teaching initiatives (Shulman, 2004), expectations in the scholarship domain were creeping upward. At the same time, faculty were either being asked to do more or wanted to do more in terms of developing and improving curricular offerings or enrichment programs such as learning communities or incorporating engaging pedagogies.

Overload

On every DEEP campus, many of the faculty and staff members we talked with mentioned that the pace and amount of their work were spiraling out of control. This was not offered as a complaint but more as a legitimate, worrisome concern that will sooner or later erode the quality of their contributions to undergraduate education. Many of the distinguishing features of DEEP schools are a function of the amount of time competent, caring professionals devote to students and other activities to maintain and improve the learning environment. Some institutions, such as Ursinus College, are studying this situation in an attempt to more effectively manage time demands that everyone agrees are escalating.

Managing the Downside of Positive Restlessness

One of the ironies of the workload issue is that another salient quality of DEEP schools—their inclination to continually improve—exacerbates the tensions and strains associated with overload. That is, positive restlessness impels people to think about how to do things better and how to individually and collectively perform at higher levels. For example, none of the DEEP institutions were completely satisfied with the experiences of members of historically underserved groups on their campus. Acknowledging that the status quo is unacceptable, new initiatives were undertaken regularly, including infusing diverse perspectives in the curriculum. A compounding factor is because there is always some aspect of work and life that can be improved, DEEP faculty and staff do not always sufficiently celebrate their collective accomplishments. Although awards ceremonies and other events acknowledge outstanding teachers, scholars, and advisors, there are few periods during which people give themselves permission to coast, catch their breath, and renew their spirit and energy. There's always something else they should be doing.

The Press to Become More Selective

We've extolled the virtues of DEEP schools because they are comfortable in their own skin, so to speak, and do good work with the students they attract. But there are pressures, many external, to get better by recruiting "better" students. The argument for "better" students—those who are well prepared academically to handle college-level work—is difficult to rebuff. Governing boards favor students with high SAT scores and high school class ranks because these indicators are familiar to others. And what faculty member doesn't want well-prepared students to work with? Even for those who are personally committed to work with and lift up historically underserved and underprepared students, there is a subtle (though probably not convincing) appeal to the argument that elementary and secondary schools should be doing a better job and by increasing admissions standards they will be pressured to do so. A more pernicious undercoating to this discussion surfaces when institutional admissions policies are reviewed. Becoming more selective can improve the academic (and ideally also the financial) profile of entering students, which could nudge the institution upward in college rankings. Stronger academic students are more likely to persist and graduate, which also affects ranking and institutional revenues. Certainly institutional missions differ and as the stories of DEEP schools show they can and sometimes should change to be responsive to the times while at the same time preserving and even enhancing educational quality. Nevertheless, the time and resources DEEP and other schools spend on considering how to enhance their student academic profile could be invested in other ways that promote student learning.

Managing Diversity for Educational Benefit

All of the DEEP colleges and universities were committed to exposing their students to diverse perspectives and various forms of human diversity, understanding that it is hard to adequately prepare students for their future roles in a diverse democracy in the absence of a diverse population of students. Some of these schools were very diverse in terms of students' age, socioeconomic backgrounds, and ethnic origins. But others were not, such as UMF, Miami, Wofford, Sewanee, and Wheaton. The schools that had less diverse populations (especially racial and ethnic background) did not discount the importance of understanding life in a pluralistic world. Indeed, all of the less diverse institutions lamented falling short in their efforts to attract a more racially and ethnically diverse student body and faculty. At the same time, faculty and staff members from several DEEP schools understood that interacting face to face with people from different backgrounds is not the only way to ensure that students gain knowledge about and develop an appreciation for diversity. In some cases, this understanding resulted in redoubling efforts to incorporate diverse perspectives into the curriculum. Class discussions and assignments featured socioeconomic class, internationalism, global consciousness, and how various perspectives could result in theoretical and practical differences in how the world is viewed and problems are solved.

At Sweet Briar, for example, students debate not only whether the institution is doing enough to realize its purported aspirations for a diverse student body and faculty, but the meaning of diversity itself. Some students are satisfied with the extent to which Sweet Briar affirms and celebrates diversity, pointing, for example, to events where foods from a variety of countries are celebrated. Other students think of diversity primarily in terms of interests, goals, family backgrounds, and home communities, not race or ethnicity, and assert that Sweet Briar "is incredibly diverse." Many staff and faculty (and some students) fear, however, that Sweet Briar's racial and ethnic homogeneity hampers preparing Sweet Briar students for productive roles in their future careers and communities.

Wofford had similar discussions about the challenges associated with attracting students of color to the campus. To no small extent, the challenge is self-inflicted because the campus did not admit African Americans until 1964. In addition, the college now emphasizes diverse perspectives throughout the curriculum. For example, the Presidential Seminar, "Religion in America," takes a pluralistic approach to religion, encouraging students to understand and appreciate religious differences by attending religious services different from their own. One student described class discussion as "so powerful that the table almost levitates." Other efforts to ensure students learn about various forms of human diversity include off-campus interim session assignments and study abroad. Still, the relative lack of structural diversity is a source of widely recognized concern.

At Miami, the desire to move beyond tolerance of diversity to construction of a pluralistic community has been a topic of serious campus discussion for more than a decade. According to many, the impact of diversity initiatives and commitments to increase the heterogeneity of the community and foster healthy dialogues about differences is "dramatic." Nonetheless, recent campus climate surveys show that much remains to be done. For example, members of minority groups (as the term is used at Miami) are significantly less likely to report that they feel a sense of belonging at Miami than are majority group members. In addition, interactions between and among members of different races have not increased over time as many had hoped. The good news, according to people who have been at Miami for decades, is the tone of conversations is different now: "Now it's an action conversation. It's about what are we going to *do*."

Multiculturalism and internationalism are two of the four pillars in Macalester College's mission. It might come as no surprise, then, that levels of interaction among students of different backgrounds and attitudes place Mac above the 90th percentile on the NSSE diversity item, which means that Mac students are well above the national average in experiences with diversity. What could be surprising is that Macalester students consistently urge the institution to become even more diverse.

DEEP institutions were committed to fostering the educational benefits of diversity. In spite of a lack of racial and ethnic diversity on some campuses, most institutions took diversity seriously. They intentionally integrated diversity experiences into undergraduate education. Multiculturalism was not simply an "add on" to the curriculum. Rather, it was incorporated into both academic and student life.

Bringing People Along, Leaving People Behind

Finally, DEEP schools also struggle with fashioning a humane way to deal with faculty and staff members who are unwilling or unable to change how they think and what they do to enhance the institution's educational effectiveness. As Jim Collins (2001) succinctly puts it, to move organizations in a different direction, it's likely that some people need to "get off the bus." Of course, this is easier said than done in institutions of higher education, especially four-year colleges, where it's not uncommon for two-thirds of the faculty to have tenure. Even if tenure isn't an issue, the collegial cultures that characterize many campuses make it difficult to confront people about the quality of their contributions. Legitimate disciplinary differences in discovering and making meaning of knowledge create their own hegemony of thought and action. In this context, the chances of personal renewal improve when people confront "disorienting dilemmas," situations in which their preferred ways of understanding or working don't fit what they are experiencing (Mezirow, 1990). Most faculty and staff are willing to do different things and even to do things differently *if* they can come to this realization themselves and receive some support for taking risks in trying out new behaviors.

SUMMARY

Each of the 20 DEEP colleges and universities has successfully implemented, maintained, and tweaked "tried and true" policies and practices. They have also invented some approaches that up to now have received relatively little attention. At the same time, what stirred them to focus on student success differ somewhat, as we discussed in Chapter Six.

The combinations of initiatives, circumstances, personalities, and many other contextual factors are numerous and complex. After spending many months studying and reflecting on what makes the DEEP schools educationally effective, we are convinced we know a lot more now than before. At the same time, there are surely other ways of looking at student success and educational effectiveness than what we've offered here. So we caution against a "hardening of the categories," or the tendency to accept what we report here as the new orthodoxy.

14

Recommendations

HIS PROJECT began with the question: What do high-performing colleges do to promote student success, broadly defined? Our visits to 20 such institutions have provided some answers. We conclude by turning to another compelling question: What should colleges and universities do if they want to increase the chances that more of their students will perform well and graduate?

In Chapter Seven we said that DEEP colleges are distinctive because the responsibility for student learning and student success is widely shared by various groups. Indeed, in an era when specialization and fragmentation are commonplace, the lesson from DEEP colleges and universities is that student success must be everyone's business in order to create the conditions that encourage and support students to engage in educationally productive activities at reasonably high levels.

This chapter presents a set of general recommendations that in one way or another have implications for just about everyone associated with a college or university, including students. Some of the recommendations are more germane to certain individuals, such as presidents and provosts, and groups, such as student affairs professionals, faculty, or librarians. Occasionally we illustrate specific applications of what these individuals and groups might do. Given the great variation in roles, responsibilities, and institutional cultures, what these ideas look like when implemented successfully will necessarily differ, depending on context-specific circumstances.

Taking Responsibility for Student Success

- Though not involved in day-to-day operations, governing board members are responsible for ensuring that the trajectory of the institution is congruent with their aspirations for the college. If student success is to be a priority for the president and others, it must be a priority for the board.

- The president or chancellor articulates the institution's vision and values, sets programmatic and financial priorities, determines the organizational structure, and evaluates the performance of senior officers. Through words and deeds, the president or chancellor demonstrates what is expected in terms of promoting student success.

- Provosts and senior academic officers have a special obligation to focus on the quality of the undergraduate experience, even though the institution may also feature graduate education and research in its mission. Thus, it is essential that senior academic officers maintain a public, steadfast commitment to institutional efforts to improve the quality of the undergraduate experience.

- The value of the out-of-class experience to student success cannot be overestimated. Any institution that wishes to make student achievement, satisfaction, persistence, and learning a priority must have competent student affairs professionals whose contributions complement the academic mission of the institution in ways that help students and the institution realize their respective goals.

- The only regular contact many students have with their institution is through the classroom. Thus, faculty members are in a key position to influence student success, not only in terms of what students learn but being able to identify students who may be struggling or whose overall performance is far short of their potential. They, along with their colleagues in student affairs, know the most about students, though their perspectives typically differ because of the settings in which they get to know students.

- Every type of institutional agent makes important contributions to student success, including those staff members at all levels of the institution who implement many of the student support initiatives as well as those whose small gestures on a daily basis affirm and support students. Represented by Miss Rita (Chapter Seven), staff members who go out of their way to make students feel "special" are institutional treasures and merit being treated as such.

As we asserted in Chapter Thirteen, no one of these recommendations by itself will likely make a substantial difference in terms of student learning and other indicators of success, whether represented by results on a survey such as NSSE, persistence and graduation rates, or various other outcomes measures. Indeed, there seems to be general agreement that to have a demonstrable impact on the nature and quality of student learning, it is necessary to do many different things *better* and more *frequently* so that one or more initiatives touch *substantial numbers* of students in meaningful ways, rather than invest vast amounts of resources, time, and energy in one large, complicated initiative (Collins, 2001; Kuh, 1996; Kuh, Schuh, Whitt, & Associates, 1991; Pascarella & Terenzini, 2005; Rhatigan & Schuh, 2003; Weick, 1984).

ORGANIZING FOR STUDENT SUCCESS

Although a uniform set of actions cannot effectively address all the issues that campuses must deal with to promote student success, two meta principles merit mention because they are essential for any campus to successfully implement strategies toward this end. They are *alignment* and *sustainability.*

Policies, programs, and practices must be *aligned* with student academic preparation and needs as well as with institutional resources and personnel in ways that complement the institution's mission, values, and culture. Alignment does not happen naturally. It requires that some persons or groups regularly monitor the efficacy of current initiatives and review proposed new efforts to determine their complementarity and potential for enhancing student success.

Attempts to improve educational effectiveness typically encounter difficulty and resistance (Engelkemeyer & Landry, 2001). Failed and faltering interventions result also because too little thought was given to where the resources or energy would come from to *sustain* the efforts beyond a first or second cycle. At the same time, the sustainability challenge cannot be allowed to paralyze institutional improvement efforts. The lesson from DEEP colleges is to move forward with eyes wide open and alternative strategies in mind to deal with possible multiple scenarios. Invariably, this will require difficult choices between continuing to support productive efforts and discontinuing those that are less effective or no longer viable so that new ideas can be weighed and implemented in a timely fashion.

Feature Student Success in the Institution's Enacted Educational Mission and Purposes

Before faculty and staff can be expected to invest time and energy fostering student success, the institution must emphasize the importance of student success to attaining its institution's mission.

- *DEEP schools featured student success in their visions of what they aspired to accomplish with their undergraduate program.*

DEEP colleges and universities made a clear, compelling case for the importance of student success by articulating a mindscape or preferred vision of the future that enabled faculty, staff, and others to see how their daily work contributes to student success. Asking questions like "What are we doing?" and "Why are we doing it this way?" helps people to determine whether established practices are still relevant to the changing needs and interests of students, evolving institutional conditions, and why and how proposed interventions would address student and institutional needs (Eckel, Hill, Green, & Mallon, 1999). Recall UTEP's use of *Moneyball* to get people to think differently in order to identify institutional obstacles that hinder student persistence. Staying focused on key objectives demands that people continually reflect on what they are trying to achieve (Eckel, Green, & Hill, 2001; Garvin, 1993; Kezar, 2001; Kezar & Eckel, 2002; Senge, 1999). This was particularly evident at Alverno, California State at Monterey Bay, Evergreen State, Ursinus, and Wheaton, where discussions about institutional mission and values are commonplace.

A common language also is essential to make the case for student success, so that people with different mental maps can more readily understand how their individual actions contribute to the "big picture" of institutional effectiveness. Evergreen is replete with institution-specific language (Chapter Three) describing its distinctive curricular components (the "Program") and processes ("seminaring"). At Alverno, every faculty member is assigned to one of the Eight Ability departments (in addition to their academic department), which brings faculty members from different academic departments together weekly to discuss student progress and related matters, all of which facilitates cross disciplinary communication. CSUMB's use of the term "Vision Students" reminds faculty and staff members of the institution's commitment to serving students whose life experiences and socioeconomic conditions have historically precluded their participation in higher education.

• *Clarify and translate the mission in plain language to stakeholders.* The institutional mission statement should emphasize and define what student success means in the local context. However, simply writing about student success is not sufficient to ensure that students will have access to and profitably use the resources they need. With so many faculty, staff, and students saying they are overextended, we should not be surprised that many people do not understand what the institution stands for and wishes to accomplish with its undergraduate program. Different groups resonate to different approaches and use different words to communicate the same concepts.

• *Ensure that the espoused mission is enacted.* As we discussed in Chapter Two, what a college writes about itself in terms of its mission may not be what it does. Systematic, period reviews of college activities, reward systems, and other operational functions are essential to maintaining fidelity between what an institution says it is about and what it actually accomplishes. The kind of process we envision focuses squarely on institutional policies and practices that foster student success. In some ways, it is akin to self-studies in advance of accreditation visits; in other ways it is quite different (Kuh, Kinzie, Schuh, & Whitt, in press).

• *Senior leaders must publicly and repeatedly champion undergraduate education.* Presidents and senior academic officers have many priorities. One of the most important is maintaining and enhancing the quality of the undergraduate experience. Indeed, DEEP presidents made it a point to remind people frequently of their institution's aspirations and high expectations for students. Provosts vigorously advocated on behalf of the undergraduate program. In multiple settings—annual state-of-the-campus reports, governing board meetings, convocations, faculty meetings, and so on—presidents and provosts underscored the institution's commitment to high-quality undergraduate education and its centrality to the institution's mission. One tactic for keeping this priority visible campuswide is to select an annual theme for an academic year around which events can be organized. Another is to establish a multiyear agenda that requires the contributions of many people, such as UMF's student work initiative.

• *Strive to appropriately balance the institution's multiple missions.* At large research universities especially, the institution can easily tip in the direction of disproportionate amounts of resources flowing toward graduate education and research. Senior academic leaders at DEEP universities such as Kansas, Michigan, George Mason, and UTEP effectively explained why balancing the research and teaching missions of the institution was crucial to maintaining high-quality undergraduate programs and support services, while at the same time illustrating how the research mission enriches the undergraduate experience. As with most matters on a college campus, carefully balancing teaching and scholarship is a perennial challenge, never completely resolved. DEEP schools spend considerable time and energy debating this important issue. And that explains in part their collective successes: they *do* deal with this and related challenges, rather than pretend the issues do not exist.

Make Talent Development a Central Tenet in the Institution's Operating Philosophy

DEEP institutions maintained a steadfast focus on students as people who are capable of learning anything the institution teaches.

• *Establish high expectations—for everyone.* People at DEEP institutions have high expectations for one another. Board members expect their presidents to be exemplary leaders. Presidents expect their cabinet members as well as faculty and staff to perform at the highest levels of professionalism. Faculty members expect a great deal of themselves, their colleagues, and their students. Such expectations are created and reinforced through judicious selection of like-minded colleagues and activities that make certain aspects of life at DEEP colleges seem "routine," such as the ethic of positive restlessness that fuels periodic curriculum reform and experimentation with promising pedagogical techniques.

• *Know your students.* DEEP colleges know a good deal about their students—where they come from, their preferred learning styles, their talents, and when and where they need help. Institutional researchers and assessment personnel frequently examine students' needs and interests and typically share the results widely with people who can use the information to make a difference. Needs assessments do not guarantee learning and student success, but it's hard to improve without collecting assessment data. At some DEEP schools faculty gained insights into students and their lives by distributing short questionnaires at the beginning of class asking students to describe their interests, goals, and out-of-class activities. Faculty use this information to tailor course assignments and the examples they use in class. In addition, the personal information students provide helps faculty members better understand the multiple commitments students must manage in addition to this particular class. More than a few faculty members routinely invite students to visit during office hours; a few regularly schedule at least two meetings a term with their students. Discussion topics vary widely, of course but most are generally related in one way or another to students' performance, such as providing additional feedback or soliciting students' views about how well the course is progressing.

• *Set performance standards for students at high but attainable levels consistent with their academic preparation.* The vast majority of students learn more when performance standards require a level of effort greater than what students would ordinarily put forth if left to their own devices. Being stretched in this way helps students cultivate habits of the mind that become the foundation for pursuing excellence in other areas of life. Challenging students to perform at optimal levels is tricky and complex. Assigning more books or more papers will not necessarily lead to higher levels of learning. It depends in part on the nature, complexity, and clarity of the assignments. Students' academic backgrounds and major fields are key factors in the equation. Classes in the sciences may use only a single text for an academic term, while students in the humanities may well read a score or more in some classes. The number of short and long papers also will vary substantially because of the learning requirements of various fields.

- *Provide generous amounts of helpful, constructive feedback.* Writing in the absence of feedback may simply become redundant exercises in mediocrity. Not only did DEEP faculty provide a good deal of oral and written feedback to their students, but generally they were also sensitive to how students would react to the feedback. Students differ in this regard, based on a variety of factors. In addition to pointing out areas where improvement is needed, faculty members typically identified strengths in the work when possible to bolster student confidence in their abilities. Some institutions, such as Alverno, used external experts to help assess the quality of student portfolios, poster projects, or research papers. This introduces an additional dimension to the evaluation process, giving students feedback about how their performance stacks up in "the real world."

- *Balance academic challenge with adequate support.* DEEP colleges provide early warning systems, redundant safety nets, and other forms of assistance and support so that if students are having trouble meeting academic and social challenges, they can learn and grow from the experience and try again. When talking about the institution's vision and values, presidents, provosts, and senior faculty members remind everyone that academic excellence is not a strain of educational Darwinism. They tirelessly advocate on behalf of responsive, learner-centered support services, such as peer tutoring, special labs for writing and mathematics, and—if necessary and appropriate, given the audiences—intrusive academic advising.

- *Use pedagogical approaches that complement students' learning styles.* Just as all faculty members do not excel at everything, neither do all students. But all students do have the capacity to learn almost anything a college teaches. Many more students would excel by using different combinations of teaching approaches and learning conditions. For example, there is some evidence that students who are "concrete learners" benefit more from active and collaborative learning approaches (Schroeder, 1993; Tagg, 2003). Students who score relatively low on standardized tests appear to benefit more in terms of learning outcomes from high-quality personal relationships, a supportive campus environment, and experiences with diversity, whereas students who score especially high on these tests may benefit less from active and collaborative learning (Carini, Kuh, & Klein, 2004). Although much more research is needed to identify the pedagogical conditions under which different groups of students learn best, it is prudent to assume that not all students will thrive using the same approach. Experience over the past two centuries using the lecture-dominated mode is ample evidence of this. To encourage more active and collaborative learning, DEEP schools tried various approaches, including reducing the size of some classes by increasing the size of others, thus increasing the odds that at least one course a semester would be small enough so that a student could actively participate. In addition, instructors were assigned to the larger classes in part because of their ability to use technology and innovative pedagogical techniques to provide an engaging learning experience.

• *Encourage the types of student-faculty interactions that pay dividends in terms of student development.* Generally, almost any form of student-faculty interaction is positively related to indicators of student success. Although student-faculty contact has salutary effects, spending too much time with one another may not be the best use of either student or faculty time, if the interactions are unrelated to intellectual or academic matters. For example, for certain activities, "occasional" student-faculty contact may be enough. Four of the six behaviors on the NSSE student-faculty interaction cluster are of this kind: discussing grades and assignments, discussing career plans, working with a faculty member outside of class on a committee or project, and doing research with a faculty member. For most students doing the first three of these once or twice a semester is probably good enough. "Occasionally" discussing career plans with a faculty member is sufficient for seeing the relevance of their studies to a self-sufficient, satisfying life after college. Working on a research project with a faculty member just once during college could be a life-altering experience, as we mentioned earlier. But in terms of prompt feedback and discussing ideas presented in readings or class discussion, it's plausible that the more frequent the behavior the better (Kuh, 2003).

Cultivate an Ethic of Positive Restlessness

For better or worse, DEEP institutions rarely engage in self-congratulatory behavior. More important, they are characteristically never quite satisfied with their performance. Rather, they are constantly looking for ways to improve the student experience and to encourage innovation by faculty and staff.

- *Steer the organization toward continuous improvement.* According to Fullan (2001, p. 75), "all successful organizations in a culture of change have been found to a certain extent to seek diversity of employees, ideas, and experiences while simultaneously establishing mechanisms for sorting out, reconciling, and acting on new patterns." People at DEEP schools constantly reminded themselves of their pursuit of excellence by periodically reviewing campus priorities, policies, and practices to ensure that what is enacted is of acceptable quality and consistent with the institution's espoused priorities and values. Such examinations were sometimes formal, such as program reviews or accreditation self-studies. The six major reports of the quality of the undergraduate experience conducted by Michigan since the mid-1980s is one such example. But many informal reviews stimulated by faculty curiosity or unease led the way to changes that enhanced student engagement.

- *Use data to inform decision making.* Typically, DEEP schools pointed to a combination of external and internal conditions to draw attention to the need to do things differently. Fayetteville State, University of Texas at El Paso, and Winston-Salem State responded to changing demographics and state mandates to graduate more students. Michigan responded to calls by national reports in the 1980s to improve undergraduate education. Ursinus, Wofford, and CSUMB used upcoming accreditation visits as a mobilizing event. Since DEEP institutions also are constantly studying and benchmarking their performance against peers, they know a great deal about the impact of their policies and practices and use this information in decision making. And DEEP schools were among the early adopters of both NSSE and the Faculty Survey of Student Engagement (FSSE), using these tools in combination to identify student and faculty behaviors that could be more effectively aligned. Whatever the means, faculty along with administrators were keen on using multiple sources of information to determine those activities worth continuing and to modify what they were doing to improve.

• *"Sunset" less effective programs and activities in order to support high-priority initiatives.* As with other institutions, DEEP schools struggled with how to gracefully terminate programs and activities that no longer seem to benefit ample numbers of students. Even so, as we noted in Chapter Thirteen, many people at DEEP institutions are teetering on the brink of overload much of the time. At one institution, faculty described their teaching load as "crushing." Thus, one of the most important questions we must answer to promote student success is not what are we going to do next, but what should we *stop doing* now so there is time and energy to invest in promising new initiatives (Collins, 2001; Kuh, 1996). Some DEEP schools are addressing this issue, such as Ursinus, which introduced its Uncommon Hour, and Evergreen, with its standing noon lunch.

• *Put someone in charge.* There is an old adage that when everyone is responsible for something, no one is accountable for it. Students at DEEP schools were advantaged because over time their schools had created a culture where the norm is shared responsibility for student learning, governance, and a variety of other complementary processes. Such cultures do not evolve in the absence of focused leadership over an extended period of time. For this reason, DEEP schools usually assigned some individual or group the responsibility for coordinating and monitoring the status and impact of its student success initiatives. Sometimes champions of change created a sense of anticipation needed to establish the momentum for change (Pritchett & Pound, 1993). Other times, current faculty and staff members with a reputation for getting things done were enlisted. Sometimes key newcomers helped to lead the way, such as a new academic dean at Sewanee. At Sweet Briar it was the new vice president of student affairs and dean of cocurricular life who was charged with pulling the in-class and out-of-class experiences on campus closer together. At Ursinus the vice president for academic affairs took the lead in organizing acculturation experiences for new faculty. At Kansas the teaching and learning center staff and provost were key players; at Wheaton it was the provost and key faculty involved in the Educational Policy Committee to promote creative thinking about the new curriculum.

The "in charge" parties were not necessarily expected to bring about the changes themselves, but to monitor, prod, and support others who also were working on the issues. The success of Miami's efforts was helped immeasurably by a partnership between academic and student affairs marked by an effective working relationship among the provost, academic deans, and the vice president for student affairs. Some institutions, such as Evergreen, established a fixed-term "think force" or other specially constituted groups of administrators, key faculty members, students, and governing board members. Such a high-profile group adds legitimacy to the initiative and can engender commitment from others by looking across the institution to connect related initiatives and individuals to create support and synergy for the change agenda.

Put Money Where It Will Make a Difference in Student Engagement

It's often said that to discover what an organization values, follow the money.

• *Invest in activities that contribute to student success.* DEEP presidents and provosts generally made it a priority to fund initiatives—often with small, token amounts of money—that promised to enhance the quality of the undergraduate experience. Such efforts took various forms, ranging from seed money to jump-start learning communities to base budget allocations to augment the number of undergraduate research opportunities with faculty members. Michigan devoted millions of dollars over a decade to various activities, building them into the base budget. Miami committed significant resources to enhance the intellectual vitality on campus through funding summer research fellowships for students and creating a minority opportunity center. In contrast, UMF could redirect only small amounts of money to most of its efforts, though when the promise was grand and the payoff immediate—such as its Student Work Initiative—the university found enough money to support it.

• *Invest in faculty members who are doing the right things.* College and university faculty members work hard. When school is in session, they average between 55 and 60 hours per week on professorial activities, depending on the discipline (National Survey of Student Engagement, 2004). The majority of that time (59%) is devoted to teaching-related tasks and contact with students. Provosts and deans at DEEP colleges are quick to recognize the effort their faculty put forth, reward those who understand and are committed to the institution's student success mission, and attempt to do their best to provide the resources and support needed to accomplish their many important responsibilities.

• *Invest in teaching and learning centers.* These units symbolize DEEP schools' commitment to instructional excellence. Moreover, with strong leadership and a modicum amount of financial support, many were hotbeds of pedagogical innovation and coordinated awards for excellent teaching and minigrants for improving teaching and learning. Instructional support staff also consult with faculty members about alternative approaches to assessing student learning and help to boost faculty morale by supporting, among other things, faculty learning communities such as those at Miami University.

• *Invest in opportunities that allow students to apply what they are learning in ways that also benefit others.* DEEP schools recognized that learning is deepened and enhanced when students apply information and practice newly acquired skills and competencies in different settings beyond the classroom, on and off the campus. Among the more powerful venues for such experiences are service learning, community activities, internships, tutoring, and a variety of paraprofessional roles. When structured appropriately, working for pay also benefited both students and the recipients of their efforts.

• *Consider a budgeting model that privileges student learning processes and outcomes.* Just as we should regularly audit the curriculum and other important institutional processes, consider experimenting with a process that allocates resources and rewards units that demonstrably contribute to student learning, persistence, and graduation. This may stimulate a college or university to annually audit and align the budget to determine whether resources are being used wisely to attain the institution's mission and educational purposes in ways that are consistent with its values and students' needs.

Feature Diversity, Inside and Outside of the Classroom

Institutions become more diverse in two ways. The most common is when demographics in the surrounding area change. The second is by determining what diversity means in the institutional context and intentionally recruiting and supporting students, faculty, and staff from historically underrepresented populations to address diversity goals.

• *Use a multifaceted, aggressive approach to diversify the student body, faculty, and staff.* Rather than allowing admissions and hiring pools to emerge naturally, DEEP institutions engage in proactive activities to diversify their members. Targeted goals for recruitment were common. Qualified candidates from institutions known to produce scholars of color were aggressively sought out. DEEP faculty are active in this process, as they realize that to attain the educational benefits of diversity (Hurtado, Dey, Gurin, & Gurin, 2003; Kuh & Umbach, 2005) they must recruit and retain both students and faculty from historically underrepresented groups. Provosts were especially active in recruiting new faculty and staff from historically underrepresented groups by working with faculty on setting annual hiring goals and contacting key Ph.D.-producing institutions.

• *Ensure that diverse perspectives are represented in the curriculum.* DEEP schools illustrate that developmentally powerful experiences with diversity transcend institutional type. In addition, there is evidence that structural diversity, or the percentage of students from historically underserved populations present in the student body, may not be as important in terms of desired outcomes of college as being exposed to different ways of thinking, either in the curriculum or through interactions with students from different backgrounds (Hurtado, Dey, Gurin, & Gurin, 2003; Umbach & Kuh, in press). Ultimately, what really matters is that students encounter in their studies perspectives that reflect a range of human experiences and that encourage them to interact with others in ways that force them to think and respond in novel, more complex ways. Indeed, students who report more exposure to diverse perspectives in their classes are also more likely to report higher levels of academic challenge, greater opportunities for active and collaborative learning, and a more supportive campus environment (Kuh & Umbach, 2005).

Attract, Socialize, and Reward Competent People

As with other aspects of institutional performance, creating a campus culture that supports student success is ultimately about the right people doing the right things.

• *Align the reward system with the institutional mission, values, and priorities.* Institutions have multiple ways to reward people, ranging from annual performance reviews and salary adjustments to public ceremonies that recognize excellence in teaching, research, and service. Because rewards and recognitions reinforce what is important at the institution, the reward system should be as transparent as is practical and operate in a manner that is consistent with what the institution through its leaders espouse to be important and valued.

• *Pick institutional leaders right for the times, campus culture, and institutional trajectory.* Many institutions plod along without strong executive, visionary leadership. This was not the case at DEEP schools. There may not be a causal relationship, but it's worth noting again that all DEEP presidents had held academic appointments before being selected for their presidency. More important, what sets most of these presidents apart from many of their counterparts is their holistic perspective on student development and the institution's responsibilities with regard to student success. They recognize that it is essential to provide a learning environment that combines high academic challenge with commensurate amounts of support. In addition, they surrounded themselves with talented colleagues—especially senior academic and student affairs officers—who worked effectively together to realize the institution's student success mission.

• *Recruit faculty and staff who are committed to student learning.* First, make certain the best people are in the pool. DEEP provosts and academic deans played a pivotal role in this process, unapologetically emphasizing the importance of high-quality undergraduate education while probing the commitment of potential faculty members to this cause. They, along with senior faculty, are primarily responsible for emphasizing institutional values. Some DEEP schools such as UMF feature an extended campus visit (three days) so that both the potential hire and institution can learn about one another in a variety of social and professional situations.

- *Emphasize student centeredness in faculty and staff orientation.* Shulman (2004) noted that new faculty members are formed into scholars during graduate school, where they are socialized to do some things and not others and to value certain ideas and views about the professoriate, teaching, and learning over others. Thus, newcomers need to be taught what the institution values. In some instances, they need to be counter-socialized. This is best done by veteran faculty with support from administrators. Such efforts must be ongoing, not relegated to only an hour during new faculty orientation. For example, as we described in Chapter Seven, the Ursinus vice president for academic affairs coordinates colloquia with a few senior faculty members present to introduce newcomers to various aspects of the college and to emphasize over time the institution's central focus on student learning and other values. Newcomers at KU hear plainly from senior faculty that they will occasionally be asked to set aside personal priorities for the good of the campus, such as when general education requirements were revised. As one veteran KU faculty member put it, "We give up a little to make the whole better."

- *Make room for differences.* Hegemony is anathema in higher education. For this reason alone, diversifying the gene pool is viewed as desirable, though challenging to accomplish and accommodate. Not every person on campus will agree with everything the president does. Dissent and disagreement typically are part of campus life. DEEP presidents welcome critical evaluation of their institutions, and take alternative points of view seriously. William Tierney (1993) has written eloquently about this challenge: "We search for commonalities while encouraging difference. We seek community through conflict. We act as leaders by following. We develop voice by listening. We learn about ourselves by trying to understand others. We develop goals by concentrating on processes. We teach about norms while we encourage new members to change them" (p. 143).

- *Ensure high-quality student support services.* Securing ongoing external funding for special support programs is difficult but worth the effort as they are—when staffed with competent professionals—especially effective in providing support for first-generation students from modest economic backgrounds or those who have disabilities. On residential campuses, residence life staff members are integral to an effective early-alert system. They see firsthand how students spend their time and directly communicate relevant information to the academic advisors and faculty members who need it. Similarly, resident assistants should be notified, as is the case at Ursinus, if students are struggling with their courses, as there may be interventions with which residence life staff can assist. Residence life staff reciprocate by informing academic advisors if they become aware of students who are having problems outside the classroom.

Encourage Collaboration Across Functional Lines and Between the Campus and Community

High-performing organizations are marked by partnerships, cross-functional collaborations, and responsive units—what some authors call "loose-tight" organizational properties (Birnbaum, 1988; Peters & Waterman, 1982; Senge, 1990; Vaill, 1989).

- *Encourage and reward cross-functional activities focused on student success.* Faculty collaboration was a key ingredient at DEEP schools, especially with regard to curriculum revision. At Wofford and Ursinus, for example, the focus on creating common intellectual experiences tended to neutralize the polarizing effects of disciplinary loyalty by compelling faculty to pull together to work on a project that benefited the whole college and enhanced the overall quality of the student experience. The dean at Ursinus described how the good ideas at the institution "spiral up from faculty" instead of vortexing down from administrative leaders. Sustainable improvements were not usually the work of a single unit. Rather, these innovations typically crossed the traditional organization boundaries, such as the collaborations between academic and student affairs on learning communities at UTEP, early-alert programs at FSU, and first-year initiatives at Miami. Moreover, they often spread horizontally to different areas, which further increased the chances that many students would be touched by the effort. Achieving this level of "spread," the degree to which a good idea is adopted by different elements of an organization (Coburn, 2003), was essential to the development and sustainability of initiatives at DEEP schools. For example, efforts aimed at enhancing undergraduate education at the University of Michigan involved administrative leaders in the president and provost offices, and was championed by the board of regents, the division of student affairs, faculty members, and students. Moreover, the commitment to improving undergraduate programs became embedded in strategic planning activities and, subsequently, policy decisions.

• *Tighten the philosophical and operational linkages between academic and student affairs.* At DEEP schools, the fundamental mission of student affairs is to support the institution's academic mission. Unlike many colleges and universities, there was no debate or confusion about this. Permeating the campus is a holistic philosophy of talent development, similar to the student development philosophy championed by student affairs professional associations. Student affairs staff were full partners in the enterprise, team-teaching with faculty members, participating in campus governance, and managing enriching educational opportunities for students such as peer tutoring and mentoring, first-year seminars, and learning communities.

• *Harness the expertise of other resources.* Educators are everywhere on DEEP campuses. For example, many librarians know a good deal about how students spend their time, what they think and talk about, and how they feel, yet they are an underused educational resource. At some DEEP schools librarians contribute to first-year seminars and orientation to college courses, academic advising, student-faculty research activities, and capstone seminars. Similarly, DEEP institutions involve information technology (IT) personnel in teaching and supporting students, faculty, and staff in their use of technology to enrich the learning environment. They also consult with faculty about the most effective ways to integrate IT into course design and delivery in order to enhance student learning.

• *Make governance a shared responsibility.* Just as DEEP schools create a climate where responsibility for student learning is widely shared, they also practice shared governance in real, practical ways. Most of the smaller colleges were exemplary in this regard; KU and Miami provide excellent examples of large schools. Students serve as members of committees, task forces, and in other forms of institutional governance, often in leadership roles. As a consequence they have a significant influence on institutional priorities by influencing both decision making and policy implementation.

- *Form partnerships with the local community.* DEEP colleges are well connected with their local communities. Advisory boards guide the development of internship opportunities, fund-raising projects, reciprocal library programs, and community service and volunteer efforts by students, staff, and occasionally presidents and provosts. Among the long-standing, formal campus-community partnerships are the Century Club at George Mason and similar initiatives at KU and Macalester. External affairs staff can help identify and coordinate such opportunities and also point to community needs that campus resources can meet in mutually beneficial ways.

Lay Out the Path to Student Success

Students will be better prepared to manage successfully the many challenges that college presents if beforehand they have an idea of what to expect and when and how to deal with these issues. It's advisable to get some of this information to students even before they start classes and then provide additional information, advice, and guidance at key points after they enroll, especially during the first weeks and months of college.

- *Draw a map for student success.* What does being a successful student look like on your campus? Many of the DEEP colleges clearly explicate what students should be thinking and doing at different points in time. Among the exemplars in this regard are Miami's Choice Matters initiative, Alverno's Eight Abilities curriculum, and FSU's University College. Winston-Salem State University reserves certain sections of its experience course for students in specific majors taught by faculty who also serve as the students' advisors for their first year. Student affairs staff teach sections for undecided students. At California State University at Monterey Bay, students design an Individualized Learning Plan (ILP) in the transition course and are expected to update it at various points in their studies, and review it formally in a major-specific ProSeminar during their junior year. Michigan provides incoming students with a compact disk that describes to students how they can get involved with faculty on research projects, as well as other forms of interaction with faculty that are encouraged on the campus.

- *Front load resources to smooth the transition.* As we said in Chapter Thirteen, DEEP schools recognized that newcomers need considerable structure and support to establish themselves academically and socially and to learn how to take advantage of the institution's resources for learning. For this reason, academic advising was a high priority at DEEP institutions. Preceptors, peer mentoring, and tutoring programs were common, with student affairs generally providing the space and infrastructure for such services and faculty members selecting and supervising peer mentors. In some cases, students, particularly those from historically underserved groups, will need additional assistance in their transition to college beyond what is provided for other students. Institutions that admit students who are not adequately prepared to perform at desired levels are morally and educationally obliged to provide opportunities for them to acquire the requisite knowledge, skills, and competencies.

- *Align the physical environment with institutional priorities and goals for student success.* Rather than putting student services on the perimeter of the campus or in out-of-the-way places, student services at DEEP institutions were centrally located and easy to find. The Johnson Center at George Mason is one such example. Also, in planning and constructing new facilities or renovating existing ones, dedicate space for "socially catalytic" interactions, areas where students and faculty can meet informally or where students can work together on projects. In addition, to the extent possible, embed cultural values in structures. Members of the Evergreen State community are mindful of the heritage of the American Indians of the Pacific Northwest every time they see the Longhouse Education and Cultural Center, which symbolizes the hospitality of the people native to the area and the institution's commitment to promoting multicultural study and understanding.

- *Teach newcomers about the campus culture.* DEEP colleges recognize that beginning college students need affirmation, encouragement, and support as well as information about what to do to succeed. They make special efforts during summer orientation and registration, fall welcome week, and events throughout the early weeks of college to teach newcomers about campus traditions and rituals and provide other information about "how we do things here and what things really mean." A key aspect of this is becoming familiar with the institution's distinctive vocabulary, or "terms of endearment" (Kuh, Schuh, Whitt, & Associates, 1991) sometimes expressed as slang, abbreviations, and other shorthand forms. At many schools, this information and other socialization activities are often introduced during a college transition course tailored to meet the unique needs of the students on the campuses.

• *Create a sense of specialness about being a student here.* One powerful way to welcome and affirm students as learners is with ceremony that formally inducts them into the institution, signifying they are full members of the community of learners. In addition, several DEEP institutions developed a campus compact or covenant that sets forth guiding principles for what's expected of members of this academic community, such as the Gentleman's Rule at Wabash College or the four "pillars" of a Macalester education. Winston-Salem State's motto—"Enter to learn, depart to serve"—is a constant reminder of the university's expectation that students enjoy many privileges and are expected to repay this debt to society by giving back after college.

• *If an activity or experience is important to student success, consider requiring it.* DEEP schools are distinctive in terms of the degree to which their students participate in one or more enriching educational experience. Some are tied to the curriculum, such as study abroad, service learning, internships, and infusion of diversity experiences. Some schools, recognizing the value of student-faculty research, now require it.

• *Develop interventions for underengaged students.* One way to use student engagement data effectively is to identify the least engaged students. Focusing on students who are already engaged at relatively high levels—say those who are in the upper third of the engagement distribution—will probably produce only marginal differences in overall institutional performance. This is not to say such students should be ignored or that they would not reap some benefit. But with limited time and resources it may make sense for many schools to target interventions toward students who are in the lower third of the engagement distribution (Kuh, 2003; National Survey of Student Engagement, 2003).

Reculture the Institution for Student Success

Efforts to enhance student success often falter because too little attention is given to understanding the properties of the institution's culture that reinforce the status quo and perpetuate everyday actions—"the way we do things here" (Kuh & Whitt, 1988).

- *Identify cultural properties that are obstacles to student success.* Among those who have written cogently about undertaking culture change (Lundberg, 1990; Schein, 1992; Senge, 1999; Tierney, 1999; Vaill, 1998) is Michael Fullan. He concluded from his studies of school performance that culture is the single most important element that must be altered and managed in order to change what an organization or institution values and how it acts: "Transforming the culture—changing the way we do things around here—is the main point. I call this *reculturing* . . . it is a particular kind of reculturing for which we strive: one that activates and deepens moral purpose through collaborative work. [We seek] cultures that respect differences and constantly build and test knowledge against measurable results—a culture within which one realizes that sometimes being off balance is a learning moment" (2001, p. 44).

- *Expand the number of cultural practitioners on campus.* Most people who survive several years in a college or university sooner or later become, in Lundberg's terms, "culturally competent." That is, they learn how to get along, what words mean when used in different contexts, what's valued and what isn't, what acceptable behavior is, and so forth. But relatively few people become astute cultural practitioners, people who "make the familiar strange" (Whitt, 1993), in the sense that they analyze the influence of norms, tacit beliefs, and other cultural properties on behavior to determine what needs to be addressed to effect change. To move an institution toward cultivating an ethos of student success, it is essential to address aspects of its culture that are antithetical to the tasks ahead.

CONCLUSION

The lengthy list of recommendations and suggestions in this chapter is a representative, though not exhaustive, analysis of the institutional conditions that we found at the 20 diverse DEEP colleges and universities.

Although these institutions were doing many things that other schools could learn from, they are not perfect. Like many gemstones, each has flaws if inspected closely. For example, as good as these institutions are, each has one or more groups of students who are not as engaged as the institution would like. Yet when viewed in context, their priorities and properties are arranged in a manner that makes them attractive on a variety of levels. Even so, faculty and staff at DEEP schools are the first to admit that they would like to be even better than they are. Indeed, this drive to improve, this sense of "positive restlessness," is one of their more distinctive and endearing characteristics. So although DEEP schools are doing many things right according to their higher-than-predicted engagement and graduation indicators, they can become even better. And so can many other institutions.

That's what makes this group of colleges and universities extraordinary. They offer the promise that in the future we will discover even more effective ideas and strategies for promoting student success.

Let's get to work.

REFERENCES

Adelman, C. (2004). *Principal indicators of student academic histories in postsecondary education, 1972–2000.* Washington, DC: U.S. Department of Education, Institute of Education Sciences.

American Association for Higher Education, American College Personnel Association, & National Association of Student Personnel Administrators. (1998). *Powerful partnerships: A shared responsibility for learning.* Washington, DC: Authors.

American College Personnel Association [ACPA]. (1994). *The student learning imperative.* Washington, DC: Author.

American Council on Education. (1949). The student personnel point of view. In G. Saddlemire & A. Rentz (Eds.), *Student affairs: A profession's heritage* (pp. 122–136). Alexandria, VA: American College Personnel Association.

Association of American Colleges and Universities [AAC&U]. (2002). *Greater expectations: A new vision for learning as a nation goes to college.* Washington, DC: Author.

Astin, A. W. (1975). *The power of protest: A national study of student and faculty disruptions with implications for the future* (1st ed.). San Francisco: Jossey-Bass.

Astin, A. W. (1977). *Four critical years.* San Francisco: Jossey-Bass.

Astin, A. W. (1984). Student involvement: A developmental theory for higher education. *Journal of College Student Personnel, 25,* 297–308.

Astin, A. W. (1985). *Achieving educational excellence.* San Francisco: Jossey-Bass.

Astin, A. W. (1991). *Assessment for excellence: The philosophy and practice of assessment and evaluation in higher education.* American Council on Education Series on Higher Education. Washington/New York: American Council on Education and Macmillan.

Astin, A. W. (1993). *What matters in college? Four critical years revisited.* San Francisco: Jossey-Bass.

Astin, A. W., & Sax, L. (1998). How undergraduates are affected by service participation. *Journal of College Student Development, 39,* 251–263.

Baxter Magolda, M. B. (1999). *Creating contexts for learning and self authorship: Constructive developmental pedagogy.* Nashville: Vanderbilt University Press.

Birnbaum, R. (1988). *How colleges work: The cybernetics of academic organization and leadership.* San Francisco: Jossey-Bass.

Boyer, E. L. (1990). *Scholarship reconsidered: Priorities of the professoriate.* Princeton, NJ: The Carnegie Foundation for the Advancement of Teaching.

Braxton, J. M. (2000). Introduction. In J. M. Braxton (Ed.), *Rethinking the departure puzzle: New theory and research on college student retention.* Nashville: Vanderbilt University Press.

Bruffee, K. A. (1993). *Collaborative learning: Higher education, interdependence, and the authority of knowledge.* Baltimore: The Johns Hopkins University Press.

Bruning, R., Schraw, G., Norby, M., & Ronning, R. (2004). *Cognitive psychology and instruction.* Upper Saddle River, NJ: Pearson Education.

Carey, K. (2004). *A matter of degrees: Improving graduation rates in four-year colleges and universities.* Washington, DC: Education Trust.

Carini, R. M., Kuh, G. D., & Klein, S. P. (2004). *Student engagement and student learning: Insights from a construct validation study.* Paper presented at the annual meeting of the American Educational Research Association, San Diego, CA.

Chaffee, E. E. (1989). Strategy and effectiveness in systems of higher education. In J. Smart (Ed.), *Higher education: Handbook of theory and research* (Vol. 5, pp. 1–30). New York: Agathon Press.

Chickering, A. W. (1969). *Education and identity.* San Francisco: Jossey-Bass.

Chickering, A. W. (1974). *Commuting versus residential students: Overcoming educational inequities of living off campus.* San Francisco: Jossey-Bass.

Chickering, A. W. (1981). *The modern American college: Responding to the new realities of diverse students and a changing society.* San Francisco: Jossey-Bass.

Chickering, A. W., & Gamson, Z. F. (1987). Seven principles for good practice in undergraduate education. *AAHE Bulletin, 39*(7), 3–7.

Chickering, A. W., & O'Connor, J. (1996). The university learning center: A driving force for collaboration. *About Campus, 1*(4), 16–21.

Chickering, A. W., & Reisser, L. (1993). *Education and identity.* San Francisco: Jossey-Bass.

Coburn, E. (2003). Rethinking scale: Moving beyond numbers to deep and lasting change. *Educational Researcher, 32*(6), 3–12.

Coffey, A., & Atkinson, P. (1996). *Making sense of qualitative data: Complementary research strategies.* Thousand Oaks, CA: Sage.

Collins, J. C. (2001). *Good to great.* New York: HarperCollins.

Creswell, J. W. (1998). *Qualitative inquiry and research design: Choosing among five traditions.* Thousand Oaks, CA: Sage.

Creswell, J. W., & Miller, D. L. (2000). Determining validity in qualitative inquiry. *Theory Into Practice, 39*(3), 124–130.

Cross, K. P. (1998). Why learning communities? Why now? *About Campus* (July/August), 4–11.

Davis, T., & Murrell, P. (1993). *Turning teaching into learning: The role of student responsibility in the collegiate experience.* ASHE-ERIC Higher Education Report No. 8. Washington, DC: The George Washington University, School of Education and Human Development.

Dweck, C. S. (2000). *Self-theories: Their role in motivation, personality, and development.* Philadelphia: Psychology Press.

Eckel, P., Green, M., & Hill, B. (2001). *Riding the waves of change: Insights from transforming institutions.* Washington, DC: American Council on Education.

Eckel, P., Hill, B., Green, M., & Mallon, D. (1999). *Reports from the road: Insights on institutional change.* Washington, DC: American Council on Education.

Education Commission of the States. (1995). *Making quality count in undergraduate education.* Denver: Education Commission of the States.

Engelkemeyer, S. W., & Landry, E. (2001). Negotiating change on campus. *AAHE Bulletin* (February 2001), 7–10.

Ewell, P. T. (1997). Organizing for learning: A new imperative. *AAHE Bulletin, 50*(4), 3–6.

Eyler, J., & Giles, D. E. (1999). *Where's the learning in service learning?* San Francisco: Jossey-Bass.

Fullan, M. (2001). *Leading in a culture of change.* San Francisco: Jossey-Bass.

Funk & Wagnalls Standard College Dictionary (Text Edition). (1963). New York: Harcourt, Brace & World.

Gabelnick, F., MacGregor, J., Matthews, R., & Smith, B. L. (1990). *Learning communities.* San Francisco: Jossey-Bass.

Gainen, J. (1995). Barriers to success in quantitative gatekeeper courses. *New Directions for Teaching and Learning, 61,* 5–14.

Gansemer–Topf, A., Saunders, K., Schuh, J., & Shelley, M. (2004). A study of resource expenditures and allocation at DEEP colleges and universities: Is spending related to student engagement? Available: http://www.indiana.edu/~nsse/pdf/DEEP_Expenditures_Schuh.pdf

Garvin, D. A. (1993). Building a learning organization. *Harvard Business Review* (July–August), 78–91.

Gladwell, M. (2000). *The tipping point: How little things can make a big difference.* Boston: Little, Brown.

Goodsell, A. M., Maher, M., & Tinto, V. (Eds.). (1992). *Collaborative learning: A sourcebook for higher education.* University Park: National Center on Postsecondary Teaching, Learning, and Assessment, The Pennsylvania State University.

Gruenwald, D. A. (2003). Foundations of place: A multidisciplinary framework for place-conscious education. *American Educational Research Journal, 40*(3), 619–654.

Guba, E. G., & Lincoln, Y. S. (1989). *Fourth generation evaluation.* Thousand Oaks, CA: Sage.

Hurtado, S., Dey, E. L., Gurin, P. Y., & Gurin, G. (2003). College environments, diversity, and student learning. In J. C. Smart (Ed.), *Higher education: Handbook of theory and research* (Vol. XVIII, pp. 145–189). Dordrecht, Netherlands: Kluwer.

Johnson, D. W., Johnson, R., & Smith, K. A. (1991). *Cooperative learning: Increasing college faculty instructional productivity.* ASHE-ERIC Higher Education Report No. 4. Washington, DC: The George Washington University, School of Education and Human Development.

Kazis, R., Vargas, J., & Hoffman, N. (2004). *Double the numbers: Increasing postsecondary credentials for underrepresented youth.* Cambridge, MA: Harvard Education Press.

Keeton, M. T. (1971). *Models and mavericks.* New York: McGraw-Hill.

Keller, G. (2001). The new demographics of higher education. *The Review of Higher Education, 24*(3), 219–235.

Kezar, A. (2001). *Understanding and facilitating organizational change in the 21st century: Recent research and conceptualizations.* ASHE-ERIC Higher Education Report, Volume 28, No. 4. Washington, DC: The George Washington University, Graduate School of Education and Human Development.

Kezar, A. (2002). Overcoming the obstacles to change within urban institutions: The mobile framework and engaging institutional culture. *Metropolitan Universities: An International Forum, 13*(2), 95–103.

Kezar, A., & Eckel, P. (2002). Examining the institutional transformation process: The importance of sensemaking, inter-related strategies and balance. *Research in Higher Education, 43*(4), 295–328.

Kimball, B. (1986). *A history of the idea of liberal education.* New York: Teachers College Press.

King, P. M. (1999). Putting together the puzzle of student learning. *About Campus, 4*(1), 2–4.

Kuh, G. D. (1996). Guiding principles for creating seamless learning environments for undergraduates. *Journal of College Student Development, 37,* 135–148.

Kuh, G. D. (2001a). College students today: Why we can't leave serendipity to chance. In P. Altbach, P. Gumport, & B. Johnstone (Eds.), *In defense of the American university.* Baltimore: The Johns Hopkins University Press.

Kuh, G. D. (2001b). Assessing what really matters to student learning. *Change,* May/June, pp. 10–17, 66.

Kuh, G. D. (2003). What we're learning about student engagement from NSSE. *Change, 35*(2), 24–32.

Kuh, G. D. (2004). Forging a new direction: How UTEP created its own brand of excellence. *About Campus, 9*(5), 9–15.

Kuh, G. D. (2005). Student engagement in the first year of college. In M. L. Upcraft, J. N. Gardner, & B. O. Barefoot (Eds.), *Challenging and supporting the first-year student: A handbook for improving the first year of college.* San Francisco: Jossey-Bass.

Kuh, G. D., Gonyea, R. M., & Williams, J. M. (2005). What students expect from college and what they get. In T. Miller, B. Bender, J. Schuh, & Associates, *Promoting reasonable expectations: Aligning student and institutional views of the college experience.* San Francisco: Jossey-Bass/National Association of Student Personnel Administrators.

Kuh, G. D., Nelson Laird, T. F., & Umbach, P. D. (2004). Aligning faculty activities and student behavior: Realizing the promise of Greater Expectations. *Liberal Education,* pp. 24–31.

Kuh, G. D., Schuh, J. H., Whitt, E. J., & Associates. (1991). *Involving colleges: Successful approaches to fostering student learning and personal development outside the classroom.* San Francisco: Jossey-Bass.

Kuh, G. D., & Umbach, P. D. (2005). Experiencing diversity: What can we learn from liberal arts colleges? *Liberal Education.*

Kuh, G. D., & Whitt, E. J. (1988). *The invisible tapestry: Culture in American colleges and universities.* ASHE-ERIC Higher Education Report No. 1. Washington, DC: Association for the Study of Higher Education.

Lave, J., & Wenger, E. (1990). *Situated learning: Legitimate peripheral participation.* Cambridge, UK: Cambridge University Press.

LeCompte, M. D., & Preissle, J. (1993). *Ethnography and qualitative design in educational research.* San Diego: Academic Press.

Lewis, M. (2003). *Moneyball: The art of winning an unfair game.* New York: Norton.

Lincoln, Y. S., & Guba, E. (1985). *Naturalistic inquiry.* Thousand Oaks, CA: Sage.

Lindquist, J. (1978). *Strategies for change.* Washington, DC: Council for Independent Colleges.

Low, L. (2000). *Are college students satisfied? A national analysis of changing expectations.* Indianapolis: USA Group (now Lumina Foundation).

Lundberg, C. C. (1990). Surfacing organizational culture. *Journal of Managerial Psychology, 5*(4), 19–26.

Martin, J., Feldman, M., Hatch, M., & Sitkin, S. (1983). The uniqueness paradox in organizational stories. *Administrative Science Quarterly, 28,* 438–453.

McLeod, W. B. (2003). Linking retention and academic performance: The freshman year initiative. Retrieved November 16, 2004, from (http://www.uncfsu.edu/chanoff/FYI01.HTM)

McKeachie, W. J., Pintrich, P. R., Lin, Y., & Smith, D. (1986). *Teaching and learning in the college classroom: A review of the research.* Ann Arbor: National Center for Research to Improve Postsecondary Teaching and Learning, University of Michigan.

Merriam, S. B. (Ed.). (2002). *Qualitative research in practice: Examples for discussion and analysis.* San Francisco: Jossey-Bass.

Mezirow, J. (1990). How critical reflection triggers transformative learning. In J. Mezirow & Associates (Eds.), *Fostering critical reflection in adulthood: A guide to transformative and emancipatory learning.* San Francisco: Jossey-Bass.

Mortenson, T. (1997, April). Actual versus predicted institutional graduation rates for 1100 colleges and universities. *Postsecondary Education Opportunity, 58.*

National Association of Student Personnel Administrators. (1987). *A perspective on student affairs.* Washington, DC: Author.

National Center for Higher Education Management Systems [NCHEMS]. (2004). Do DEEP institutions spend more or differently than their peers? Available: (http://www.indiana.edu/~nsse/pdf/DEEP_Expenditures_NCHEMS.pdf)

National Survey of Student Engagement [NSSE]. (2003). *Converting data into action: Expanding the boundaries of institutional improvement.* Bloomington: Indiana University Center for Postsecondary Research.

National Survey of Student Engagement [NSSE]. (2004). *Student engagement: Pathways to collegiate success.* Bloomington: Indiana University Center for Postsecondary Research.

Nelson Laird, T. F., & Kuh, G. D. (in press). Student experiences with information technology and their relationship to other aspects of student engagement. *Research in Higher Education.*

Noel-Levitz Inc. (2003). *2003 National student satisfaction report.* Available at: (http://www.noellevitz.com/pdfs/2003_SSI_Report.pdf)

Orrill, R. (Ed.). (1997). *Education and democracy: Re-imagining liberal learning in America.* New York: The College Examination Board.

Pace, C. R. (1979). *Measuring outcomes of college: Fifty years of findings and recommendations for the future.* San Francisco: Jossey-Bass.

Pace, C. R. (1980). Measuring the quality of student effort. *Current Issues in Higher Education, 2,* 10–16.

Pascarella, E. T. (2001). Identifying excellence in undergraduate education: Are we even close? *Change, 33*(3), 19–23.

Pascarella, E. T., & Terenzini, P. T. (1991). *How college affects students.* San Francisco: Jossey-Bass.

Pascarella, E. T., & Terenzini, P. T. (2005). *How college affects students: A third decade of research* (Vol. 2). San Francisco: Jossey-Bass.

Patton, L., Morelon, C., Whitehead, D., & Hossler, D. (2004). *Campus-based retention initiatives: Does the emperor have clothes?* Paper presented at the Association of College Personnel Administrators, Philadelphia, PA.

Patton, M. Q. (1990). *Qualitative evaluation and research methods.* Thousand Oaks, CA: Sage.

Peters, T. J. (1987). *Thriving on chaos: Handbook for a management revolution.* New York: Harper & Row.

Peters, T. J., & Waterman Jr., R. H. (1982). *In search of excellence: Lessons from America's best run companies.* New York: Harper & Row.

Pike, G. R. (1993). The relationship between perceived learning and satisfaction with college: An alternative view. *Research in Higher Education, 34*(1), 23–40.

Pike, G. R. (1995). The relationship between self reports of college experiences and achievement test scores. *Research in Higher Education, 36,* 1–21.

Pike, G. R., & Killian, T. (2001). Reported gains in student learning: Do academic disciplines make a difference? *Research in Higher Education, 42,* 429–454.

Pike, G. R., Kuh, G. D., & Gonyea, R. M. (2003). The relationship between institutional mission and students' involvement and educational outcomes. *Research in Higher Education, 44,* 241–261.

President's Commission on the Undergraduate Experience. (2002). *The second chapter of change: Renewing undergraduate education at the University of Michigan.* Retrieved from (http://www.umich.edu/pres/undergrad/)

Pritchett, P., & Pound, R. (1993). *High-velocity culture change: A handbook for managers.* Dallas, TX: Pritchett.

Rhatigan, J. J., & Schuh, J. H. (2003). Small wins. *About Campus, 8*(1), 17–22.

Richards, L. (2002). *Using N6 in qualitative research.* Melbourne, Australia: QSR International.

Rose, M. (1989). *Lives on the boundary: The struggles and achievements of America's under-prepared.* New York: Free Press.

Schein, E. H. (1992). *Organizational culture and leadership* (2nd ed.). San Francisco: Jossey-Bass.

Schroeder, C. C. (1993). New students: New learning styles. *Change, 25*(4), 21–26.

Senge, P. M. (1990). The leader's new work: Building learning organizations. *Sloan Management Review* (Fall), 7–23.

Senge, P. M. (1999). *The dance of change: The challenges of sustaining momentum in learning organizations.* New York: Currency/Doubleday.

Shapiro, N. S., & Levine, J. (Eds.). (1999). *Creating learning communities: A practical guide to winning support, organizing for change, and implementing programs.* San Francisco: Jossey-Bass.

Shulman, L. S. (2004). *Teaching as community property: Essays on higher education.* San Francisco: Jossey-Bass.

Smith, B. L., MacGregor, R., Matthews, R., & Gabelnick, F. (2004). *Learning communities: Reforming undergraduate education.* San Francisco: Jossey-Bass.

Sorcinelli, M. D. (1991). Research findings on the Seven Principles. In A. W. Chickering & Z. F. Gamson (Eds.), *Applying the Seven Principles for Good Practice in undergraduate education, New Directions for Teaching and Learning* (pp. 13–25). San Francisco: Jossey-Bass.

Stake, R. E. (1995). *The art of case study research.* Thousand Oaks: Sage.

Strauss, A. L. (1987). *Qualitative analysis for social scientists.* Cambridge, UK: Cambridge University Press.

Study Group on the Conditions of Excellence in American Higher Education. (1984). *Involvement in learning.* Washington, DC: US Department of Education.

Tagg, J. (2003). *The learning paradigm college.* Bolton, MA: Anker.

The Evergreen State College. (2001). *Evergreen advising handbook, 2001–2002.* Olympia, WA: Author.

Tierney, W. G. (1993). *Building communities of difference: Higher education in the twenty-first century.* Westport, CT: Bergin & Garvey.

Tierney, W. G. (1999). *Building the responsive campus: Creating high performance colleges and universities.* Thousand Oaks, CA: Sage.

Tinto, V. (1993). *Leaving college: Rethinking the causes and cures of student attrition* (2nd ed.). Chicago: University of Chicago Press.

Upcraft, M. L., Gardner, J. N., & Barefoot, B. O. (Eds.). (2005). *Challenging and supporting the first-year student: A handbook for improving the first year of college.* San Francisco: Jossey-Bass.

Vaill, P. B. (1989). *Managing as a performing art: New ideas for a world of chaotic change.* San Francisco: Jossey-Bass.

Vaill, P. B. (1998). *Spirited leading and learning: Process wisdom for a new age.* San Francisco: Jossey-Bass.

Waldrop, M. M. (1992). *Complexity: The emerging science at the edge of order and chaos.* New York: Simon & Schuster.

Weick, K. E. (1984). Small wins: Redefining the scale of social problems. *American Psychologist, 39*(1), 40–49.

Whitt, E. J. (1993). Making the familiar strange: Discovering culture. In G. D. Kuh (Ed.), *Cultural perspectives in student affairs work* (pp. 81–94). Lanham, MD: American College Personnel Association: Distributed by University Press of America.

Whitt, E. J., & Kuh, G. D. (1991). Qualitative research in higher education: A team approach to multiple site investigation. *Review of Higher Education, 14,* 317–337.

References

APPENDIX A

Research Methods

THIS SECTION BRIEFLY summarizes the research methods used in the Documenting Effective Educational Practice (DEEP) project, a two-year study carried out under the auspices of the National Survey of Student Engagement Institute for Effective Educational Practice at the Indiana University Center for Postsecondary Research.

Colleges and universities are complicated organizations with multiple layers of culture, diverse structures, and different curricular arrangements. The DEEP project aimed to develop a comprehensive understanding of what 20 strong-performing institutions do to promote student engagement and student success, broadly defined. To do this, a research team was assembled and used a qualitative case study design (Merriam, 2002) to discover and document the policies, programs, and practices at these institutions as well as related factors and conditions that were associated with student success. A case study method was especially suitable for examining phenomena bounded by time and place, such as programs, events, activities, and individual and group behaviors in the context of different institutions. Done well, qualitative case studies can yield detailed, thick descriptions to illustrate what these institutions do to foster student success.

ASSEMBLING AND PREPARING THE RESEARCH TEAM

To conduct an inquiry of this scope required multiple investigators. The DEEP research team consisted of 24 people with different areas of expertise (see Appendix B). Some were primarily scholars; others were current or former academic and student affairs practitioners. Many had combinations of these and related experiences. Everyone on the team including the advanced graduate students had several years of experience working in a collegiate setting. This variation in backgrounds and perspectives was intentional, given the nature of the assignment. The team was large enough to be able to conduct two multiple-day site visits to each school (for a total of 40 visits) between fall 2002 through winter 2004.

Coordinating 24 investigators from different locations across the country presented certain challenges. Project management and coordination tasks were done by National Survey of Student Engagement (NSSE) Institute staff, primarily the DEEP project director George Kuh and DEEP project manager Jillian Kinzie. To fully comprehend the purposes of the project and become familiar with the research methods and with one another, DEEP team members met for three days in August 2002. During this time, we reviewed the research process and preferred case study method, discussed site visit procedures and logistics, and developed data collection protocols. Equally important, this meeting allowed team members to become better acquainted, establish trust, and build common understandings so they could work effectively together in the field and later, during the data analysis and interpretation phases of the project. Following the August 2002 team meeting, the data collection protocols for the first and second visits were finalized.

After the first few round-one site visits in early fall 2002, the team conferred by conference call to review site visit procedures and to tweak the data collection protocols. The team met three additional times during the data collection phase of the project: one day in November 2002, three days in August 2003, and another day near the conclusion of the second-round site visits in November 2003. Also, site visit teams communicated regularly via e-mail and conference calls during and following the site visits to keep people informed and to discuss data analysis procedures and emerging interpretations. These training sessions and meetings were essential to acquainting investigators with the project and to making decisions about various aspects of our work as it moved along, from the selection of sites, creation of interview protocol, to data analysis. For example, the second site visit protocol was revised extensively, based on what we were learning from the first-round visits.

SELECTION OF INSTITUTIONS

We used an ideal-typical case selection process, whereby we tried to find institutions that represented "models" or desirable examples of colleges and universities with demonstrable track records for promoting student success (LeCompte & Preissle, 1993). Only four-year colleges and universities that participated in the NSSE between 2000 and 2002 were eligible for selection. From this pool of more than 700 institutions, we flagged those that had both higher-than-predicted student engagement results and higher-than-predicted six-year graduation rates. That is, these schools arguably "added value" to the student experience in that their engagement scores were better than expected on the five NSSE clusters of effective educational practice (Chapter One) and outperformed what they were predicted to do in terms of student graduation rates, taking into account student and institutional characteristics. Regression models were used to calculate the predicted student engagement scores and graduation rates.

The regression model for *higher-than-predicted NSSE cluster scores* considered the following institutional and student characteristics, which were obtained from fall 1999–2000 IPEDS data: (a) public/private, (b) admissions selectivity from *Barron's Profiles of American Colleges* (2001), (c) Carnegie Classification, (d) undergraduate enrollment, (e) urbanicity, (f) proportion full-time, (g) proportion female, (h) proportion of different races/ethnicities, (i) proportion of different student-reported major fields, (j) mean student-reported age, and (k) proportion of students reporting on-campus residence. The results yield a set of scores that NSSE refers to as an "Institutional Engagement Index." This index is provided annually to participating schools and represents the degree to which students do more or less than expected in terms of engaging in the five areas of effective educational practice, after statistically adjusting for the types of students attending the institution and other institutional characteristics.

The regression model for *higher-than-predicted graduation rates* was calculated for first-year and senior students (see Mortenson, 1997) and included the following variables: (a) public/private, (b) admissions selectivity from *Barron's Profiles of American Colleges* (2001), (c) undergraduate enrollment, (d) urbanicity, (e) proportion full-time, (f) proportion of different races/ethnicities, and (g) proportion of students reporting on-campus residence. The Common Data Set compiled by Wintergreen/Orchard House on behalf of The College Board, Thomson Learning, and *US News & World Report* was used to verify better-than-predicted graduation rates for the high performing schools.

As expected, the number of institutions that met these two criteria exceeded the target of 20 schools, which was the maximum number project resources (financial, personnel, time) could accommodate. At this point NSSE Institute staff narrowed the list of eligible institutions by considering such additional criteria as institutional size, type (for example, four-year institution), control (for example, public or private), and geographic locale (region of the country, rural or urban) with the goal of including a diverse set of institutions in the study. Given limited degrees of freedom, the site selection process yielded a group of colleges and universities that served a broad spectrum of students and were "good enough" from which to learn some valuable things about promoting student success. That is, we do not claim that these institutions are the "best" in the country or that they have the highest student engagement scores and graduation rates. Nevertheless, they were outperforming what they should be doing, given a variety of institutional and student characteristics. Thus, something worth learning about was, in all likelihood, going on at these places.

DATA COLLECTION

Each of the 20 institutions identified someone to be its DEEP site visit coordinator. This person (and their assistants) facilitated our work in many ways, including gathering relevant documents for team review and scheduling interviews and focus groups.

For the first round of site visits, teams of three to five researchers visited each of the 20 DEEP schools. To prepare in advance, the site visit team reviewed hundreds of written or Web-based documents, such as institutional histories, catalogs, admissions materials, recent policy statements, student handbooks, organizational charts, student newspapers and other campus publications or videos, accreditation reports and institutional self-studies, and other relevant information about students, academic and student support programs, and institutional resources. Reviewing campus Web sites helped alert the visiting team to current issues and events prior to arriving on campus. In addition, research team members studied the institution's NSSE survey data, including means and frequency reports, benchmark results, and respondent characteristics. These data suggested possible lines of inquiry and exploration when talking with different groups on campus. Team members also collected additional information during the institutional site visit.

Once on site, the research team focused on obtaining as much information as possible from many different people about the programs, policies, and practices that contributed to student success. One conceptual map we used to guide our inquiry was the five NSSE clusters of effective educational practice: level of academic challenge, active and collaborative learning, student-faculty interactions, enriching educational experiences, and supportive campus environment (Chapters One, and Eight through Twelve). We systematically asked students, faculty members, staff, and others about these areas of institutional and student performance. In addition, we also sought to discover programs, policies, and practices that were not necessarily encompassed by the NSSE framework but that our respondents indicated were related to student engagement and success in their context. For example, cultural properties of institutions emerged as especially relevant, such as their history, traditions, and physical artifacts as did the educational philosophies and leadership approaches of key individuals and groups.

By the end of the second day of a site visit, research team members were testing assumptions with other team members and respondents. Indeed, team members were encouraged to challenge one another at the end of a day of field work to share evidence that supported or contradicted emerging themes and interpretations.

Most site visits concluded with a debriefing meeting that minimally included the site visit campus coordinators during which attendees posed and answered questions and addressed "loose ends." These meetings were the first of many efforts to share findings with key informants for feedback and verification purposes.

Following the first round of site visits, the respective site visit teams drafted an "interim report" for each institution. Averaging between 40 and 50 pages, the purpose of the interim report was to describe the college or university and its context as well as feature relevant policies, programs, practices, and other institutional factors and conditions that respondents and other data sources suggested were related to student success. The report also summarized tentative themes that warranted additional consideration and identified unanswered questions and topics for exploration during the second visit. The team sent the interim report to the campus site visit coordinator with the request that it be distributed widely to various groups on campus such as faculty members, students, and administrators as well as beyond the campus, if appropriate, such as to selected graduates or governing board members. The purpose was to solicit feedback as to our interpretation and to correct factual errors. Essentially, we wanted to know "Did we get it right?" (Stake, 1995). Some institutions posted their report on an internal Web site or sent a copy to all campus e-mail addresses to invite comments and suggestions as to topics and issues about which the team needed to learn more to better understand effective educational practice in that context. Most of the DEEP schools compiled feedback on the report, and this information was shared with both the first and second site visit team members.

Second site visit teams were usually composed of two or three people, at least one of whom was a member of the first site visit group and one of whom was new to the campus. This approach insured both continuity and "fresh eyes," allowing the team to probe more specifically into areas identified in the report that lacked clarity or specificity and to generate alternative interpretations about what was going on. Typically, during the first day of the second visit the research team conducted debriefing meetings with groups of faculty, students, staff, and others. The purpose of this session was to discuss the substance of the interim report, correct any errors of fact, and to identify areas of educational practices that needed further attention. In a variant of snowball sampling, team members also sought out people who, they learned from others on campus, might hold different or potentially instructive views. Following the second visit, the site visit teams produced a "final" report that was sent to each institution with a request for additional feedback and commentary. This document also became the primary source for data analysis.

Although all 20 site visit reports had a common introduction and employed some organization of data using the five NSSE clusters of effective educational practice, each team devised its own organizational framework. Most reports followed Lincoln and Guba's (1985) substantive case report recommendations, incorporating a thorough description of the context, the processes observed in the site, and explication of elements explored in depth. In addition, both the interim and final site visit reports included descriptive and interpretive material. Interpretations were essential so that readers could make explicit connections between the goals of the study, the findings, and emerging themes, thus minimizing the chance for misinterpretation (Merriam, 2002).

In all, we talked individually or in groups with more than 2,700 people—including about 1,300 students, 750 faculty members, and 650 "others" (such as administrators, student affairs professionals, librarians, and instructional technology staff). We met with some of these people more than once. In addition to traversing these campuses on foot and by bus and auto, we also sat in on about 60 classes, attended more than 30 campus events, including faculty senate meetings, lectures, candlelight vigils, campus forums, and student government meetings, dined in about 20 campus locations, and visited student centers at least two dozen times.

DATA ANALYSIS

Analyzing qualitative data from multiple sites must be an iterative process (Coffey & Atkinson, 1996). As mentioned earlier, we began to think about what we were learning from the very first interviews on a campus. Subsequently, we became more systematic in our analysis as each site visit team collected more data and compiled and compared field notes from interviews and summaries of observations and institutional documents at the end of a site visit. After about half of the first-round site visits, a subset of the research team came together to debrief their visits, recommend modifications to the data collection protocol, identify additional potentially instructive questions and sources of information, and discuss emerging themes. Different combinations of the DEEP research team also met throughout the course of the data collection when circumstances allowed, such as at professional meetings, to fine-tune the data collection procedures. This iterative, emergent design allowed us to continually improve the amount and quality of the information we were gathering.

NSSE Institute staff members took the lead on designing the coding and data management systems and invited other research team members to recommend additions and revisions to these approaches. Research team members brought different analytic perspectives to the data analysis tasks, and we attempted to use their strengths, interests, and creativity to full advantage (Strauss, 1987). For example, some researchers concentrated on basic descriptions, some quickly organized data into categories that comported with the NSSE effective practices framework, while yet others experimented with alternative interpretive frameworks. Through this hermeneutic and dialectic process (Guba & Lincoln, 1989), different interpretations, claims, concerns, and issues (including etic and emic views) could be shared, understood, considered, critiqued, and acted upon. The objective was to elicit ongoing interpretive impressions from research team members and institutional stakeholders—honoring but at the same time testing their constructions and interpretations of tentative claims against the collected evidence.

Within-Site Analysis

Site visit team meetings were the origins of initial within-site analysis. From here, analysis proceeded variously. Most investigators shared field notes which allowed teams to organize and manipulate the data according to various categories, such as the NSSE clusters of effective educational practices. Teams typically assigned a team member one or more of the NSSE clusters of effective educational practice to use as a lens through which to organize and interpret data and begin to develop an understanding of the more relevant institutional policies and practices, as well as other institutional conditions that were associated with student success.

Team members aggregated instances from the data that were congruent with these clusters and merged them with the work of other team members. Equally important, teams sought to better understand how these practices came about, including the cultural contexts in which they emerged, the role of leadership and strategic planning, and other catalytic conditions for using effective educational practices and promoting student success. As needed, site visit teams devised new categories of findings to account for additional data and then analyzed these findings to discern overarching themes that characterized the respective institution. Site visit teams then assembled detailed descriptions of their analyses and interpretations for each DEEP school and shared these reports with the other research team members.

Cross-Site Analysis

The cross-site data analysis approach we adopted was a fusion of perspectives consistent with best practices in qualitative data analysis. The interim and final site visit reports are the case records for cross-site analysis in that they contain and organize much of the major information in common reporting formats (Patton, 1990). In one sense, the final site visit reports are a form of "pre-interpreted" field notes for the cross-site analysis.

A "whole team" approach was employed to conduct cross-site analysis. Team members began by chunking out key data elements from the reports (Lincoln & Guba, 1985), seeking the smallest units—phrases, sentences, paragraphs—that stood alone and revealed meaningful information. To manage documents and conduct common qualitative analysis tasks such as text search and retrieval of cases, paragraphs, or coded segments using complex text search expressions, we used NUD*IST/INVivo software (Richards, 2002). In addition to organizing data, NUD*IST required us to read through data line by line and think about the meaning of each word, sentence, and idea (Creswell, 1998). About half of the research team participated in this phase of the data analysis and intimately familiarized themselves with chunks of the smallest units of data. While coding data for NUD*IST required considerable time, the relative ease of retrieving data offsets the initial time and energy spent on data input.

We conducted a formative cross-case analysis after about half of the second-round site visits were done. At this meeting, the team generated and discussed working themes and identified areas that needed additional information and interpretation. This was a key step in triangulating data elements and establishing empirical support for emerging themes as well as acknowledging alternative perspectives and interpretations.

Establishing Trustworthiness

To establish the trustworthiness of the data, we used triangulation, peer debriefing, member checking, and searching for disconfirming evidence to establish credibility (Creswell & Miller, 2000; Lincoln & Guba, 1985). We tested preliminary hypotheses and challenged assumptions and interpretations with peer debriefings during site visits and afterward via e-mail and conference calls. In addition, NSSE Institute staff reviewed every interim report to scrutinize data and preliminary interpretations. Finally, NSSE Institute staff distributed interim and final reports as they became available to the entire research team to help inform their data gathering at upcoming site visits. We also shared interim and final reports with respondents so they could confirm or challenge the accuracy and credibility of the information.

We were sensitive throughout the project to connect whenever we could what we were learning from one setting to our findings from other institutions (Lincoln & Guba, 1985). The site visit reports include thick, rich descriptions of the institutions and their policies, programs, and practices. In reporting the findings and conclusions, we included the broadest and most thorough information possible within prudent confidentiality limits. To provide evidence that our inquiry decisions were logical and defensible, we established an audit trail (Lincoln & Guba, 1985; Whitt & Kuh, 1991), including raw data such as tapes, interview notes, and documents; such products of data reduction and analysis as field notes, interview and document summary forms, and case analysis forms; such products of data synthesis as multiple drafts of site visit reports; evidence of member checking through written feedback from the institutions; and materials relating to the intentions of the research team including notes of debriefings and staff meeting minutes and correspondence.

APPENDIX B

Project DEEP Research Team

Robert W. Aaron

Robert Aaron is a project associate with the National Survey of Student Engagement (NSSE) Institute for Effective Educational Practice and is a doctoral student in higher education administration at Indiana University Bloomington. Prior to attending IU, Aaron was director of First-Year Student Services at Virginia Commonwealth University. He received an M.A. in higher education and student affairs from The Ohio State University and a B.A. in music from the University of Rochester, where he studied piano at the Eastman School of Music.

Charles Blaich

Charles Blaich is the director of inquiries at the Center of Inquiry in the Liberal Arts at Wabash College. He earned his Ph.D. in psychology from the University of Connecticut. Blaich joined Wabash College in the fall of 1991 and taught in the psychology department for 10 years. In addition to teaching psychology at Wabash, Blaich served as the cochair of Wabash's core interdisciplinary course, Cultures and Traditions, for two years. Blaich received the college's McLain-McTurnan-Arnold Excellence in Teaching Award and two National Science Foundation grants. He also received teaching awards from the University of Connecticut and Eastern Illinois University.

Anne Bost

After completing a B.S. in biology at Rhodes College in Memphis, Tennessee, Anne Bost moved to Nashville where she received a Ph.D. in microbiology and immunology at Vanderbilt University. She subsequently joined the infectious diseases research team at Eli Lilly & Company in Indianapolis, where she worked for two years. She currently serves as research fellow at the Center of Inquiry in the Liberal Arts at Wabash College. There her interests include identifying different ways in which student/faculty research collaborations are structured at liberal arts colleges, whether these structures are correlated with different student gains, and understanding which types of out-of-class interactions with faculty are most effective for individual types of students.

Larry A. Braskamp

Larry Braskamp received his B.A. from Central College and Ph.D. from the University of Iowa. Currently he is professor of higher education at Loyola University Chicago, where he served as the senior vice president for academic affairs. Braskamp held administrative positions at the University of Nebraska-Lincoln, University of Illinois at Urbana-Champaign, and University of Illinois at Chicago. He served as the first executive director of the Council for Higher Education Accreditation. He is the coauthor and coeditor of six books including *Assessing Faculty Work* and *The Motivation Factor: A Theory of Personal Investment,* and has published numerous research articles.

Edward K. Chan

Edward Chan is director of the Sophomore-Year Experience Program and assistant professor of English in the Department of University Studies at Kennesaw State University. He received his Ph.D. in English at the University of Rochester. In addition to first-year seminars, he has taught writing, literature, and film courses at the University of Rochester, the Rochester Institute of Technology, Wabash College, and Kennesaw State. His research interests include sophomore programs, 20th-century American literature and culture, utopian science fiction, race studies, cultural theory, and film.

Arthur W. Chickering

Arthur Chickering is special assistant to the president of Goddard College. He is the author of many publications, including *Education and Identity*, *The Modern American College: Responding to the New Realities of Diverse Students and a Changing Society*, and *Getting the Most Out of College* (with Nancy Schlossberg). He has received the E. F. Lindquist Award from the American Educational Research Association, the Outstanding Contribution to Higher Education Award from the National Association of Student Personnel Administrators, the Distinguished Contribution to Knowledge Award from the American College Personnel Association, the Distinguished Service Award from the Council for Independent Colleges, and the Howard R. Bowen Distinguished Career Award from the Association for the Study of Higher Education.

D. Jason De Sousa

Jason De Sousa is assistant vice president for academic affairs at Morgan State University, serving the university as director of the Institute for Student Leadership and Character Development, chair of the university's Student Retention Advisory Committee, and adjunct faculty member in the Department of Advanced Studies, Leadership, and Policy. He was formerly vice president for student affairs at Savannah State University and director of the Center for Leadership and Character Development. He also served as assistant vice president for student affairs at Alabama State University and director of the Career Development Center at Tuskegee University. He earned a B.S. from Morgan State University, an M.A. from Bowling Green State University, and an Ed.D. from Indiana University.

Elaine El-Khawas

Elaine El-Khawas is professor of education policy at George Washington University. Previously she served as professor of higher education at UCLA and as vice president for policy analysis and research at the American Council on Education. She holds master's and doctoral degrees in sociology from the University of Chicago. She is a past president of the Association for the Study of Higher Education, serves on editorial boards of several international journals in higher education, and is on the board of trustees at Emmanuel College.

Sara E. Hinkle

Sara Hinkle is a former project associate with the NSSE Institute for Effective Educational Practice at Indiana University Bloomington (IUB). She currently serves as associate director for orientation and transition issues at New York University. She received a B.A. in psychology from Gettysburg College, an M.S. in counseling from Georgia State University, and a Ph.D. in higher education from IUB. Hinkle has also worked in student affairs at IUB, Oglethorpe University, Brenau University, Kennesaw State University, and Georgia State University, as well as with the Semester at Sea program.

Mary Howard-Hamilton

Mary Howard-Hamilton is associate dean for graduate studies in the School of Education at Indiana University (IU). She previously served two years as associate professor in the Department of Educational Leadership and Policy Studies at IU. She also held the positions of associate professor and coordinator for the University of Florida's Student Personnel in Higher Education Program and held an affiliate faculty position at the Center for Women's Studies and Graduate Research. Howard-Hamilton earned her Ed.D. from North Carolina State University and her M.A and B.A. from the University of Iowa.

Bruce A. Jacobs

Bruce Jacobs is the vice chancellor of auxiliary services and programs at Indiana University Bloomington. Jacobs has held positions at SUNY Brockport, Dutchess Community College (New York), Southwest Texas State University, Gettysburg College, Rutgers University, and Indiana University (IU). He has worked in residence halls, student activities, Greek affairs, special events, judicial affairs, student unions, and orientation. Jacobs also holds an adjunct assistant professor position in the Higher Education and Student Affairs (HESA) program at IU. In addition, he has served as the coordinator of the HESA master's program at IU. His B.S.

and M.S. degrees are from SUNY Brockport, and his doctorate is from IU in higher education and student affairs.

Adrianna Kezar

Adrianna Kezar is associate professor at the University of Southern California. Her research interests include leadership, organizational change, governance, and diversity. Her most recent books include: *Understanding and Facilitating Organizational Change in the Twenty-First Century: Recent Research and Conceptualizations* (Jossey-Bass) and *Taking the Reins: Institutional Transformation in Higher Education* (ACE-ORYX Press). Kezar holds Ph.D. and M.A. in higher education administration from the University of Michigan and a B.A. from the University of California, Los Angeles.

Jillian Kinzie

Jillian Kinzie is associate director of the NSSE Institute for Effective Educational Practice and project manager of the Documenting Effective Educational Practices (DEEP) initiative. She earned her Ph.D. in higher education at Indiana University Bloomington. Prior to this, she held a visiting faculty appointment in the Higher Education and Student Affairs Department at Indiana University and worked as assistant dean in an interdisciplinary residential college and as an administrator in student affairs. In 2001, she was awarded a Student Choice Award for Outstanding Faculty at Indiana University. Kinzie has coauthored a monograph on theories of teaching and learning and has conducted research on women in undergraduate science.

George D. Kuh

George Kuh is Chancellor's Professor of Higher Education at Indiana University Bloomington. He directs the Center for Postsecondary Research which is home to the National Survey of Student Engagement (NSSE) and related surveys for faculty members and law school students, the NSSE Institute for Effective Educational Practice, and the College Student Experiences Questionnaire Research Program. A past president of the Association for the Study of Higher Education, Kuh has written extensively about student engagement, assessment, institutional improvement, and college and university cultures and has consulted with more than 150 educational institutions and agencies in the United States and abroad.

Richard A. Lynch

Richard Lynch was a research fellow at the Center of Inquiry in the Liberal Arts at Wabash College. He taught for two years at Wabash College as a visiting assistant professor of philosophy and for three years prior to that as a teaching fellow at Boston College, where he earned the Donald T. White Teaching Excellence Award. He is currently completing his doctorate in philosophy at Boston College and holds an M.A. from Northwestern University in philosophy and a B.A. from the University of Texas at Austin. His publications include scholarly articles on Hegel, Habermas, Foucault, and others, as well as translations from French.

Peter Magolda

Peter Magolda is an associate professor in the Miami University College Student Personnel program. He teaches research and educational anthropology courses. His research interests include ethnographic studies of college students and qualitative program evaluation. He earned a Ph.D. in higher education from Indiana University. His M.A. is in college student personnel from The Ohio State University and his B.A. is in psychology from LaSalle College. Prior to joining the Miami University faculty in 1994, he worked for 14 years in student affairs at The Ohio State University, the University of Vermont, and Miami University.

Kathleen Manning

Kathleen Manning has taught at the University of Vermont since 1989 in higher education and student affairs. A 2003 Fulbright Fellow at Beijing Normal University and Fulbright Senior Specialist in 2004, Manning has received various teaching and service awards. Her interests include organizational theory, research methodology, and cultural pluralism. Her published books including *Research in the College Context: Approaches and Methods* and *Rituals, Ceremonies and Cultural Meaning in Higher Education*. She holds a Ph.D. in higher education from Indiana University, an

M.S. in counseling and student personnel from SUNY Albany, and a B.A. from Marist College.

Carla Morelon

Carla Morelon is a project associate with the NSSE Institute, and her responsibilities include the Documenting Effective Educational Practice (DEEP) and Building Engagement and Attainment for Minority Students (BEAMS) projects. During her tenure at IU, she has been actively involved in the higher education and student affairs department, orientation, practicum facilitation, and other outreach activities. In 2002, she received the Wade Fellowship and was nominated for the ASHE Graduate Student Policy Seminar. Most recently, Morelon created and now facilitates a doctoral student research team interested in issues of access and retention for graduate students of color. She is currently working on her dissertation and plans to graduate in May 2005.

Shaila D. Mulholland

Shaila Mulholland is a former project associate with the NSSE Institute. She is currently pursuing her Ph.D. in higher education administration at New York University and is a research assistant with the Alliance for International Higher Education Policy Studies, a Ford-funded project researching state higher education performance. Her research interests are student access to higher education, educational equity, and college choice. She earned her B.A. in biology and M.S. in higher education and student affairs from Indiana University.

Richard Muthiah

Richard Muthiah is director of the Academic Learning Center at George Fox College in Newberg, Oregon. Previously he worked as a project associate for the NSSE Institute and the College Student Experiences Questionnaire (CSEQ). Muthiah also worked at the Center for Service and Learning at Indiana University-Purdue University Indianapolis and in several student affairs roles at Taylor University. He completed a B.S. in psychology/systems analysis at Taylor University in Upland, Indiana, an M.A. in counseling at Ball State University, and a Ph.D. in higher education at Indiana University Bloomington.

Charles C. Schroeder

Charles Schroeder received his B.A. and M.A. from Austin College and his doctorate from Oregon State University. He has served as the chief student affairs officer at Mercer University, Saint Louis University, Georgia Institute of Technology, and University of Missouri-Columbia. In 2001, he became a professor of higher education in the educational leadership and policy analysis department at the University of Missouri-Columbia. He served as president of the American College Personnel Association in 1986 and as executive editor of *About Campus: Enriching the Student Learning Experience* in 1993. Schroeder has authored over 60 articles and published a book in 1994 with Phyllis Mable entitled *Realizing the Educational Potential of Residence Halls*. In January 2004, he joined Noel-Levitz, a national higher education consulting firm, as a senior executive specializing in retention management systems.

John H. Schuh

John Schuh is distinguished professor of educational leadership at Iowa State University. Previously he has held administrative and faculty assignments at Wichita State University, Indiana University Bloomington, and Arizona State University. He earned his B.A. in history from the University of Wisconsin-Oshkosh and his M.C. and Ph.D. in counseling from Arizona State. He is the author, coauthor, or editor of over 200 publications and is the editor of the *New Directions for Student Services* sourcebook series and associate editor of the *Journal of College Student Development*.

Mary Beth Snyder

Mary Beth Snyder is vice president for student affairs, including enrollment services, at Oakland University. She also teaches in the educational leadership Ph.D. program. Snyder earned her B.A. from Western Michigan University and her M.A. from The Ohio State University where she worked for seven years in student affairs. She completed her Ph.D. in higher education at UCLA, after which she joined the president's office of the University of California for six years as the chief policy analyst on all issues that affected student life across the nine-campus system. Following that, Snyder served for a number of years as dean of students at Iowa State University where she also taught in the higher education program.

Elizabeth J. Whitt

Elizabeth Whitt is a professor in the College of Education at the University of Iowa and coordinator of graduate programs in student affairs administration. She received a B.A. from Drake University, M.A. from Michigan State University, and Ph.D. in higher education administration and sociology from Indiana University. Whitt served on the faculties at Oklahoma State University, Iowa State University, and University of Illinois at Chicago. She also worked in student affairs administration at Michigan State University, University of Nebraska-Lincoln, and Doane College (Nebraska). Whitt is associate editor of the *New Directions for Student Services* monograph series. In 2002, the American College Personnel Association named her a senior scholar for her contributions to student affairs research and practice.

National Survey of Student Engagement

T HE NATIONAL SURVEY of Student Engagement (NSSE) provides colleges and universities with valuable information about students' views of collegiate quality by annually administering a specially designed survey, *The College Student Report.* The NSSE project was established with a generous grant from The Pew Charitable Trusts and is cosponsored by The Carnegie Foundation for the Advancement of Teaching and the Pew Forum on Undergraduate Learning. Today, the survey is entirely supported by institutional participation fees. Additional support for related research and development efforts has been provided by Lumina Foundation for Education and the Center of Inquiry in the Liberal Arts at Wabash College.

The NSSE survey instrument, *The College Student Report,* is a versatile, research-based tool for gathering information that focuses local and national conversations on learning-centered indicators of quality in undergraduate education. *The Report* is useful in several ways:

- Institutional improvement—as a diagnostic tool to identify areas in which a school can enhance students' educational experiences and student learning

- Benchmarking instrument—establishing regional and national norms of educational practices and performance by sector

- Public accountability—documenting and improving institutional effectiveness over time

Designed by national experts, *The College Student Report* asks undergraduate students about their college experiences—how they spend their time, what they feel they've gained from their classes, their assessment of the quality of their interactions with faculty and friends, and other important indicators. Extensive research indicates that good educational practices in the classroom and interactions with others, such as faculty and peers, are directly related to high-quality student outcomes. *The Report* focuses on these practices.

The Report is administered each spring to random samples of first-year students and seniors at public and private four-year colleges and universities. Over the first five years of the NSSE project (2000–2004), more than 620,000 students at 850 different four-year colleges and universities completed the survey, which can be administered either via a traditional paper questionnaire or on the World Wide Web. A demonstration of the Web version and a copy of the paper version of *The Report* are available at (http://www.iub.edu/~nsse).

The random sampling method ensures that the results are comparable, meaningful, credible, and usable for institutional self-study and improvement efforts, as well as consortium comparisons and national benchmarking. After institutions provide a student data file and customized invitation letters, NSSE handles the sampling and all aspects of the data collection, including mailing surveys directly to students; collecting, checking, and scoring completed surveys; and conducting follow-ups with nonrespondents. Guidance for the NSSE project is provided by a national advisory board of distinguished educators (http://www.iub.edu/~nsse/html/advisory_board.htm.).

INDEX

A

Aaron, R. W., 337

Academic challenge, 177–192; individualized plans for, 114, 115; level of, 11; NSSE components of, 177; and peer support, 248–251; and scholarship celebrations, 190–191; senior culminating experiences, 188–189; and student performance expectations, 178–182, 268, 300; and success skills, 196, 243, 244, 250; and support services, 302, 306, 312; writing centers, 185–187; writing courses, 183–185

Academic Skill Achievement Program (ASAP), 250

Accountability, 348; state-level requirements for, 152–153, 275–276

Accreditation, 20, 145, 201, 265, 299, 304

Acculturation, 111–113, *See also* Cultures, institutional

Activism. *See* Leadership

Addictive substances, avoiding, 199

Adelman, C., 7

Administrative support. *See* Services, student; Student affairs

Administrators, 333; escalating overload of, 290, 305; leadership by senior, 158–161, 299–300; monitoring students at risk, 128, 166–167; reorganization of, 277–278; respect for, 160–161; teaching by, 46

Admission: early, 242–243, 253, 286; policies, 14, 290–291; and student body diversity, 291–293, 308

Adult students, 30, 254–255, 277

Advisors, academic, 116–117, 127, 128–130, 213–214, 224, 231, 244, 268, 278–279; First Peoples' Advising program, 254; four-year student notebooks, 129–130; importance of, 314; living on campus, 106–107, 259; networks of, 246–248, 260; and student affairs, 166–167, 278, 311, 313; tag teams of, 251; teams with, 129, 246–247, 251

Affirmative action, 49, 98, 254, 257

African American colleges and universities, 14, 34–35, 55–57, 105

African American faculty, 163–164

African American students. *See* Color, students of

Ages of students, 30, 226

Collins, J. C., 18, 133, 158, 293, 297, 305

Color: faculty of, 163–164; students of, 14, 34–35, 36, 55–57, 105, 196, 212, 220, 221–222, 225, 253–254, 292, 306

Common Intellectual Experience (CIE) course, Ursinus, 52, 118, 145, 161–162, 164, 180–181, 187, 245, 258, 287

Communication abilities, 184

Community college students, 19, 255–256

Community, local: collaborative learning in the, 200–204, 307; Mexico-U.S. border, 225–226; partnerships, 313

Community service. See Service to society

Commuter institutions, 14, 91, 101, 104–105, 254–255, 277

Compact or covenant, campus, 315

Comprehensive Studies Program (CSP), 67, 76–77, 254

Contracts: internship, 238; learning, 33, 205

Cormier, P., 159

Courses: and assignments, 301; and curriculum development, 150–151, 153, 203; and diversity experiences, 220–221; electronic technology use in, 72–74, 231, 282–283; experiential learning, 202–204, 214–215; for first-year students, 107, 113, 116–117, 138–139, 179–181, 243–244; infusion and connection in, 151, 220–226; interdisciplinary, 142–143, 146–147, 164, 176, 187; international experienced linked to, 227–228; leadership minor, 239; load reductions of, 144, 183, 272; re-enrollment in, 181–182; required writing, 183–185; requiring enriching, 315; in Spanish, 221, 250; "super-size" gateway, 74–75;

titles of, 221, See also Curriculum development; particular school names

Creating Higher Expectations for Educational Readiness program (CHEER), 117

Creative or artistic projects, 190–191

Creswell, J. W., 335, 336

Criticism. See Feedback

Cross-cultural experiences, 222, 226–229, 240, See also Study abroad

Cross, K. P., 109, 198

CSUMB. See California State University, Monterey Bay (CSUMB)

Culture of evidence, 265, 278–279, 301; for DEEP project data collection, 331, 336

Cultures, institutional, 21, 272–275, 313–315, 331, 335; reculturing, 316; teaching newcomers about, 111–113, 117, 314–315, See also Traditions and rituals; particular school names

Cultures, other. See Study abroad

Curriculum development, 150–151, 153, 155, 161, 203; and adoption, 162; and diversity, 220–226, 292, 308; gender-balanced, 55, 223–224, 276, 287; and international experiences, 227–228, 315; liberal and practical arts, 286–287; and reform, 37, 125–127, 311–312; student advice on, 168, See also Courses; Seminars, student

D

Data collection. See DEEP project; The College Student Report (NSSE)

Davis, T., 175

Decision making: informed by data, 152–155, 156, 278–279, 304; student participation in, 119, 141, 168–170, 210–211, 247, 312, See also Governance, campus

DEEP project, 10–18; cross-site data analysis, 335–336; data analysis, 18, 333, 334–335; data collection protocols, 18, 328, 330–333; data trustworthiness, 336; interim and final reports, 332, 333, 336; primary purpose of, 18; qualitative case study method, 327; recommendations and suggestions, 295–317; research team, 18, 328–329; secondary purpose of, 18; selection of institutions, 18, 329–330; selection philosophy, 175; site visits, 18, 274, 328, 330–331, 336; statistics, 18, 333; summary and recommendations, 263–264; team meetings, 328–329, 331–332, 334–335; Web site, 13, 18

DEEP schools (overviews): academic challenge at, 177–178, 191–192; acculturation to, 111, 123; active and collaborative learning at, 193–194, 206; alignment infrastructures, 123–131, 281–282; Common Data Set, 330; community links of, 200–204; commuter institutions, 14, 101, 104–105, 254–255, 277; and curriculum development, 150–151; disagreement in, 58–59, 293–294; diversity or homogeneity of, 14, 223, 291–293; documents reviewed, 18, 331; EECQ questions about, 4–5; enriching educational experiences of, 219–220, 239–240; environments of, 91–93, 105–106, 108, 175–176, 241–261; as examples, 18–19, 21, 266, 294, 317–318; features of, 10, 11–13, 14, 18; feedback on DEEP reports, 332; focus on student learning by, 62, 88–89, 109–110, 118–119, 131, 173–175; four-year sector, 19, 348; gemstones analogy, 23–24, 317; improvement initiatives at, 133–134, 138–140, 146–150, 153–154, 155–156, 159, 263,

276, 304–306, 311, 317; Institutional Engagement Index (NSSE), 329; institutional philosophies of, 27–28, 58–62; introduction to, 14, 18, 28–29; as learning organizations, 133–134; organizational structure of, 277–278; as outperforming expected scores, 330; perennial challenges at, 287–294; positive restlessness of, 146–150, 265, 276, 290, 300, 303–306, 317; in Project Pericles, 41, 203–204; public and private, 14; quiz and answers, 4–5, 63; religious affiliations, 29, 36, 37–39, 51, 61, 112, 170, 292; selection criteria, 14, 329–330; shared responsibility at, 157–158, 171–172, 305–306; single sex, 26, 29–30, 44–45, 52–54, 257, 276; single sex then coeducational, 39, 54–55; six features of, 24; statistical data table, 15–17; student-faculty interaction at, 207–208, 217–218; two characteristics of, 25, 58–59; types of, 14, 15–17, *See also particular school names*

Demographics, major changes in, 50, 134–136, 159–160, 275, 304

De Sousa, D. J., 339

Dey, E. L., 308

Disciplines: collaboration across, 311–313; residence halls by major, 258; writing in the, 184, 186

Discussion: campus listserv, 60, 282; campus roundtables, 224; class, 71, 194, 248; DEEP team visits, 18, 333; dining and student-faculty, 210, 224; electronic, 216; of mission, 49, 60–61, 298–299; public dialogues and, 59; serious, 219, 310; of stopping programs, 305; "Suite Talk," 258, *See also* Decision making

Dissent and dialogue, space for, 59–61, 310

Diversity: affirming, 37, 49, 116–123, 220–226; awareness initiatives, 12–13, 100; the educational value of, 220–221, 239; faculty and staff, 163–164, 308; importance of, 49, 220–221, 304, 310; infusion into courses, 151, 220–226, 290, 315; of learning styles, 32, 117, 204–205, 217, 223, 285, 302–303; out-of-class experiences of, 20–21, 96, 224–226; of student ages, 30, 226; student body, 36–37, 40–41, 219, 223, 291–293, 308

Documenting Effective Educational Practice. *See* DEEP project

Domain, 43, 93–95, 114, 121, 200, *See also* Sewanee: University of the South

Duderstadt, J. J., 138

Dunlap, B. B., 142

Dweck, C. S., 285

E

Early warning systems, 127–128, 251–252, 260, 268, 269, 311

Eating and gathering facilities, campus, 98–99, 210, 224

Eckel, P., 276, 297, 341

Ecology and agriculture study, 203

Educationally Effective Colleges Quiz (EECQ), 3; answers, 63; questions, 4–5

Educational practices, "sticky," 24, 269, 284–285, *See also* Pedagogies, engaging

Education Commission of the States, 9, 173

Effective education practices, 11–13, 19–20, 173–175, 264, 284–285

Ehrenreich, B., 179

Electronic technologies. *See* Technologies, electronic

El-Khawas, E., 339–340

El Paso. *See* University of Texas El Paso (UTEP)

E-mail, student-faculty, 83–84, 208, 216–217, 231, 282

Engelkemeyer, S. W., 297

Enriching educational experiences, 219–220, 239–240; cluster questions, 12–13; cocurricular leadership, 44, 238–239; infusion of diversity in, 151, 220–226; internships, 236–238; opportunities and use of, 9–10; study abroad and international, 40–41, 224, 226–229; and technologies, 72–74, 229–233, *See also* Learning; Study abroad

Enrollment: percentages among students, 308, 329; size challenges, 36, 276, 287–288, 304

Entering students. *See* First-year students

"Environmental residents," 259

Environments: and community connections, 101–104, 119, 313; community service, 234; cross-cultural U.S., 229; of DEEP schools, 91–93, 283; DEEP schools and city, 19, 36, 37–38, 40–41, 102, 103, 104; international, 221, 226–229, 256; and location challenges, 104–105; natural resources, 93–95, 200; off-campus learning, 196, 202, 228, 229, 233–236, 236–238, 237, 287, 307; scavenger hunt, 72; socially catalytic, 209–210, 218, 242–243, 283, 314; supportive campus, 13, 241–261, 314; for teaching and learning, 8–9, 93–106, 195–196, *See also* Architecture at DEEP schools; Residences, campus

Evergreen State College. *See* The Evergreen State College

Ewell, P. T., 273

Examinations: comprehensive, 124–125, 189; senior comprehensive, 188

Excellence: celebrations of, 190–191, 290; institutional, 9, 159, 304; student academic, 60, 302; teaching, 48, 130–131

EXCEL program (Excellence through Connected and Engaged Learning), 73–74, 141, 191, 230, 232–233

Expectations of students, 113–116, 168, 187–188, 270, 300; about academic work time, 182–183; and academic challenge, 178–182, 268, 300, *See also* Students

F

Faculty, 333; accessible and responsive, 58, 208–213, 259, 261, 280–281; alliances with students, 170; collegiality, 161, 293; of color, 163–164; course assessments by, 146–148, 152–155; course-load reductions, 144, 183, 272; development, 46, 66, 223, 232; Disappearing Task Forces (DTFs), 147, 162; diversity, 163–164, 222; evaluations by students, 1, 87–88, 125; external evaluation of, 289; feedback communication, 83, 84–88, 125, 216–217; full-time and adjunct, 170; HBCU exchange of, 164; importance of student meetings with, 116; Integrated Learning, 142; intellectual connections among, 145–146, 311–312; investment in, 306–307; lunch rooms and meetings, 98, 149; named professorships for, 131, 139; notes to students, 85, 208, 251, 269; overload problems, 290, 305; performance standards setting by, 124–125; recruitment, 46, 118, 130, 163–164, 170, 172, 211, 218, 267, 281, 300, 308, 309; reward systems, 130–131, 309; as role models, 70–71; scholarship expectations of, 288–289, 300; socializing new, 118–119, 164, 281, 309; and student affairs partnership,

159, 164–167, 281, 286, 311; student interaction questions, 12; student spaces near, 209–210; summer workshops, 144; task forces, 138, 147, 162, 278–279, 306; tenure, 51–52, 293–294; time for students, 80–84, 208–213; women, 164; workshops, 144, 223, 279; writing center seminar, 186, *See also* Advisors, academic

Faculty Colloquium, 118, 146, 164, 310

Faculty development, 46, 66, 223, 232

Faculty Learning Committee (FLC), 68, 147–148

Faculty mentors. *See* Mentoring

Faculty-student relationships. *See* Student-faculty interaction

Faculty Survey of Student Engagement (FSSE), 284, 304

Farmington. *See* University of Maine at Farmington (UMF)

Fayetteville State University (FSU), 14, 21, 155, 209, 214, 274, 275, 288, 304; about, 34–35; AUTOS group, 254; Bronco Cohort, 35; Careers on the Move, 237; Center for Personal Development, 258; Chancellor's Scholars, 35; CHEER program, 117; community programs learning, 201; cross-cultural study, 228; diversity experiences, 220; Early Alert System, 127, 181, 251, 269; electronic feedback at, 216, 231; experimental instruction at, 70; Extension Grade policy, 181–182; Freshman Year Institute (F.Y.I.), 137, 220; and NC-LSAMP, 196; operating philosophy, 28, 267, 278; Professional Image Day (PID), 244–245; statistics, 15, 35; student development at, 77, 78–79, 109–110, 128, 136–138, 198, 258; Student Government Association (SGA), 251; University College, 213–214, 244, 313

culture of, 149, 191; Johnson
Center, 97, 98–99, 221, 283, 314;
New Century College (NCC), 195,
198, 202, 222, 227; Robinson
Scholars program, 130–131; slogan,
36; STAR Center, 74, 232;
statistics, 15, 36; student advisory
committees, 211, 247; student
assessment at, 127, 205; technology
access at, 230, 231; Technology
Assistants Program (TAP), 233;
University 100 courses, 237, 243,
248; Writing Across the Curriculum
program, 183–184

Gladwell, M., 284

Globalism, study of, 222

Gonyea, R. M., 174, 182

Gonzaga University, 14, 20, 208, 226;
about, 37–39; community service,
101, 149–150, 202, 235; Core
Curriculum, 38, 287; faculty
advisors, 214; GEL recruitment
program, 112; Jesuit tradition of,
61, 112, 170; mission, 38, 61,
169–170, 276; Positive Choice
living, 199; social justice core
requirement, 203; statistical profile,
15; Unity House, 98

Goodsell, A. M., 9

Governance, campus, 46, 47, 168–170,
210–211; and community service,
234; shared, 312; Student
Government Association (SGA),
251, See also Decision making

Graduate teaching assistants
(TAs), 46

Grants. See Investment

Green, M., 297

Group learning, student, 71–72,
75–76, 168; active, 11, 193–194;
affiliations, 144; peer networks and,
249–250; physical facilities for, 30,
72, 95–99; study groups, 195–196;
via electronic discussions, 216,
See also Collaborative learning;
Peer learning

Gruenwald, D. A., 92

Guba, E., 333, 334, 335, 336

Gurin, G., 308

Gurin, P. Y., 308

H

Hawthorne effect, 274

HBCU (Historically Black College or
University), 14, 34–35, 55–57,
105; faculty exchanges, 164

High schools, student presentations
to, 202

Hill, B., 297

Hinkle, S. E., 340

Hispanic students, 14, 50, 134–136,
159–160, 221, 225–226, 250, 256;
institutions serving, 14, 31–32,
49–51

Hoffman, N., 8

Hossler, D., 286

Howard-Hamilton, M., 340

Hurtado, S., 308

I

Indiana. See Wabash College

Indiana University Center for
Postsecondary Research, 327

Information technology personnel.
See Technologies, electronic

Infusion principle. See Courses;
Diversity

Institutional Engagement Index,
NSSE, 329

Integration of ideas, student, 174

Intelligence, self-theories
about, 285

International experiences. See Study
abroad

Internships, 102–103, 176, 190, 215,
236–238, 307, 315

Interviews: DEEP project, 18, 333;
NSSE project, 348; of seniors by
faculty, 152

Investment: in assessment, 141; in community service, 234–236, 307; in course-based technology, 72–74, 232; and enrollments, 288; in faculty, 306–307; grants (received and denied), 135, 143, 148, 215, 279; in learning communities, 143, 144, 148, 272; mission-related, 150, 271–272, 279; in student engagement, 306–307, 315; student-managed, 200; in student support services, 310–311; in teaching and learning, 68, 149, 307; in undergraduate programs, 67, 68, 127, 138–139, 140; in undergraduate research, 54, 55, 215

J

Jacobs, B. A., 340–341
Jayhawk Boulevard. *See* University of Kansas (KU)
Jesuit traditions. *See* Gonzaga University
Jobs: peer mentor, 197, 233; work study on-campus, 48, 73, 127, 272, 306, 307
Johnson, C., 57
Johnson, D. W., 9
Johnson, R., 9
Juarez, Mexico, University of, 225–226
Judiciary, campus, 211

K

Kalikow, T. J., 140, 141
Kansas. *See* University of Kansas
Kazis, R., 8
Keeton, M. T., 25, 266
Keller, G., 8
Kezar, A., 276, 297, 341
Killian, T., 174
Kimball, B., 287
King, M. L., Jr., 225
King, P. M., 109

Kinzie, J. L., 299, 341
Klein, S. P., 302
Knowledge: celebrations of, 190–191; construction of, 194
Kuh, G. D., 8, 9, 25, 33, 134, 136, 173, 174, 182, 221, 266, 277, 282, 284, 297, 299, 302, 303, 305, 308, 315, 316, 336, 341–342
KU. *See* University of Kansas

L

Landry, E., 297
Language: institution-specific, 298–299, 315; Spanish, 221, 250; study of, 227, 229
Lave, J., 277
Leadership, 43, 158–163; citizen, 159, 234; cocurricular, 44, 238–239; development, 56, 225–226, 234, 250–251; distributed, 161–163; of senior administrators, 21, 134–135, 136–137, 140, 141, 142, 158–161, 270–271, 299–300, 305–306, 309, 335; shared institutional, 157–158; student, 239, 250–251, 250, 312; and student activism, 98, 168–170; training, 250–251, *See also* Presidents and provosts, institutional
Learning: active and collaborative, 11, 69–72, 75–76, 80–81, 88–89, 202; contracts, 33, 205; enriching educational, 219–220, 239–240; experiential, 200–204, 214–215, 236–238, 240; four streams of practice encouraging, 65; to learn actively, 194; outcomes and learning styles, 32, 204–205, 217, 223, 285, 302–303; via electronic technologies, 72–74, 231–232
Learning communities (LCs), 49, 76, 217, 272, 287, 288, 311; and course clustering, 142–144, 148, 176, 199; first-year student, 135, 199, 259

Mexico, U.S. students in, 225–226, 229

Mezirow, J., 294

Miami University, 14, 20, 28, 74, 92, 187, 188, 194, 274, 282, 291, 312; about, 41–43, 272; architecture applications, 201; campus abroad, 226; "Choice Matters" initiative, 126, 165, 313; diversity at, 292–293; faculty advisors, 213; Faculty Learning Committee, 68, 147–148, 307; First Year Institute (FYI), 179, 311; improvement momentum, 153–154, 155, 306; living-learning residences, 101, 106–107, 129, 247, 258, 286; Miami Plan Core Curriculum, 42, 287; mission statement, 42; statistics, 16, 42; Summer Scholars programs, 190, 215; teaching and scholarship, 288–289

Michigan Community Scholars Program (MCSP), 14, 100, 198–199, 274, 282; mission, 48

Michigan. *See* University of Michigan

Miller, D. L., 336

Minority students, 55–57, 105, 196, 212, 225, 253–254, 292, 306; Hispanic students, 14, 31–32, 49–51, 134–136, 159–160, 221, 225–226, 256

Missions, operating, 25–27; balancing teaching and, research, 54, 55, 59, 116, 118, 130–131, 288–289, 300; campus compact or covenant, 315; challenges to, 58–59, 61, 275, 310; changing and reaffirming, 59–61; and changing demographics, 134–135, 159–160, 275; espoused and enacted, 26, 266–268, 298–300; importance of, 21, 62, 151, 156, 217; language of, 299; living, 266–268; reward systems aligned with, 130–131, 309; statements, 31, 42, 299; and student affairs, 164–166, 281–282;

and student success, 266–268, 298–300; variations in, 26–27, *See also* Alignment infrastructure; Philosophies, institutional

Mistakes, freedom to make, 123

Model Institutions for Excellence (MIE), NSF-funded, 135

Monterey. *See* California State University, Monterey Bay (CSUMB)

Morelon, C., 286, 343

Mortenson, T., 330

Mottos and slogans, DEEP school, 36, 50, 56, 112, 234, 315

Mulholland, S. D., 343

Multiculturalism, commitment to, 40, 221–223, 291–293, 314

Multimedia uses, 73, 83, 232

Murrell, P., 175

Muthiah, R., 343

N

Natalicio, D., 134, 160

National Association of Student Personnel Administrators, 281

National Coalition Building Institute (NCBI), 151, 222

National Endowment for the Humanities (NEH), 148

National Science Foundation (NSF) grants, 135, 143, 215

National Survey of Student Engagement (NSSE) Institute, DEEP project management and coordination, 328, 334, 336

National Survey of Student Engagement (NSSE) survey, 18, 125, 152, 304, 307, 315; clusters of effective educational practices, 10, 11–13, 173–175, 264, 329, 331, 334; clusters summary (table), 11–13; collaborative learning practices, 193; enriching

Q

Questions on your college or university, 20

Quiz, DEEP schools, 4–5, 63

Quizzes, class, 74, 249–250

Quotes from students. *See* Students

R

Race relations, 151, 163–164, 220–226, 291–293; faculty discussions on, 222, *See also* Diversity

Reading programs: incoming class common, 1, 57–58, 179–180, 194, 245; intensive, 187–188

Real-world experience. *See* Internships; Service to society

Recommendations and suggestions to readers, 295–317; general, 295, 297–316

Recruitment programs: competent people, 309–311; faculty, 46, 118, 130, 163–164, 170, 172, 211, 218, 267, 281, 300, 308, 309; of students, 89, 112, 290–291; underserved students, 253, 291

Reculturing the institution, 316

Reisser, L., 8, 173, 288

Religious affiliations, DEEP school, 29, 36, 37–39, 51, 61, 112, 170, 292

Reports on institutional performance, public, 278, 304, 332

Reports, project. *See* DEEP project

Requirements, learning, 114–115, 183–185, 203; student time spent on, 182–183

Research: balancing teaching and, 54, 55, 59, 116, 118, 130–131, 288–289, 300; celebrations of, 190–191; institutional, 125, 147, 152–155, 162, 278–279; needed, 302–303; student-faculty collaborative, 12, 54, 55, 174, 303; undergraduate, 45–46, 82–83, 116, 190, 197, 214–215, 306; universities, 100, 138–140, *See also* Surveys and studies

Research, DEEP. *See* DEEP project

Residence life staff: RAs (assistants), 100, 161, 166–167, 310–311; technology assistants, 73, 233, 259

Residences, campus, 14, 45, 99–101, 199; advisors living in, 247, 252, 259; apartment-style, 108; career services at, 237; Freshman Centers, 115, 258; human scale, 106–108, 288; Language Houses, 227; living-learning, 101, 106–107, 129, 198–199, 247, 258, 282, 286; major-related, 39, 40, 258; supportive environments in, 257–259, 261; for theme communities, 99, 101, 148, 198–199, *See also* Environments

Retention. *See* Persistence and graduation rates, student

Reward systems, 190–191, 309; teaching awards, 48, 130–131, 290

Rhatigan, J. J., 297

Richards, L., 335

Rita, Miss, 171

Rituals. *See* Traditions and rituals; *particular school names*

Robes, academic, 122

Robinson Scholars. *See* George Mason University

Ronning, R., 73

Rose, M., 285

S

Safety nets, multiple, 251–252

Schein, E. H., 27, 316

Scholarship: celebrations of student, 190–191; expectations of faculty, 288–289, 300; programs, 117

Schraw, G., 73

Schroeder, C. C., 302, 344

Speakers, keynote, 225

Sports and teams, 41, 43, 276

Staff, 137, 309, 312; cultural practitioners on, 316; diversity, 308; importance of supportive, 170–171, 172; library, 312; professional advising, 246–248, *See also* Student affairs

Stake, R. E., 332

STAR (Student Technology Assistance and Resource) Center, 74, 232

State mandates: and accountability, 39, 152–153, 275–276; and enrollments, 288, 304

Statistics: campus living, 31, 257; college graduation rate, 7; DEEP project, 18, 333; DEEP schools (table), 15–17; institutional and student characteristic, 329; NSSEE project, 348; on undergraduate research participation, 214, *See also particular school names*

Stories, traditional campus, 119–120

Strauss, A. L., 334

Structure, organizational, 277–278, *See also* Alignment infrastructure

Student affairs, 161–162, 226, 278, 333; internships support, 236–238, 239–240; partnerships with faculty, 159, 164–167, 281, 286, 304, 312, 314; and student success, 164–167, 281–282; support for civic engagement, 234–236, *See also* Services, student

Student engagement, 29, 95–99, 306–307, 315, 331; indicators set, 8, 24, 347; and student success, 8–10, 13, 264, *See also* Civic engagement

Student-faculty interaction, 28, 83, 119, 170, 207–208, 217–218; and academic advising, 213–214, 278–279; and correspondence, 279; and electronic technologies, 216–217, 230–231, 282–283; and faculty accessibility, 208–213, 259,

261, 280–281, 282–283, 301; friendships, 81; NSSE cluster questions, 12; ratios for, 15–17; on research projects, 214–215; and student development, 303

Students, 333; achievement emphasis, 52, 290–291; adult, 30, 254–255; at risk, 127–128; of color, 14, 34–35, 36, 55–57, 105, 196, 212, 220, 221–222, 225, 253–254, 292, 306; commuter, 14, 91, 254–255, 277; demographic changes in, 50, 134–136, 159–160; diversity or homogeneity of, 220–226, 223, 291–293; engagement of, 8–10, 29, 264, 306–307, 315, 331; entering, 135, 199, 245, 279, 290–291; faculty focus on, 118–119; feedback to faculty, 152, 153, 168–170; first-generation college, 30, 35, 50, 212, 228, 242–243, 310; fostering the agency of, 167–170; Hispanic, 14, 31–32, 50, 134–136, 159–160, 221, 225–226, 256; initiative by, 116; international, 36, 40–41, 221; interventions for underengaged, 315; interviews of, 18, 152, 333, 348; IPEDS data characteristics, 329; knowing the, 301; making time for, 80–84; marginalized, 270; NSSE interviews of, 348; paraprofessional, 280; part-time, 14, 15–17; pathways to success of, 109–110, 116, 131, 136–138; as preceptors, 167–168, 197, 246, 249, 280, 314; quotes from, 1–2, 30, 43, 75, 204, 240, 243, 245, 254, 257; as role models, 250, 251, 258; scholarship celebrations, 190–191; selection of, 290–291; self-evaluations by, 125, 154, 198; Spanish-speaking, 221, 250; survival of, 116; suspension of, 182; "tag teaming" the, 251; teaching students, 167–168; as technology experts, 73–74, 232–233; traditions and rituals connecting, 119–123, 190–191, 273; transfer, 15–17, 252,

University of Maine at Farmington (UMF), 20, 21, 77, 109, 181, 184, 197, 275, 291; about, 47–48, 92; community connections, 102, 224, 230; early admission, 242–243; EXCEL program, 73–74, 141, 191, 230, 232–233; faculty, 208–209, 210, 309; institutional renewal at, 140–141, 149; operating philosophy, 28, 47; practicum experiences, 236; rural environment of, 19, 91–92, 95, 118; Spring Symposium, 190, 215, 229; statistics, 17, 48; student governance at, 211; Student Work Initiative, 48, 306; Summer Experience, 180

University of Michigan, 20, 21, 208, 273; about, 48–49, 138–140, 272; Center for Research on Learning and Teaching (CRLT), 67, 223; compact disks, 286, 313; Comprehensive Studies Program, 67, 76–77, 254; "Diag" gathering place, 97–98; Ginsberg Center for Community Service and Learning, 67, 235; institution-wide improvement agenda, 138–140, 155, 159, 306, 311–312; International Center, 256; living learning programs, 198–199, 282; mentoring at, 67, 212, 250; POSSE program, 116; Project Community, 203; reports on the undergraduate experience, 66–67, 304; research at, 116, 288, 300; residence communities, 67, 107, 198–199; Science Learning Center, 195–196; statistics, 17, 48; study groups at, 76, 195–196; Thurnau Professors, 131, 139; undergraduate focus and programs at, 66–67, 82–83, 181; UROP (program), 49, 67, 82–83, 100, 126, 190; writing center, 186

University of Texas El Paso (UTEP), 14, 21, 77, 101, 109, 150, 278, 287, 288, 300; about, 49–51;

Bhutanese architecture of, 92, 107; changing demographics and the mission of, 50, 134–136, 155, 159–160, 275, 304; collaborative learning at, 71–72, 103, 135, 199, 311; commuter students, 254–255, 277; course clustering, 199; Entering Student Program (ESP), 135, 245; faculty, 214; freshman seminars, 181; Mexican-American and Hispanic students, 50, 134–136, 159–160, 221, 225–226, 256; mission, 28, 59, 267, 275; off-campus learning, 202; slogans, 50; statistical profile, 17; student affairs at, 167; Student Leadership Institute (SLI), 250; Tutoring Learning Center (TLC), 196–197, 280; Undergraduate Learning Center (ULC), 68, 107; UNIV 1301 program, 50–51, 68, 71–72, 103, 135, 220–221; University College, 68; U.S.-Mexico student commuters, 91, 225–226, 229

University of Virginia. See George Mason University (GMU)

Untraveled students, 228

Upcraft, M. L., 286

Upside Down Degree program, 33, 255

Ursinus College, 20, 95, 98, 155, 183, 202, 236, 269, 286, 304; about, 51–52; Bridge Program, 116–117, 251; campaign change metaphor, 52; campuswide intellectual community of, 145–146; Common Intellectual Experience (CIE) course, 52, 118, 145, 161–162, 164, 180–181, 187, 245, 258, 287; faculty, 163–164, 209, 289, 290; Freshman Centers, 115, 258; Independent Learning Experience (ILE), 51, 214–215, 227; Laptop Initiative, 216, 230; Leadership Scholars Program, 238–239; mission, 52, 298; a Project Pericles